100 THINGS
BUCKEYES FANS
SHOULD KNOW & DO
BEFORE THEY DIE

Andrew Buchanan

TRIUMPH
BOOKS

The Library of Congress has catalogued the previous edition as follows:

Buchanan, Andrew, 1966–
    100 things Buckeyes fans should know and do before they die / Andrew Buchanan.
    p. cm.
    Includes bibliographical references.
    ISBN-13: 978-1-60078-097-4
    ISBN-10: 1-60078-097-0
    1. Ohio State Buckeyes (Football team)—Anecdotes. 2. Ohio State University—Football—Anecdotes. 3. Ohio State Buckeyes (Football team)—Miscellanea. 4. Ohio State University—Football—Miscellanea. I. Title. II. Title: One hundred things Buckeyes fans should know and do before they die.
    GV958.O35B82 2008
    796.332'630977157—dc22
                                                              2008014152

This book is available in quantity at special discounts for your group or organization. For further information, contact:
    Triumph Books LLC
    814 North Franklin Street
    Chicago, Illinois 60610
    (312) 337-0747
    www.triumphbooks.com

Printed in U.S.A.
ISBN: 978-1-60078-989-2
Design by Patricia Frey
Photos courtesy of AP Images

*For my dad, who instilled in us a love of sports,
but more importantly, a curiosity for—and
appreciation of—all the wonders of life.*

Contents

Foreword

I don't think it's outlandish at all to say that I was a Buckeye from the first day of my life. I was born in a hospital on campus here, and that particular hospital has a wonderful view of Ohio Stadium. Although I can't say for sure, I've always thought there's little doubt I probably caught a glimpse of that special place in the first few moments of my life.

Since then, I've developed a great passion for Ohio State and its football program. When I was a kid, guys like Rex Kern and Paul Warfield were people who I looked up to. I loved listening to them strut their stuff on WVKO radio here in Columbus. In those days, you always had Burt Charles and Buckeyes Heisman Trophy winner Vic Janowicz calling the games. Those guys did a great job of conveying the excitement and importance of Buckeyes football. When they called a game, you could just hear it in their voices. They cared, and their audience most certainly did.

My father was one of the guys in that audience who carried a great love of the university. He really enjoyed the team, and I could tell that he saw their successes as a point of pride, as many people do. I can't say he ever thought he'd have one of his sons play for the Buckeyes (let alone a few of them), but I don't doubt he hoped that would happen.

And most folks didn't think I would play for Woody Hayes at Ohio State. Although I had an excellent high school career at Eastmoor High here in Columbus, I didn't really fit the prototype of the running back people thought Woody wanted most. I was smaller and quicker, and in that day and age, Woody had some of his greatest successes with bigger, fullback types. But the day came when Woody did come calling. I was so excited and thrilled and just couldn't wait to meet the man.

When we finally sat down for our first discussion, I actually came away a little disappointed. Woody didn't talk about football at all. He talked about life and academics and about doing whatever you do the right way. I went home after the visit with my head hung low, convinced that Woody had just given me a courtesy visit. But my dad set me straight. He told me that Woody cared about me as a person and that was more important than football. Like many other times, my dad was correct, and a period of time later, I committed to the Buckeyes.

This is probably the time when I started to really learn about being a Buckeye and about the greatness of our program. I still remember running out onto the field at Ohio Stadium for the first time. It really took my breath away, hearing the hearty cheers that came from the packed stadium. The sound was one that I'd be quite familiar with for the rest of my life.

Looking back, I am pretty satisfied with the way my college career played out. I feel blessed to have been able to win two Heisman Trophies, four Big Ten championships, and perhaps best of all, never lost to Michigan. But I am not naïve enough to think that those accomplishments were my own. I've always said that I was in the right place at the right time with the right people. My successes were the direct result of playing with great players and for great coaches. Those are the people who put me in a position to succeed, and we worked together to create one of Ohio State football's most wonderful eras.

Once I left the school, my appreciation for how special the Buckeyes are just grew. It seemed that wherever I'd go I'd find some representative from Buckeye Nation just waiting there with a kind word for me. And in the locker rooms and playing fields of the National Football League, I found camaraderie from former Buckeyes who were also playing professionally, and I rediscovered good-natured rivalries with players from other Big Ten institutions.

When my pro days were over, I had little doubt that I'd return home. I was fortunate enough to have the opportunity to start working in the athletics department at Ohio State. I worked there for many years, and in 2004 took over as president and CEO of our Alumni Association.

Through all these years and all these interactions with fellow Buckeyes, I've had plenty of time to think about our football program and what makes it special. There are a lot of teams out there that win games, and there's no question our on-field successes have helped us gain our stature. However, I don't think it is wins alone that really sets Ohio State apart and defines it as the best college football program in the nation.

To me, that definition comes from two places: our people and our traditions.

The traditions are what link our glorious present to our storied past. Years and years of Buckeyes fans have been coming to our games and participating in the timeless rituals of an Ohio State game day. There's the Skull Session at St. John Arena the morning before the game, where the fans, band, and team all get together and get pumped up for the game. There's the walk from the arena to the stadium, where thousands of fans line the road and cheer our guys on. There's our band—"the Best Damn Band in the Land," by the way—spelling out Script Ohio. And then there's the ceremonial singing of "Carmen Ohio" after another Buckeyes victory.

Just writing about these things gives me chills. But they are far from the only great traditions we have here at Ohio State. We have the gold pants, a small charm given to each Ohio State player after they beat Michigan. We have the Buckeye leaf stickers on our helmets that signify excellent play. And, of course, we have our great tradition of outstanding players and coaches. From Coach Hayes to Earle Bruce to Jim Tressel to Urban Meyer, we've always had outstanding and virtuous men leading our programs. And they've coached guys like Kern, Bill Willis, Eddie George, and many, many others. Some of the greatest players in college football have played here, and those players are another reason we are set apart from other programs.

But it's not really the players and coaches I am talking about when I talk about the people who make our program special. Certainly they play a role, but the people who most drive Buckeye Nation are our alumni and fans. I've really gained an appreciation for this power, particularly since I started here at the Alumni Association.

One of the best parts of my job is the fact that I get to meet Buckeyes on a daily basis. It never fails to amaze me the passion and pride so many of our alumni and fans have in our football program. These are the people who are supporting the team year in and year out. The coaches and players may come and go, but our fans are consistent. They're always there, they're always loud, and they always love their Buckeyes.

That is truly a special thing, and I've seen it exhibited time and time again. I've traveled the world, and it doesn't surprise me anymore when someone hollers "*O-H*" at me from across the street in a foreign country. I always respond "*I-O*" with the same passion and excitement I'd show when I'm watching an Ohio State game with my friends. Wherever you go in the world, the feeling is the same. The thrill of Ohio State football is everywhere.

As I've moved on in life, I've really come to have a great appreciation for what this all means. As a young man, I enjoyed the camaraderie of my teammates and the exuberance we exhibited playing games in Ohio Stadium. But today, I realize that it is about much more than games. It's about family and bonding and finding a common thread that can draw so very many people together.

Certainly there are more important things in the world than football, but I don't think you can overlook the incredible power of our football program. It goes past the field into the lives of countless people who pull on a scarlet jersey each fall Saturday and cheer their Buckeyes on to a win.

This book, *100 Things Buckeyes Fans Should Know & Do Before They Die,* captures that spirit with its stories about the great teams and players and incredible history of Ohio State football, and also with its descriptions of the traditions surrounding Buckeyes football that fans should experience in their lifetimes. I've experienced many of them and continue to do so all the time, and it never gets old.

I enjoyed reading the stories about the excellent Buckeyes teams I was lucky enough to play for, the legacy and complexity of Coach Woody Hayes, and the fascinating anecdotes from over the years. And I like the unique format of ranking stories from 1 to 100, as it provides a starting point for discussions among Buckeyes fans on the history and significance of this great program.

I feel incredibly fortunate that I've been able to be a small part of this great tradition. It is a special thing and something that I cherish every day of my life.

—Archie Griffin

Acknowledgments

I attended my first game at Ohio Stadium about 40 years ago and have been watching Ohio State football and going to games and reading about and talking about the Buckeyes ever since. I also have written a guidebook to Ohio Stadium, the *Wise Guide Ohio Stadium.* So, much of the material for this book, particularly about game day at Ohio State and all that surrounds it, comes from my own personal experiences and observations.

I relied on several sources for many of the unique stories about Buckeyes football going back decades, as well as the finer points like scores and statistics and important dates in Ohio State history: Ohio State *Football Media Guides;* the Ohio State athletics department website, www.ohiostatebuckeyes.com; as well as the websites of other schools, the Big Ten, and the NCAA. Two books come in for special mention: *"Then Tress Said to Troy…": The Best Ohio State Football Stories Ever Told* by Jeff Snook (Triumph Books, 2007), which has the same publisher as this book, and *The Official Ohio State Football Encyclopedia* by Jack Park (Sports Publishing L.L.C., 2003). Park is the foremost Ohio State football historian, and I had the opportunity to interview him. His encyclopedia was indispensable.

The DVD *The History of Buckeye Football* (Intersport and Collegiate Images, 2005), which contains interviews with several Buckeyes greats, was insightful. And, in a sign of the times, the Internet was also incredibly helpful. Rather than just read about or try to recall moments from classic Buckeyes games over the past 40 years or so, I could often watch video of them posted by fans.

I also want to thank those who were open to discussing their experiences with Ohio State football and who provided invaluable insight. First among them is Archie Griffin, who also provides the foreword for this book.

Introduction

One of my favorite stories about Ohio State football involves the inmate who agreed to plead guilty the week of the 2003 Michigan game, on the condition that he be allowed to stay in the local lockup through the weekend, where he knew he could watch the game before being transferred to prison. If he could see the Buckeyes win (they didn't), he said he'd "be on cloud nine for a few months that I'm incarcerated."

The judge granted the request with a simple explanation: "It's Michigan week, and it's Columbus, Ohio."

Yes, it's just a game, but anyone who's ever lived in Ohio or experienced Ohio Stadium on a fall Saturday knows there is so much more. In fact, while there are wonderful college football traditions at places like Texas, Nebraska, LSU, Florida, USC, Notre Dame, and Michigan, it would be hard to argue that anywhere does it better than Ohio State.

There are the fans who make game day a festival, pack Ohio Stadium for every home date, and travel to see the Buckeyes on the road and in bowls, turning stadiums 1,000 miles from home into a "sea of scarlet." There is the band, which has the temerity to call itself the best anywhere, and who would argue after watching them make their Ohio Stadium entrance or perform Script Ohio? And of course there are the Buckeyes of Woody Hayes and Archie Griffin and Chic Harley and Jim Tressel, the national championships and Heisman Trophy winners and All-Americans, the great games and teams and names, and the rivalry with that school up north.

I grew up in Columbus and of course recall going to games as a young child and being enthralled by the experience: the crowds and the colors, the band entrance, and the players running onto the field and piling on top of one another with their index fingers raised (why don't they do that anymore?). Life in central Ohio then and now seems to come to a standstill when the Buckeyes play, and it was impossible not to be captivated by the Ohio State Buckeyes.

I remember my excitement when Corny Greene and a couple of other players came to my youth football banquet and signed autographs. As a teen I hopped the gates one time at Ohio Stadium with friends and played touch football, thrilled at the experience and amazed at the Astroturf field, hard as asphalt. I remember the Michigan game in 1982, when Ohio State knocked off the Wolverines, 24–14, and my little brother and I stormed the field with other fans. I realized it was a bad idea almost immediately as I lost my brother, then 12 years old, amid the sea of fans, and some frightening moments ensued. And I'll never forget the day Hayes, several years removed from his days on the Buckeyes sideline, spoke to my school. He talked about American history, and I don't think he once mentioned football.

Some two decades later there have been many thrilling games and experiences since, which have only deepened my respect for and appreciation of Buckeyes football. This book endeavors to capture the tradition and history of Ohio State football and give an overview of a program that has captivated millions of fans over more than a century of football. There are stories on the greatest players ever to wear the scarlet and gray, the history-making teams and those that came close, and the many dramatic moments that have occurred both on the field and off.

And there are anecdotes and stories that I think will surprise even the most devoted Buckeyes fans: Hayes wasn't Ohio State's first choice as coach and almost never got the job, Script Ohio was apparently first performed by the Michigan band, Ohio State's first Heisman Trophy winner didn't even play football the year before, and Griffin came to Ohio State with the goal to "make the varsity" and then fumbled on his very first carry.

There are also stories on the great traditions that surround the game—the band's ramp entrance, the tailgating scene on game day, the Varsity Club, Ohio Stadium, and other Buckeye shrines that fans should experience.

Ohio State football is a part of the fabric of life in Ohio and for Buckeyes fans far and wide, and this book hopefully illustrates what it has meant and continues to mean to so many people.

1 Woody Hayes

Woody Hayes molded one of the greatest programs in college football history in his blunt, tough image. He was a disciplinarian and a demanding coach who would rip into a player he thought wasn't giving his best, but he was also a master motivator who would build that player back up and have him ready to run through a brick wall on Saturday. He was a fierce competitor obsessed with winning, but he told his players that education came first. He had a titanic temper but would spend off hours visiting the local children's hospital cheering up the sick. He could be compassionate one moment and maddeningly obstinate the next, and his famous temper eventually cost him his job and, to some degree, forever tarnished his legacy.

One of his longtime assistant coaches at Ohio State, Esco Sarkkinen, put it best: "You don't describe Woody Hayes in one word, one sentence, or one paragraph. You describe him with chapter after chapter."

For mostly better and sometimes worse, Woody Hayes was and is Ohio State football.

Born on Valentine's Day 1913, in Clifton, Ohio, Wayne Woodrow Hayes played football at Denison University. He went back there to coach after a stint in the U.S. Navy in World War II, where he rose to the rank of lieutenant commander. After instant success as head coach at Denison and then at Miami of Ohio University, Hayes was off to Columbus in 1951.

The Buckeyes were 4–3–2 that first season, and Hayes came under some heavy criticism for his record and his use of the new T formation. Two 6–3 seasons followed, and Hayes was thought to be on shaky ground as the 1954 season opened. He later said he heard the whispers, and they made him work all the harder. The result was a 10–0 record for the Buckeyes and Hayes' first national title. He would win another three years later, and he earned at least a share of a national title five times in his career, including the consensus championship in 1968.

Hayes' overall record at Ohio State was 205–61–10, and he won or shared 13 Big Ten titles and took teams to eight Rose Bowls, winning four. In 28 seasons he only had a losing record twice, compared to four teams that went unbeaten. Hayes was fanatical about the University of Michigan rivalry, particularly during his "10-Year War" with former colleague Bo Schembechler. Hayes hit a relative rough patch in the mid-1960s, and rumors again swirled that his time might be up in Columbus. Hayes blamed it on the school's decision not to allow his unbeaten 1961 team to go to the Rose Bowl and said that ruling damaged his ability to recruit, particularly in Ohio.

So Hayes responded the only way he knew how: he worked harder than ever and hit the out-of-state recruiting trail, bringing in stars from around the country for the first time. What followed was a national title in 1968 with the so-called "Super Sophs," a class considered by some to be the greatest in college football history. Hayes earned a share of the title two years later and had a miraculous run from 1968 to 1977 that saw the Buckeyes win a share of a Big Ten title in nine out of 10 seasons.

"Nobody despises to lose more than I do," Hayes once said. "That's what got me into trouble over the years, but it also made a man with mediocre ability a pretty good coach."

Hayes did find trouble occasionally, and stories of his temper are legendary. Some of them make him sound petty and childish. He would frequently explode in anger and fire assistant coaches, only to rehire them hours later or the next morning when he'd cooled off. Players often felt his wrath verbally as well as with a swift punch to the gut. One time he came to practice with welts

The legendary Woody Hayes, shown here during the 1954 season, did not get off to the smoothest of starts as coach of the Buckeyes.

on his own face after pummeling himself in a fit of rage. He was known to throw or stomp on anything within reach, and equipment managers reportedly kept empty water jugs on his desk for him to bash.

He became a caricature to many people outside Ohio after some of the more public of these incidents. Once he ran onto the field to protest a call in the 1971 Michigan game and ripped up yard markers, and more than once he shoved reporters and cameramen. The worst of these incidents was the last one, when on national television he punched a Clemson University player who had intercepted a pass near the end of the 1978 Gator Bowl to seal the loss for the Buckeyes. It was the end of a frustrating season for the Buckeyes, and some people close to Hayes say it was his diabetes and his failure to keep up with his medication more than anything that led to the outburst. He was fired the next morning.

It was a sad end to an incredible career, but to those who had played for him and were close to him, the incident did not define the man. The stories they remember about Hayes are ones that never made headlines: the frequent trips to hospitals to visit the sick, his devotion to his players and former coaches even long after they'd left Ohio State, an openness that saw him recruiting and starting African American players years before many other major college programs, his consistent refusal of raises and requests that the money instead be distributed among his assistants, and his emphasis on education and insistence that his players get their degrees.

"He was a very, very caring man," says Archie Griffin, his biggest star. "He was tough, but he was fair. That's all you can really ask; you got a coach that cares about you and that you know was going to be fair. But he was tough, no question."

Tom Skladany, a Buckeyes punter and kicker in the mid-1970s, describes the "emotional roller coaster" of playing for Hayes. "You were afraid of him as a freshman. You hated him as a sophomore. You liked him as a junior, and you loved him as a senior."

Hayes had a great love of American and military history and would often weave anecdotes into pep talks. He was good friends with former president Richard Nixon, who said he would often want to talk football while Hayes wanted to discuss foreign policy. It's hard to imagine something similar being said about a coach today. When Hayes died in 1987, Nixon delivered the eulogy at his funeral.

Bo Schembechler frequently clashed with Hayes when Schembechler was an assistant at Ohio State and then later as the head man at Michigan, but he recalled how Hayes sent him a nice letter after he'd had a heart attack in the 1970s and then came to visit him at his home. Schembechler said that despite his flaws, Hayes was a fascinating person whom people loved being around. "If you want to find fault with him, I can too—bad temper and he doesn't listen and all that," Schembechler said years later. "But that guy was a helluva man. You want him on your side."

2 Ohio Stadium

More than 90 years after it was christened with an Ohio State win, Ohio Stadium remains the nexus of game day in Columbus, drawing more than 100,000 fanatics who cram into the old Horseshoe along the banks of the Olentangy River to cheer on the Buckeyes. But the stadium is, and always has been, more than just an arena to the university and its proud football program. From its inception, when many questioned the need for and appropriateness of such a large facility dedicated to football, Ohio Stadium remains the beating heart of Buckeye Nation. And to many near and far, it has become the definitive symbol of Buckeyes football and Ohio State University itself.

Ohio Stadium is called "the House that Harley Built" in honor of Ohio State's first superstar, Charles "Chic" Harley, who, with his teammates, brought unprecedented success and overflow crowds to old Ohio Field. With fans hanging from trees and standing atop nearby buildings to get a glimpse of Harley and his championship teams starting in 1916, it was evident a new stadium was needed. University administrators began to see that Ohio State football required a modern, much larger home.

The idea for a new football facility had been floated even before Harley's arrival on campus. Ohio State had joined the Western Conference in 1913 (the precursor to the Big Ten), and the program was obviously on the rise. And the location of Ohio Field along High Street left little room to expand. That property was considered too valuable for athletic uses.

Important proponents of the plan to build a new stadium included school president William Oxley Thompson, Professor Thomas French, known as the "Father of Ohio Stadium," and athletics director Lynn St. John.

Howard Dwight Smith, an Ohio State alumnus and faculty member in the school of architecture, came up with the unique horseshoe shape and upper deck—no other stadium at the time had one—to pack in as many fans as possible and keep them close to the action. Smith's design won him a gold medal from the American Institute of Architects for "excellence in public work," and the stadium was later listed on the National Register of Historic Places.

French was said to be quite upset when he found out the university would not contribute any funds to the project. But he and others turned the disappointment into a positive by declaring that the stadium belonged to all of Ohio and was a potential economic boon for the city and state. Thompson, too, had grand plans for the university, and he wanted a stadium that matched his vision.

A campaign was launched in the fall of 1920 to raise $1 million that drew on the vast (even then) alumni network and Columbus

Horseshoe Doesn't Bring Good Luck
Ohio State was justly proud and excited at the opening of Ohio Stadium in 1922, but the stadium did nothing for the fortunes of the football team. The Buckeyes were 3–4 that season, their first losing season in more than two decades, and they followed that up by going 3–4–1 and 2–3–3. Those years mark the only time in the history of Ohio State football that the Buckeyes have posted three consecutive losing seasons. In fact, since 1922–24, they haven't even had two losing seasons in a row, and it's only happened one other time, 1897–98.

business leaders such as Simon Lazarus and Samuel Summer. The success of the Buckeyes from 1916 to 1920 helped keep investors interested, and there were even creative initiatives that promised donors of certain monetary amounts access to game tickets (sound familiar?).

A little more than a year later the funding goal had been reached, although the athletic board also would have to borrow several hundred thousand dollars to cover all costs, which reached approximately $1.5 million. The design was finally approved by the board of trustees in May 1921, and ground was broken on August 3 of that year.

There were vocal critics in the Ohio State community, however, who argued that such a large structure would overshadow, literally and figuratively, the school's academic mission. And besides, such a huge venue would never be consistently filled, they said.

The latter concerns seemed justified when only approximately 25,000 fans saw the opening game on October 7, 1922 (only 14 months after ground was broken), against Ohio Wesleyan University, a 5–0 Ohio State win. An even smaller crowd of about 17,000 was on hand the following week for a win over Oberlin College. However, the dedication game a week later against the University of Michigan, a 19–0 Wolverines win, drew a crowd of 72,500, with thousands more turned away. More than eight decades later, millions of fans have seen games at the Horseshoe, and sellouts have become the norm.

The official capacity of Ohio Stadium when it opened was 66,000, so it has undergone various expansions and renovations over the years, the most significant from 1999 to 2001. That $194 million project included a new concrete shell that emulated but also encased Smith's original design and expanded capacity to more than 102,000.

It is maybe impossible to quantify what Ohio Stadium has meant to Ohio State football and its fans, but some images help: the incredible sea of scarlet that almost seems ready to swallow up the field at every game, the wide-eyed look of young children at their first game, band members with tears streaming down their faces on their final march into the stadium, and the current and former players who describe the incomparable feeling of emerging from the tunnel and running out onto the field before a game.

"Literally, my feet didn't touch the ground that first time in my freshman season," former Buckeyes wide receiver Cris Carter says. "When I got into pro football, that feeling made me love Ohio State even more. You wind up chasing that feeling again for the rest of your life."

3 The Michigan Rivalry

Archie Griffin is the only player in history to win college football's top prize, the Heisman Trophy, twice. It's not how he wants to be remembered.

"I never lost to Michigan," Griffin says, "and I take more pride in that than I do winning two Heisman Trophies."

Ohio State–Michigan. Just the mere mention evokes strong emotions from those who played in the games and from rabid fans in both states. It's a rivalry that has featured some of the greatest players and teams in the history of college football. The matchups pit two proud universities against one another in an annual, end-of-season contest, usually with a conference and sometimes a national title hanging in the balance. Heck, there's such a passion for supremacy that Ohio State and Michigan fans could have a spirited argument over who has the better band and stadium.

College football has gotten incredibly complex, with expanded schedules and conference championship games and so many bowl games, that some old-school rivalries like Oklahoma-Nebraska and Pitt–Penn State have been sacrificed. Not Ohio State–Michigan. Simply put, it's the rivalry of rivalries.

"Let me tell you, there is nothing—and I mean nothing!—as intense as Ohio State–Michigan," says former Ohio State coach Earle Bruce.

The feeling is mutual.

"Back in those days 10–1 is not good enough," longtime Michigan coach Bo Schembechler once said about a particularly intense stretch of games in the first half of the 1970s. "If that one is Ohio State, that's not good enough. We can't accept that."

ESPN.com rated Ohio State–Michigan the top rivalry in all of sports, with Muhammad Ali–Joe Frazier second, but it wasn't always so. The two teams first played in 1897, and in the first 15 games, Michigan won 13, with two ties. Ohio State finally broke through in 1919, when Chic Harley led the Buckeyes to a 13–3 win in Ann Arbor, Michigan, setting off a huge celebration in Columbus.

Animosity between the states actually predates that big win in 1919. Ohio and Michigan almost went to war during the 1830s in a border dispute over some land near where Toledo is located. The matter was resolved without any bloodshed when the federal government intervened, but some historians peg the later gridiron hostility as an extension of this early confrontation.

It is doubtful that many Ohio State and Michigan players know the facts of the so-called Toledo War, but it doesn't matter.

"No game meant more to me," former Ohio State linebacker Chris Spielman says. "I pride myself on being ready to play every game, but when it comes to playing Michigan, I was ready on Monday. When you grow up in Ohio, it is kind of in your blood."

No one did more to raise the level of rancor between the schools than Woody Hayes. He was obsessed with Michigan. Legendary is the story of the time Hayes ran out of gas on a recruiting trip to Michigan but pushed his car across the border rather than spend a dime in the state. At least that's how one version has it. In reality, Hayes just said that's what he'd do.

Either way, his hatred of Michigan was about as subtle as his "three yards and a cloud of dust" offense. He called Michigan "that state up north" rather than utter the word. In one of his most famous quotes, Hayes explained why he went for two points after a late score in the 1968 rout of Michigan, won by the Bucks 50–14: "Because I couldn't go for three!" he said.

That story, too, has been distorted over the years. First of all, the attempt failed, so the notion that he was trying to reach 50 to rub it in is false. Also, according to players who were there, it was not planned but had more to do with a foul-up in personnel that prevented the Bucks from kicking. But that's how deep Woody's animosity ran: even when the perceived slight was unintentional, he wanted it to seem deliberate.

Hayes went 16–11–1 against Michigan, and he and Schembechler engaged in a so-called 10-Year War from 1969 to 1978, during which time one of the teams either won or shared the Big Ten title every year. It started when Schembechler, in his first year in Ann Arbor, upset undefeated and top-rated Ohio State in 1969. It may have been Hayes' worst loss ever. Ohio State gained

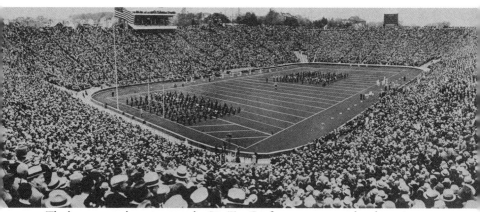

The largest crowd to ever attend a Big Ten Conference game watches the action in 1933 at Michigan Stadium in Ann Arbor, as Michigan plays Ohio State. The crush was so great that two spectators had fatal heart attacks during the game.

revenge the following year, with an emotional 20–9 win that capped off a perfect regular season for the Buckeyes. Then there was the three-year stretch from 1972 to 1974: OSU 14, UM 11; OSU 10, UM 10; OSU 12, UM 10. Michigan won every other game on its schedule during those three seasons.

"Coach [John] Cooper doesn't believe me, but when I was here we practiced for Michigan all the time," Griffin once said. "Our spring practice was all Michigan. Sometimes the first week of practice was all Michigan. It was just something you thought about all the time."

It's not clear Coach Cooper was listening. He compiled a sterling .715 winning percentage at Ohio State (1988–2000) but found himself out of a job because he couldn't beat Michigan (2–10–1).

When Jim Tressel was hired to replace Cooper, Tressel knew the score. In a statement that became both famous and prophetic, Tressel promised that fans would be "proud" of his team the next fall in Ann Arbor. Ohio State won that game and went 9–1 against the Wolverines in the Tressel era.

Michigan still leads the series, 58–45–6, mostly because of its early dominance; the Buckeyes have had the edge, 34–28–2, since 1950. The game has been the season finale since 1935.

Quarterback Rex Kern was 2–1 against Michigan from 1968 to 1970, and that one loss sticks with him. His reaction, decades later, shows what this rivalry means: "It was, without question, the worst loss I ever experienced. When did I get over it? I haven't."

4 Chic Harley

It is difficult some nine decades out to understand and appreciate the impact Charles "Chic" Harley had on Ohio State football. It is also hard to overstate it. Harley was a three-time All-American as a running back and also was an excellent passer, played defense, and punted and kicked. He led Ohio State to its first conference title in 1916, to a repeat one year later, and to an overall mark of 21–1–1 in his three seasons.

Just as important is what came with this on-field success: fans, lots of them. Buckeyes supporters packed into old Ohio Field to see Harley and his teammates play. University administrators, who had been considering a new stadium already, watched this phenomenon for a couple of years, and it persuaded them that the spectacle Ohio State football had become needed a much larger, more modern home. Designs were in the works for "the House that Harley Built."

So although Ohio State had been playing football for 25 years by the time Harley suited up, he is considered the most influential player in its early emergence. He is credited with not only creating the winning tradition that exists almost a century later, but

Harley Stays in Columbus

When Charles "Chic" Harley was a star football player at Columbus' East High School, the Tigers were racking up unbeaten seasons and playing before larger crowds than Ohio State was drawing to Ohio Field. But, prior to Harley's senior season, his parents decided they wanted to move to Chicago, where Chic was born. The family had moved to Columbus when he was 12 years old, and his parents wanted to return with Chic and his three brothers and three sisters.

But East High principal John Harlor and football captain John Vorys talked to the Harleys to try to convince them to let Chic stay for his final season at the school. Chic's parents relented, much to the relief of his teammates and East High fans. East would lose only once with Harley in uniform—his final game, against Columbus' North High School—and East's football field was later named for him.

Generations of Buckeye fans should be grateful for his parents' decision, too. It is doubtful that Harlor and Vorys knew the impact their lobbying would have on the future of Ohio State football. But if not for their efforts, maybe it would be the University of Illinois or Northwestern University that would now boast all those Big Ten titles and Heisman Trophy winners and a landmark of a football stadium that is recognized nationwide.

with being the motivating force behind the construction of Ohio Stadium, a college football shrine more than 85 years after it was built.

Harley, out of Columbus' East High School, was small, about 5'9" and weighed less than 160 pounds, but he was elusive and fast and a superior all-around athlete. While at Ohio State he also lettered in basketball, baseball, and track. In his initial year of play, Harley led Ohio State to a 7–0 record and the school's first conference title. The Buckeyes beat Oberlin College that year, 128–0, in the most lopsided score in Ohio State history.

"If you never saw him run with a football, we can't describe it to you," wrote Bob Hooey, longtime sports editor of the *Ohio State Journal*. "It was a kind of a cross between music and cannon fire, and it brought your heart up under your ears."

Teammate Gaylord "Pete" Stinchcomb used another metaphor for Harley in Wilbur Snypp's book, *The Buckeyes*. "Chic was like a cat," Stinchcomb said. "You know how hard it is to catch a cat? It usually takes more than one person. It always took more than one player to catch Harley."

In 1917 Ohio State was again unbeaten, the only blemish on the record a 0–0 tie with Auburn, and the Buckeyes again won the conference. World War I was raging at the time, and Harley and many of his teammates missed the 1918 season because of military service. Ohio State fell to 3–3. He returned the following year to lead the Bucks to six straight wins, including their first victory over Michigan in 16 tries, before a season-ending 9–7 loss to Illinois. It was the only game Harley lost as a collegian.

By the middle of his first season, Ohio State and Harley had started receiving national attention, and Ohio Field was seeing overflow crowds. More than 12,000 packed into the grandstands and surrounding areas for a big midseason game against the University of Wisconsin in 1916, roughly three times as many fans as had seen the season opener. By the end of the season the audience count was closer to 15,000, with fans climbing trees and crowding the windows on the top floors of buildings to catch a glimpse of this marvel in cleats. Such crowds became the norm during Harley's time on campus as Buckeyes football had become a happening in Columbus.

The *Ohio State Journal* described a game in 1917: "The stands resembled a living, throbbing, nervous mass which lost all consciousness when Ohio State gained some slight advantage."

Harley's play even inspired Columbus' most famous writer, James Thurber, to pen a poem about Ohio State football, the final two lines of which are: "But admit there was no splendor in all the bright array / Like the glory of the going when Chic Harley got away."

The Ohio State Board of Trustees came to the conclusion that Ohio Field could no longer contain the madness and decided, against the objections of many at the school, to build a new stadium for the Buckeyes. They started raising money from private sources, with the help of Harley, and in the fall of 1922 Ohio Stadium opened.

Harley was voted a first-team halfback on the Associated Press All-Star team for the first half of the 20th century, with Jim Thorpe, but ahead of Red Grange, who was voted to the second team. One voter explained his thinking this way: "Red Grange was a great runner, but that's all he was. Chic Harley was a great runner, a great passer, a great kicker, and a great defensive back. That's why he's on my first team."

Harley was a charter member of the College Football and Ohio State halls of fame, and his No. 47 was retired in 2004. He actually wore other numbers, too, but he was No. 47 for his final game, which, ironically, was the only game he lost in his career.

He passed away in 1974 at the age of 78, and the pallbearers at his funeral were starters on that year's Ohio State team, including junior running back Archie Griffin.

5 Archie Griffin

Archie Griffin made his first appearance in an Ohio State uniform late in the 1972 season opener, with the Buckeyes well ahead of Iowa. The very first play was a pitchout to him, and he violated the golden rule of all sports: keep your eye on the ball. "I was so shocked at the size of the hole and the quarterback pitched the ball to me, and I fumbled it," he says.

The Buckeyes recovered, and the play had no bearing on the outcome of the game. He was concerned it would, however, have great impact on his status with his coaches. "I didn't think I'd get another chance because I was a freshman and was working the scout squad," he says.

That routine continued the following week, and he was not among the top 60 or so players who stayed at a hotel the night before the North Carolina game. So, the next day he took his spot on the bench not expecting to see the field. But then, with North Carolina holding an early lead, a call came up: "Griffin!"

"I didn't think they could be yelling for me. I was really shocked," he says. "I went up there, and Woody [Hayes] grabbed me by the shoulder pads and said 'Get in there!'"

Griffin took a few steps onto the field before stopping. "In all the excitement I forgot to take my helmet with me," he says. "But I got myself together."

Boy did he ever. He would run for a then-school record 239 yards that day as Ohio State won, 29–14. Over the next four seasons he would break every significant school rushing record and many NCAA ones, too. The Buckeyes would go 40–5–1, win four Big Ten titles, and go to four Rose Bowls, with Griffin starting every one (another of his records). He would run for 5,589 yards, an NCAA record that has since been topped by several players. It is still the Ohio State record and more than 1,800 yards ahead of the next player (Eddie George). Griffin scored 26 touchdowns and averaged an astounding six yards per carry over his career. He still holds the NCAA record with 34 career 100-yard games and 31 straight regular-season games of 100 yards or more. He was a three-time All-American and is still the only player to win the Heisman Trophy twice, which he did in 1974–75.

The ever modest Griffin says he didn't see any of it coming. He was a star at Columbus' Eastmoor High School but didn't think Ohio State wanted him. "The first time [Hayes] talked to

Archie Griffin smiles as he poses with the 1975 Heisman Trophy in December 1975, in New York City. Griffin, who already won in 1974, is still the only player to ever win the prestigious award twice.

me he never mentioned one thing about football. He talked about getting an education and how important that was," says Griffin. He thought Hayes was trying to deliver a subtle message, one that he was hearing from others: "You're too small to play at Ohio State, so concentrate on the books." Griffin says: "I didn't think he was interested in me playing football."

Ohio State came through with a scholarship, and Griffin arrived on campus with his ego in check. "My first goal was to try to make the varsity team," he says.

That he did, and despite his small stature he was soon tearing up defenses. Griffin was maybe 5'9", 180 pounds or so, but he was

Mr. Buckeye

A Sports Illustrated story prior to his senior season said of Archie Griffin, only half in jest, "He's God's gift to impressionable youth, the most wholesome influence since Pat Boone."

Woody Hayes didn't dispute it. "He's also the most popular player we've ever had, by far. In fact, we value Archie's attitude more than his football ability," Hayes said. "Which is saying something, because he can do everything. He's a great blocker, a great faker, and a great broken-field runner, one of those rare backs who can run over you and around you."

Griffin didn't duplicate his college success at the pro level, but he played for the Cincinnati Bengals for seven seasons, rushed for 2,808 yards in his career, and also caught 192 passes for 1,607 yards. After retiring, he came home.

Griffin is currently the president of the Ohio State University Alumni Association and also served as assistant athletics director. He is in the Ohio State and College Football halls of fame, his No. 45 was the first number retired by the school, and he wears his Buckeyes love on his sleeve.

"I played in front of maybe 2,000 people in high school, and you'd hear stories about what it would be like to play in Ohio Stadium," he says. "To go out there in front of 86,000 people at the time was mind-boggling. You see all that scarlet and gray out there. It's just an awesome thing."

quick, elusive, tough, and had incredible balance. He would spin out of the grasp of defenders, and would-be tacklers would bounce off him. He gained 867 yards that first season, and as a sophomore he would break his own single-game rushing record by going for 246 yards against Iowa. He finished with 1,577 yards on the season. He ran for 1,695 yards in 1974, which remains the third highest single-season total in school history, and he earned 1,450 yards as a senior.

Griffin no doubt benefited from being on some dominant teams, and he is the first to admit it. "That success could not happen individually without being part of a great team," he once said. "I was fortunate to be in the right place at the right time with the right people."

It's that humility and Griffin's role as an ambassador for the school that has made him Mr. Buckeye to Ohio State fans. The two Heismans help, too. "He's a better young man than he is a football player, and he's the best football player I've ever seen," Hayes said about Griffin.

The Class of 1970

Woody Hayes was incensed by the Ohio State faculty council decision in 1961 to reject an invitation to that season's Rose Bowl, and he was convinced it had damaged his ability to recruit top players in ensuing years, particularly in his home base of Ohio. The ever-paranoid Hayes just knew that rival recruiters were using the decision to steal players from his back yard.

But for the man who constantly preached hard work and perseverance, this was just one more challenge. Hayes and his staff continued to recruit hard in Ohio but, for the first time, also made a concerted effort to reach beyond the borders of the state. In the freshman class of 1967, Ohio State landed Jack Tatum from New Jersey, Jan White from Pennsylvania, and Tim Anderson from West Virginia. The three would become All-Americans and would be joined in that year's class by future Buckeyes legends Rex Kern, Jim Stillwagon, and John Brockington. The class also included Mike Sensibaugh, Bruce Jankowski, Larry Zelina, Doug Adams, Mark Debevc, and Ron Maciejowski, who filled in at quarterback for the oft-injured Kern.

It would prove to be the greatest class in the history of Ohio State football and maybe of all college football. This class, 1971 academically but known as the class of '70 by football historians, put together the greatest three-year run in Ohio State history. They went 27–2, won two outright Big Ten titles and shared a third, and won one consensus national title and shared another. They won 18 straight games at one point, never lost at Ohio Stadium, and had seven first-team All-Americans.

And it couldn't have come at a more important time for Hayes and the program. Whether that 1961 decision really had the impact Hayes claimed, several uncharacteristically mediocre seasons had followed. By 1967 there were rumbles around town that maybe it was time that Hayes moved on.

"It was a turning point I think for Ohio State," says Stillwagon, an All-American middle guard. "That team, if you can say anything, it turned the tide for the tradition of Ohio State and started a dynasty. Instead of 'good-bye Woody' it was 'here he comes again.'"

Freshman weren't eligible then, and certainly there was not the publicity surrounding recruiting that there is today. But stories circulated among Buckeyes backers in 1967 that these youngsters were giving the regulars fits in practice, and there was much anticipation as the 1968 season dawned.

Fans would not be disappointed as these "Super Sophs" would lead Ohio State to a 10–0 record, a win over USC in the Rose Bowl, and a consensus national championship. They followed that in 1969 by ripping off eight straight wins, allowing no team to come closer than 27 points, before being upset 24–12 in the season finale by Michigan and Bo Schembechler. Hayes called his squad that year "probably the best team that ever played college football," and it was a crushing loss.

Hayes and his returning seniors were committed to making sure it didn't happen again. The 1970 team defeated number-four-ranked

Michigan at Ohio Stadium, 20–9, to go 9–0 in the regular season. The Buckeyes were then beaten by Stanford University and Heisman Trophy–winning quarterback Jim Plunkett in the Rose Bowl, 27–17, with Plunkett leading two fourth-quarter scoring drives for the come-from-behind win.

That 1970 team was still named the national champion by the National Football Foundation, finished at number two in the final United Press International poll, and was voted to the number-five spot by the Associated Press, the Buckeyes' lowest ranking in that three-year stretch. Six players were named All-Americans that season, and nine were All–Big Ten selections. The Rose Bowl loss was disappointing, but that class accomplished more than any before or since and was the backbone of three of the greatest teams in Ohio State history.

7 The Best Damn Band in the Land

There are 225 students who make it through auditions and can call themselves members of the Ohio State University Marching Band, but that doesn't mean they're marching into Ohio Stadium on Saturdays. Only 192 members get that honor, and they have to earn it each week. In a practice designed to keep the band sharp and ensure that the top 192 members are on the field, each of the 33 alternates challenges a regular band member every week in a 20–minute repeat of tryouts. No wonder they call themselves the Best Damn Band in the Land.

It takes a great deal of audacity to refer to yourself as such, and at Ohio State it's not done casually. The declaration is on T-shirts and all sorts of memorabilia around campus. The band's Web address is www.tbdbitl.osu.edu. And, when Ohio State won the national championship in 2002, Coach Jim Tressel crowed: "We've always had the best damn band in the land; now we've got the best damn team in the land!"

Outsiders, especially those from schools that take great pride in their own bands, could be forgiven for being suspect of the TBDBITL claim, if not downright annoyed. One Saturday in Ohio Stadium would cure that. When the pride of the Buckeyes makes its dramatic entrance from the ramp at the north end of the stadium—with more than 100,000 fans on their feet and clapping along as the drummers beat out their rapid cadence and the 192 members file in two by two before striking up the "Buckeye Battle Cry"—it's enough to give a Michigan fan goosebumps.

Fans also can hear the band at the Skull Session in . John Arena a couple of hours before every home game, and, of course, there's the halftime show that often, but not always, includes the famous Script Ohio. During the game, the band fires up fans with frequent versions of the two Ohio State fight songs (especially if the Bucks are racking up the points), as well as its signature tune, "Hang on Sloopy."

The band is so popular and elicits such strong emotions from fans that there's a feeling sometimes that Ohio State would just like a football team its band can be proud of. Tressel has made it a point to introduce his players to many of the traditions surrounding Buckeyes football, and he brings the team to the band's Skull Session before every home game. Woody Hayes also had deep respect for the band, sometimes bringing it to practice for an informal Script Ohio with players following along, says Archie Griffin. And if the coach felt his players weren't giving their best, he would often point to the band. "Woody used to tell us when he'd get mad at us, 'You're not working! You want to see somebody working? You go over and watch that band!'" Griffin says.

The band was formed in 1878 as a 12–piece military band, but by the end of the century it had expanded in size and begun

OSU snare drummers step high during the pre-game show before the 2002 Michigan– Ohio State game in Columbus.

marching at school athletic events. In 1973, women were first admitted and, in 1976 it was expanded to its current size of 225 members. It is all brass and percussion, which gives it its crisp, incomparable sound.

Just as the football team spends a sweaty summer in training for the season, so to does the band. There are preseason try-outs, and the lucky 192 and alternates who make the cut receive class credit. Members go through difficult summer sessions in preparation for opening day, and practices are held throughout the season.

If it sounds like a steep investment, arrive early to Ohio Stadium, where you'll literally see, feel, and hear the passion for the Best Damn Band in the Land.

8 The 2003 Fiesta Bowl: The Greatest Game

The University of Miami was just too good. Anybody outside Ohio who had followed college football in 2002 or over the preceding couple of seasons could see that the Fiesta Bowl national championship game was a mismatch. Ohio State may have run up a 13–0 record that season, but it had looked less than impressive in many of those wins, almost half of which came by one touchdown or less.

Miami? The defending national champions were riding a 34-game winning streak and had a roster loaded with talented players who looked ready for the NFL. The Hurricanes were 13-point favorites, and many so-called experts didn't think it'd be nearly that close.

"The week before the Fiesta Bowl, you would have thought Miami was out there just for the joy of it," said Ohio State linebacker Cie Grant. "It was a given that they would be crowned national champions again."

Then January 3, 2003, arrived. Sun Devil Stadium filled with rabid Buckeyes fans—a "sea of scarlet" as one player saw it, with Ohio State supporters making up 80 percent or more of the crowd, according to some estimates. The band, the pride of the Buckeyes, cranked up the noise, and a fast, swarming Ohio State defense attacked from the opening kick. This would be no cakewalk for the Hurricanes.

The Ohio State defense, led by Grant, middle linebacker Matt Wilhelm, safety Mike Doss, and a host of others, set the tone early and maintained its strength throughout, sacking Miami quarterback Ken Dorsey four times and forcing five turnovers. Meanwhile, unheralded Buckeyes quarterback Craig Krenzel was keeping Miami off balance by running the ball and would finish as the game's leading rusher with 81 yards.

Ohio State had built a 14–7 lead and was close to adding to it in the third quarter, when Krenzel threw a pass that was picked off by Miami's Sean Taylor in the end zone. Taylor ran it out and streaked up the sideline, but then came a play that has to be on the all-time Ohio State highlight reel. Freshman running back Maurice Clarett chased Taylor down and tackled him, while at the same time ripping the ball from Taylor's arms. The two players tumbled to the turf with Clarett in possession of the ball. Mike Nugent kicked a 44-yard field goal four plays later, and the Buckeyes led 17–7.

But that was just one of several key plays that night. The Hurricanes came back and tied the game with a field goal on the final play of regulation, then scored first in overtime to take a 24–17 lead. Ohio State got its turn with the ball, but moved backward instead of forward. In a season full of miracles, the Buckeyes would need a couple more. The Bucks faced a fourth-and-14 on the Miami 29-yard line when Krenzel hit Michael Jenkins on a 17-yard pass play.

Then, faced with another fourth down at the Miami 5, Krenzel threw an incomplete pass to Chris Gamble in the end zone. Miami players began to celebrate, pouring onto the field from the sideline, and fireworks erupted.

"I fell to my knees," said Ohio State running back Lydell Ross. "Then I heard the announcer say, 'Flag on the field.'"

Yes, a late flag came in penalizing Miami's Glenn Sharpe for interfering with Gamble. The Buckeyes were alive.

Miami fans and many commentators complained about the call, especially the fact that it came late. Field judge Terry Porter didn't help the situation by first signaling holding, then interference. Buckeye fans argued it was both, Miami fans, neither. In the end it was interference, and Ohio State had first and goal on the 2.

Krenzel plunged over on the third play, Nugent added the extra point, and the game was headed to a second overtime.

Ohio State got the ball first this time, and Clarett finished off the drive with a five-yard run and dive into the end zone to put the Bucks up 31–24. Miami, benefiting from a couple of Buckeyes penalties, then moved the ball to the 2-yard line, where it had first down. Three plays garnered just one yard, and Miami was facing a fourth-and-goal with the national championship on the line. Dorsey dropped back to pass, but Grant was on him immediately and the quarterback's hurried throw fell incomplete.

Ohio State was the consensus national champion for the first time in 34 years, and Buckeyes fans celebrated as if they'd been counting the days since the previous title. Ohio State was the only team in college football history to go 14–0, and coach Jim Tressel reached iconic status in just his second season.

"We've always had the best damn band in the land; now we've got the best damn team in the land!" the normally reserved Tressel shouted afterward.

That Fiesta Bowl is frequently referred to as the greatest college football game ever, but that's more because of the context and the ending than because of the play throughout. There were simply too many key penalties, too many turnovers (seven), and too little offense (the Bucks had fewer than 275 yards of total offense, and offensive MVP Krenzel completed seven of 21 passes with two interceptions). But with two undefeated teams battling for the national title and dramatic moment piled on top of dramatic moment, this certainly was one of the greatest games of all time.

Krenzel and his teammates reacted with the composure that had served them well throughout that roller-coaster ride of a season. "That's the way it's been all year," he said. "We make plays in the big games when we have to."

"That team fought from beginning to end," Tressel added,

although he could have been talking about the entire season. "And in the end, they had what it took to be champions."

9 The Fans

When undefeated and number-one-ranked Iowa came to Ohio Stadium on November 2, 1985, for a showdown with eighth-ranked Ohio State, the Hawkeyes brought with them a potent offense led by quarterback Chuck Long, a Heisman Trophy candidate, and running back Ronnie Harmon. But a fired-up Buckeyes defense limited Long to 169 yards passing and picked him off four times, two by linebacker Chris Spielman, and Ohio State pulled off a 22–13 win.

Although it was a rainy and dreary day, the Buckeyes also had a 12th man: a then–Ohio Stadium record crowd of 90,467 that was rockin' throughout the game. In fact, Iowa coach Hayden Fry complained after the game that his players couldn't hear Long call his plays, and Fry acknowledged that his star quarterback was rattled.

"It's a realistic fact that happened," Fry said. "He became mentally disturbed for the first time since he's been a starter for us because of his inability to communicate."

After experiencing Ohio Stadium that day, Fry suggested sound meters be used and teams penalized when the home crowd got too loud.

Spielman also said he'd never experienced a game like that. "It felt like the stadium was shaking that day, from the start of the game to the end of the game," he says. "It was a miserable, cold, rainy day, but it was the most alive that I've ever experienced in any football game that I've ever played in."

Fans are the lifeblood of any college football program, but Buckeyes fans come in for special mention. They sell out Ohio Stadium for every home date and have drawn more than 100,000 fans for every game there, dating back to September 2002. Ohio State led the nation in attendance 21 times from 1951 to 1973, including 14 consecutive years, from 1958 to 1971, and since 1949 attendance has never been lower than fourth nationally. More than 36 million fans have passed through the turnstiles at Ohio Stadium since it opened.

And Buckeyes fans may travel more than any fans in the nation—the 2003 Fiesta Bowl against the University of Miami looked like an Ohio State home game. Heck, the Buckeyes get more fans for their spring game than most schools do for their regular games.

The Iowa game in 1985 was far from the only time it seemed the fans had become a 12th man for the Bucks. Fans who were there swear the Horseshoe shook during Ohio State's dramatic come-from-behind win over LSU in 1988, and the win over Michigan in 2002 that sent Ohio State to the national title game set off a celebration like no other.

The south end of the 'Shoe is often the most raucous as that's where the band is situated and where the Block *O* student section is located. There are the frequent *O-H-I-O* chants that make their way around the stadium, and the band makes its dramatic entrance when it seems all 100,000-plus fans are on their feet and clapping along.

"I played in several big games during my pro career, including the Super Bowl," says former Buckeyes running back Eddie George. "Nothing compares to walking out in front of 100,000 fans in a sea of scarlet and gray. Playing in the Horseshoe in that atmosphere is the best experience any football player can imagine, even better than the Super Bowl. I miss those days."

Former linebacker Stan White echoes those feelings as he recalls intercepting a pass late in the 1970 win over Michigan. "I played for 21 years, including 13 in pro football, and you know what? On that interception it was the only time I ever heard the crowd late in the game," White says. "As I jumped to catch the ball, I was struck by the booming explosion of the crowd. The moment is seared in my memory."

10 Jim Tressel

When Ohio State was experiencing some instability and inconsistency in the middle of the last century, they handed the program over to a relatively unknown young coach from Miami of Ohio University. That move looked brilliant when Woody Hayes turned the Buckeyes into a national power over the next three decades and games at Ohio Stadium into the biggest happening in the state.

Half a century after that hire, Ohio State again turned to an up-and-coming coach from a smaller Ohio college, this time Youngstown State, entrusting him to restore the team to national prominence and honor the great traditions of Buckeye football. Again, they got it right. Although he left the school under a cloud, what Jim Tressel accomplished in his tenure as coach at Ohio State was truly exceptional. In 10 seasons, Tressel won one national championship and qualified for the title game two other times, won or shared seven Big Ten titles, had eight seasons of at least 10 wins, and compiled an overall record of 106–22. And Tressel's teams went 9–1 against Michigan.

For many Ohio State fans, that last stat is the most telling. John Cooper compiled an impressive record at Ohio State but was 2–10–1 against the rival Wolverines, and Ohio State fans and the administration were—to put it mildly—tired of the losing. And no one understood that more than Jim Tressel. Just hours after he was hired in January 2001, he appeared at an Ohio State basketball game to address fans and made his now-famous statement: "I can assure you that you'll be proud of our young people in the classroom, in the community, and especially in 310 days in Ann Arbor."

Not exactly a Namath-like guarantee but bold nonetheless. And when a mediocre Buckeye team went up to Michigan the next fall and sprung a 26–20 upset on the Wolverines, it was prophetic. Tressel, like Hayes before him, put tremendous emphasis on the rivalry, and it was never far from his thoughts. He was famous for keeping most everything close to his (sweater-) vest, from his own personality quirks, if there are any, to game plans and the general goings-on of his players and team. But one anecdote is revealing: no matter what time of year it was, Tressel could reportedly tell you the exact number of days until the Michigan game.

Tressel grew up in suburban Cleveland and attended Baldwin-Wallace College, where he played quarterback for his head coach father. He worked as an assistant at Ohio State for three seasons (1983–85) coaching the quarterbacks and receivers before accepting the head job at Youngstown State. He won four Division I-AA national championships there and more games than any team in the country in the 1990s at that level.

After a 7–5 record in 2001 in his first season at Ohio State, a lightly-regarded Buckeyes team rolled to a 14–0 record in 2002 and the school's first consensus national championship in 34 years. Tressel was a legend in just his second season on campus. He took Ohio State to the Bowl Championship Series title game twice more in the next five years, both losses, and there were the Big Ten titles, bowl wins, and all those victories over Michigan.

There were some bumps along the road, starting with those two BCS defeats. The 2006 team roared to a 12–0 record and was favored in the title game with Florida, but Tressel had no answers for the Gators in a stunning 41–14 loss. The following year, Ohio

State jumped out to a 10–0 lead over LSU but then surrendered 31 straight points on the way to a mistake-filled 38–24 loss. The critics were circling and included some Buckeye fans who questioned everything from the coaching staff's preparation and in-game strategic decisions to the team's discipline. Or maybe Ohio State was just overrated and benefited from a soft schedule and a weak Big Ten, they said.

Jim Tressel sings "Carmen Ohio" with his team after defeating Indiana 45–17 in their Big Ten opener in September 2002.

But Tressel had taken a team with many question marks and led it to an 11–2 record and another top five finish. At the close of the 2007 season Ohio State had won 30 of its previous 33 games, and Tressel held a 29–9 record against top 25 teams and was 8–4 versus the top 10. As *Columbus Dispatch* sports columnist Bob Hunter observed following the second BCS loss, Tressel and Ohio State were "having both too much success and not enough success at the same time."

Following the 2008 BCS loss in New Orleans, Tressel said he was deeply disappointed but proud that his team had always played hard. When asked the day before the game about his program's reputation in light of the previous year's failure, he said he wouldn't concern himself with what others thought. "What's most important is how you feel about yourself.... So the biggest goal we have is to play as good as we can possibly play...," he said. "If you worry about much more than that, then I think you have things out of perspective."

He also came in for criticism from fans of Ohio State opponents who swore that behind the sweater-vest and "aw-shucks" attitude was a calculating man whose only concern was winning football games. This theory gained strength after some of his players found trouble, including Maurice Clarett, the star freshman running back from his national championship team who never played again for Ohio State and eventually ended up in prison.

And then there was the way it ended. Tressel resigned in May 2011—he was likely to be fired—after becoming embroiled in a scandal that also led the school to vacate all the wins from the 2010 season, when the Buckeyes went 12–1 and won the Sugar Bowl. An investigation found that Tressel had learned about a scheme in which star quarterback Terrelle Pryor and some other players were exchanging Ohio State football memorabilia—including championship rings—for free tattoos, and had failed to notify school officials of the NCAA violations. Tressel maintained he didn't share the information he had with authorities because he feared for his players' safety and also didn't want to jeopardize an FBI investigation involving the owner of the tattoo parlor.

But the evidence against him was pretty damning, and the fact he continued to play Pryor and others throughout the 2010 season led to the decision to vacate those wins. So Tressel's official record as Buckeyes coach is actually 94–21.

The scandal certainly tarnished Tressel's reputation and legacy. But Heisman Trophy–winning quarterback Troy Smith is one who bought into Tressel heart and soul.

"It is more about my life than football," Smith says. "I got there as a boy and left there as a man. There are plenty of reasons, but the biggest reason? Coach Tressel."

Tressel says he learned the most important lesson on coaching from his father, who won a Division III national title and is in the College Football Hall of Fame, but who understood that winning wasn't paramount. "My dad was one of the great coaches because he cared about every player," Tressel has said. "He knew the most important thing the player was concerned with was 'Do you really care about me?'"

Also important to Buckeye fans was the fact Tressel completely embraced the history and traditions of Ohio State football, and added a few of his own along the way. Under Tressel, the team started visiting the band's Skull Session at St. John Arena before walking over to the stadium, and after the game, win or lose, gathered in front of the band and student section to sing the alma mater.

"I wake up every day and count my blessings that I am in a situation like this…," Tressel once said. "It is very hard for me to imagine being anywhere better than Ohio State."

11 Script Ohio and Dotting the *i*

The University of Tennessee has "Rocky Top," and Florida State has a flaming spear thrown into the turf. At the University of Southern California it's a white horse, and Notre Dame has those gold helmets and that fight song. The University of Georgia has its bulldog, Louisiana State University has its live tiger, and Clemson University a rock. But is there any tradition in all of college football to match Script Ohio by the Ohio State University Marching Band and the dotting of the *i* by a sousaphone player?

Buckeye fans would give that a thunderous "No!" and so would probably anybody else on hand to see them performed at Ohio Stadium. Script Ohio was first performed by the band on October 10, 1936, during a game against Pittsburgh, but no one at the time knew it was a formation that decades later would be considered one of the greatest traditions in all of college football.

"We knew that we did something different, not started a tradition," says John Brungart, a trumpet player who dotted the *i* that day and three more times that season. "I wasn't picked to dot the *i*, I was just in the right place at the right time."

More on that later. First, there is Script Ohio itself, which starts with the band in a three-deep block *O* formation and unwinds in single file as members play the French march "Le Regiment." The drum major leads the way, and the resulting word *Ohio* is complete when they escort a high-stepping sousaphone player (no, it's not a tuba) out to dot the *i*. The sousaphone player then executes a kick turn and bows deeply to each side of the stadium.

Brungart the trumpet player was the first to do it, but that changed the next fall when band director Eugene Weigel suddenly ordered a sousaphone player, Glen Johnson, out there one day during fall rehearsal. A new tradition was born. Another, the *i* dotter's bow, was a spur-of-the-moment movement by Johnson.

"It was an impulse reaction when drum major Myron McKelvey arrived three or four measures too soon at the top of the *i*," Johnson says. "So I did a big kick, a turn, and a deep bow to use up the music before "Buckeye Battle Cry." The crowd roared when this happened, and it became part of the show thereafter."

The honor of dotting the *i* goes to a fourth- or fifth-year sousaphone player. Only a few non-band members have been given this

Though he is hard to see, that's alum Jack Nicklaus waving to the crowd after "dotting the i" in the Ohio State marching band's signature maneuver, Script Ohio, at halftime of an October 2006 home game.

Script Ohio by Michigan?

It sounds like the height of sacrilege, but there's a story that the University of Michigan band actually first performed Script Ohio and thus provided the idea for the Ohio State band's most famous formation.

While the Ohio State University Marching Band's first Script Ohio came in 1936, the Michigan band did a version of it four years earlier at the Ohio State–Michigan game as a tribute to the Buckeyes. According to the Michigan band's website, "The University of Michigan Band created the first [their emphasis] 'script Ohio'—predating a similar formation now made famous by the OSU Band." The Michigan band then supposedly gave Ohio State band director Eugene Weigel the band's charts for the formation.

The Ohio State band first performed it at halftime of the Pittsburgh game on October 10, 1936. The Buckeyes' band website tells of the tradition but makes no mention of its origin. But a site about the Ohio State–Michigan rivalry that is sponsored by the libraries from both schools, as well as the Ohio State University Archives, acknowledges that Michigan may indeed have performed it first, but that Weigel and Ohio State added the important touches, such as the revolving block O at the beginning, the dotting of the "i" by the sousaphone player, and the traditional music, "Le Regiment." The site (http://library.osu.edu/sites/archives/OSUvsMichigan/osuvsmichigan.htm) concludes:

"So which marching band performed a script Ohio first? Michigan. Which marching band created Script Ohio? Ohio State."

privilege, including Woody Hayes, Bob Hope, Jack Nicklaus, and the seniors from the 2002 national championship team.

Sousaphone player Brian Thompson from Loveland, Ohio, dotted the *i* in 2004 and described the "awesomeness" of the experience. "I was really keyed up, and it was really exciting. It had been building up that entire year," Thompson says. "If you zoom in on my face, I'm screaming my head off at the top of the *i* because of the relief of all that tension and everything that built up."

He says it was "no walk in the park" to strut out to his position. "My biggest fear when I went out there was falling down. Doing the struts, that's not an easy thing to do with a 40-pound instrument on your back."

Thompson says that just as young boys throughout Ohio dream of playing for the Buckeyes one day, there are little boys and girls who dream of dotting the *i*.

"It's the sole reason why many people in the sousaphone rows are here in this band," he says.

12 The 1968 National Champions

In the fourth row, all the way on the end, is the future star middle guard. Directly to his left is the defensive back who would lead the team in interceptions. Three spots over is the quarterback who would become an All-American and the team's unquestioned leader. All the way at the top, in the last row, is the defensive back later known as one of the best ever.

When the team picture was taken on the Ohio Stadium turf prior to the 1968 season, no one knew that these underclassmen relegated to the back rows would be front and center in possibly the greatest season in Ohio State history. Jim Stillwagon, Mike Sensibaugh, Rex Kern, Jack Tatum, and other Super Sophs would lead Ohio State to a surprising 10–0 record and a national championship—the school's first in 14 years.

Freshman weren't eligible in those days, so there were many questions about how much success the team would have coming out of training camp in the fall of 1968. At least some of those questions were answered with a season-opening, 35–14 win over Southern Methodist University, during which Kern completed eight of 14 pass attempts for 227 yards. The defense picked off pass-happy SMU, then coached by Hayden Fry, five times. So, the Bucks had themselves a quarterback and a defense. Not a bad start.

A win over the University of Oregon followed and then another during a visit from number-one ranked Purdue University, which had blown out the Buckeyes the previous year, 41–6. That had been the worst loss in Woody Hayes' career at Ohio State, and he made sure his team was ready for the rematch. The Ohio State defense was maturing into the nation's best, and it completely shut down the Boilermakers. Hard-hitting defensive back Tatum helped smother Purdue's All-American running back Leroy Keyes, and Buckeye Ted Provost intercepted a Mike Phipps pass in the third quarter and returned it for a touchdown. Ohio State backup quarterback Bill Long, on the field for an injured Kern, scrambled for another score, and Ohio State won 13–0.

There were some close calls in the coming weeks—31–24 over the University of Illinois, 25–20 over Michigan State, and 33–27 over the University of Iowa—but Ohio State entered the season finale against Michigan on November 23 a perfect 8–0 and ranked second in the nation. A Big Ten title, a Rose Bowl berth, and a possible national title were all on the line as Ohio State took on the Wolverines, who were number four in the country.

They may as well have been number 400. Ohio State rolled to a 50–14 win that day before 85,371 fans, the largest crowd in Ohio Stadium history at the time. Fullback Jim Otis rushed for 143 yards and four touchdowns, and Kern added 96 yards on the ground and two scores. Michigan actually led 7–0 early and Ohio State was up just 21–14 at the half, but the Bucks rolled in the second half.

In the Rose Bowl, Ohio State took on number-two-ranked USC and its Heisman Trophy–winning tailback O.J. Simpson. Simpson scored on an 80-yard touchdown run as the Trojans built a 10–0 first-half lead. But the Buckeyes' sophomores had been playing like seasoned veterans all season, and this day would be no different.

They calmly climbed back into the game, tying the score at 10 by halftime. A field goal and two fourth-quarter touchdown passes by Kern to running backs Leo Hayden and Ray Gillian put the score at 27–10. USC scored a touchdown with less than a minute to play for the final score, 27–16.

Kern was named the Rose Bowl's Most Valuable Player after completing nine of 15 passes for 101 yards and the two touchdowns, and Ohio State had a perfect season and national championship.

Certainly the praise didn't belong only to the sophomores, though. Otis, the leading rusher, was a junior. The offensive line was anchored by seniors Dave Foley, Rufus Mayes, and John Muhlbach. Defensive standouts included senior linebacker Mark Stier, the team's Most Valuable Player, and junior back Provost. And the coaching staff not only had Hayes at its head, but Earle Bruce and a young Lou Holtz coaching the defensive backs.

"It just seemed like it was a cast of different characters," Stillwagon remembers. "We had a lot of different people who could do a lot different things."

But by season's end an amazing 13 sophomores were playing regularly, including starters Kern, Stillwagon, Sensibaugh, Tatum, running back John Brockington, end Jan White, and defensive back Tim Anderson. It was the Super Sophs who were the heart of this team and the reason the 1968 Buckeyes are remembered by many as the greatest Ohio State team ever.

13 Hopalong Cassady

As a young boy growing up in Columbus, Howard Cassady used to sneak into Ohio Stadium to see the Buckeyes play. He later would go on to star for Ohio State as a halfback and defensive back, winning the Heisman Trophy and helping lead them to a national championship.

It sounds like something out of a Hollywood script, too fanciful to be true. Cassady even had a catchy nickname, "Hopalong." But although he got that handle from a famous Hollywood cowboy of the day, Cassady's story was real.

A star at Columbus Central High School, the slightly built Cassady made an immediate impact upon his arrival at Ohio State. He came off the bench in his first game as a freshman in 1952—freshman were eligible then—and scored three touchdowns to help the Bucks bring down Indiana University, 33–13.

Hopalong, or Hop, as Columbus sportswriters started calling him, was a speedy and elusive running back and an excellent defensive back. In 1954 the junior would rush for 701 yards and lead the team in receiving with 13 catches. That year the Buckeyes went 10–0 and captured Woody Hayes' first national title. In a big game against number-two ranked Wisconsin at Ohio Stadium that season, with the Badgers up 7–3 and threatening late in the third quarter, Cassady picked off a pass and returned it 88 yards for a touchdown. In the Rose Bowl win over USC he led the Bucks with 92 yards rushing.

Cassady rushed for 958 yards and 15 touchdowns during his senior year as the Buckeyes won their second-straight Big Ten title. Cassady was named All-American for the second consecutive year, won the Heisman Trophy, and was named the Associated Press Male Athlete of the Year. He averaged nearly six yards per carry in his final three seasons and was Ohio State's career leader in rushing (2,466 yards), all-purpose yards (4,403), and scoring (37 touchdowns for 222 points) when he left.

He has been surpassed in all three categories but remains near the top of the list of greatest Buckeyes of all time. He is also a sentimental favorite of longtime Ohio State fans who remember his

It almost seemed like Howard "Hopalong" Cassady, shown here in a 1953 photo, was destined to star for the Buckeyes.

electrifying presence at Ohio Stadium. In 1955 the Horseshoe drew more than 80,000 fans for every home game for the first time. An incredible athlete, Cassady was also the starting shortstop on the Ohio State baseball team for three years.

Cassady earned his nickname for his unique running style but also as a nod to Hopalong Cassidy, the western star of the day

Hop's Stolen Heisman

The Heisman Trophy is the most cherished award in all of college football, but Howard "Hopalong" Cassady's ended up broken and in a trash bin. It may have been lost forever if not for a sharp-eyed garbage collector. Cassady was on the road when a thief broke into his Columbus, Ohio, home in the 1980s and made off with all sorts of hardware, including the Heisman Cassady won in 1955.

Apparently the thief valued the silver he snatched over the 25-pound bronze bust, so he dumped it in a trash bin. The garbage collector later spotted the hand and arm of the trophy—its signature stiff-arm pose—poking out of a bag in the bin. Some fingers had been broken off, but otherwise it was in good shape. He pulled it out and called the school, and the trophy was fixed and returned to Cassady.

The first Cassady heard about the break-in and the missing Heisman was when police called to tell him it had been recovered. It now resides with Cassady at his home in Florida.

played by William Boyd, who was also from Ohio. The two met before the 1955 Rose Bowl and posed for photos, with Cassady in his Buckeyes uniform and Boyd in his cowboy getup, pistols drawn.

Cassady went on to a productive career in the NFL, mostly with the Detroit Lions. He was primarily a defensive back but also rushed for more than 1,000 yards and 24 touchdowns rushing and receiving in his career. A good friend of New York Yankees owner George Steinbrenner, he worked for the Yankees organization for years as a coach and scout, including a stint as first-base coach for the Triple A Columbus Clippers.

"It's something how time passes," he told the *St. Petersburg Times* in a 2005 story about the 50th anniversary of his Heisman win. "You start out up there on the podium. And each year, people pass away, and you move a little closer to the end of the bench. I'm getting a little too close to the end of the bench now."

Troy Smith

Plenty of questions swirled around Troy Smith as he battled for—and eventually won—the starting quarterback position in his sophomore season in 2004. When Smith came out of Cleveland's Glenville High School it wasn't even certain he would play quarterback at Ohio State. Smith was an excellent athlete, and as a freshman, with Craig Krenzel entrenched at quarterback, was used occasionally as a kick returner. Some saw Smith as a possible multithreat player who would come in and throw defenses off because of his ability to run, catch, and throw the ball—kind of like what the Pittsburgh Steelers attempted with athletic quarterback Kordell Stewart, nicknamed 'Slash' for his many roles.

There was one person who didn't see things that way: Troy Smith. He wanted to be the starting quarterback, no slash needed, and set about making himself just that. He worked extremely hard, studied reels of film, and absorbed everything thrown his way. When starting quarterback Justin Zwick went down with an injury midway though the 2004 season, and with the Buckeyes struggling, Smith got his chance. He won four of the five games he started, including a 37–21 victory over Michigan.

The maturation process for Smith continued both on the field and off after he was suspended from the Buckeyes' bowl game that year and the 2005 season opener for accepting $500 from a booster. Zwick started those games as well as the second game of the 2005 season, a much-hyped contest with the University of Texas, although Smith did play in the game against the Longhorns.

After the loss to Texas, Smith was back as starter for good, and the Buckeyes were back as a national power. They would win 21 of their next 23 games, including a 34–20 Fiesta Bowl victory over

After being installed as the starter in 2005, Troy Smith led the Buckeyes to wins in 21 of their next 23 games.

Notre Dame after Smith's junior year. He was named that bowl's MVP. The Buckeyes were co–Big Ten champs with Penn State that season and won the title outright the following season as they rolled to a 12–0 regular-season record.

In 2006 Smith was named the sixth Ohio State player, and first true quarterback, to win the Heisman Trophy. Smith, with a powerful and accurate arm and athletic enough to avoid the rush and run when needed, put up some phenomenal numbers that year. He threw for 2,507 yards, completed 67 percent of his passes, and had 30 touchdowns with just five interceptions. One of his frequent targets was his high school teammate, wide receiver Ted Ginn Jr.

Just as important, Smith matured into a team leader who became extremely close with coach Jim Tressel and embodied Ohio State football in the century's first decade. Besides the Heisman and Big Ten titles, Smith beat Michigan three times as a starting quarterback, the only Ohio State player ever to accomplish that feat.

As the undefeated and favored Buckeyes headed into the national championship game against the University of Florida at the end of the 2006 season, all Smith needed was one more win to solidify his status as one of the greatest Buckeyes of all time. Anticipating a win and a national title, along with all his other accomplishments, it was easy to foresee his No. 10 going up on the Ohio Stadium facade with the other Ohio State legends.

Florida wasn't ready to follow that script, however, and the Gators trounced Ohio State, 41–14. Smith was far from the only culprit in the shocking rout, but he looked sluggish and confused and finished the game having completed just four of 14 passes for only 35 yards, with an interception and a fumble. He was also sacked five times and spent much of the night running from Florida defenders.

It was an unfortunate end to an incredible career, kind of like an award-winning Broadway star who puts on a dazzling performance and then trips and falls on his face in the climactic scene. No matter how good it was until then, it's hard to get over the ending. Ohio State has retired the numbers of the five other Buckeyes who won the Heisman, so some time and distance may provide the perspective that will get Smith the same honor.

Pro scouts said Smith's draft status plunged following the Florida game, and his height (approximately 6', a bit short for an NFL quarterback) didn't help. He was selected by Baltimore in the fifth round and began his rookie season in 2007 as the third-string quarterback, although he was elevated to starter for the final two games because of injuries. He started six games for the San Francisco 49ers in 2010, and joined the Montreal Alouettes in 2013, leading them to the Canadian Football League playoffs.

15 The 1942 National Champions

With Ohio and the nation distracted by war and with low expectations for a young, inexperienced Buckeyes team, just 22,555 fans showed up for the season opener at Ohio Stadium in the fall of 1942. But under the guidance of a 34-year-old coach named Paul Brown, Ohio State routed a service team from the Fort Knox army base that day, 59–0, and immediately gave notice that this would be a special season.

Brown was at Ohio State just three seasons, but it was long enough to foreshadow his becoming one of the most famous names in the history of American football. In 1942 Ohio State had lost its entire starting backfield from the year before, had only 11 lettermen return, and had only three seniors on the team. Brown wasn't one to dwell on the past, though, and he had the Bucks playing like a cohesive unit from the season's opening kick.

J.T. White

J.T. White had one of the most unique careers in the history of Ohio State and all of college football. White experienced the Ohio State–University of Michigan rivalry from both sides as a player and, incredibly, won national championships with both schools, too.

White was an end on Ohio State's 1942 national title team, the school's first, and helped the Bucks defeat Michigan, 21–7. He then joined the military and served during World War II. After the war ended, White enrolled at Michigan, where he was the starting center on the 1947 Wolverines team that beat Ohio State, 21–0, and captured the national championship.

The team was led by quarterback and captain George Lynn; halfbacks Paul Sarringhaus (an All-American), and Les Horvath, who would win the Heisman Trophy two years later; and fullback Gene Fekete, who led the Big Ten in rushing and scoring that season. On the line were Bill Willis, All-American guard Lin Houston, and eventual team MVP Chuck Csuri, a tackle and another All-American.

The Buckeyes rolled up 507 yards in total offense compared to Fort Knox's negative five yards in the opener and followed that with wins over good teams from Indiana University and the University of Southern California. By then Ohio Stadium was leading the nation in attendance, with crowds hovering around 50,000—excellent for the time, considering the war and gasoline shortages—and the Buckeyes had risen to number one in the Associated Press poll. Another couple of wins, over Purdue University and Northwestern University, and Ohio State took a train to Madison for a showdown with the 5–0–1 University of Wisconsin.

Many Buckeyes fans over the years believe it was what happened on the train, and not the field, that most led to Ohio State's only loss of the season. The drinking water on the train was bad, and several players got sick and were at less than full strength at kickoff. Wisconsin won that day, 17–7, in what became known at

Ohio State as the "bad-water game," and the Buckeyes dropped to number six in the nation.

Brown quickly got them back on track, though, as the Buckeyes trounced the University of Pittsburgh 59–19 the following week and then beat the University of Illinois 44–20 at Cleveland's Municipal Stadium (a "home" game for Illinois that was moved there because of poor attendance at games in Champaign). Ohio State then defeated Michigan 21–7 before a crowd of 71,896 at Ohio Stadium and a national radio audience. It meant the Big Ten title for the Bucks as Wisconsin had been upset by Iowa a couple of weeks prior.

Ohio State closed the season with a win over the Iowa Pre-Flight Seahawks, another of the service teams that were common at the time. The Seahawks were a strong team and had rolled to a 7–1 record, but the Buckeyes romped over them, 41–12. While this was happening, two teams ahead of the Buckeyes in the polls, Boston College and the Georgia Tech, were being upset. When the dust settled, Ohio State was the top team in the country according to Associated Press voters, the first national championship in school history.

"We have had many great Ohio State teams but in my humble opinion, none better than this outstanding team," Tippy Dye, an assistant coach in 1942, would say later. "There was great camaraderie, very much like family. They played together so well."

The Buckeyes had frequently been among the better teams nationally, but that first title elevated them to the elite of college football. As for Brown, he coached another year in Columbus but then was called into the military and became coach at the Great Lakes Naval Training Center. He of course would then move on to a Hall of Fame coaching career in the NFL, the 1942 season having been a small but significant chapter in his career.

Bill Willis

Bill Willis was not only one of the greatest linemen ever to put on an Ohio State uniform, but he also was a pioneer as one of the first African Americans to play for the Buckeyes and the first African-American All-American in school history. Willis earned that status in both his junior and senior years, 1943 and 1944, and as a sophomore he was a mainstay on Paul Brown's 1942 national championship team.

The 6'2", 215-pound Willis, a Columbus native who attended East High School, played on both the offensive and defensive lines and was known for his quickness and his aggressive, relentless play. Playing tackle, he cleared the way for Heisman Trophy–winner Les Horvath in 1944, when the Buckeyes went 9–0 and captured a Big Ten title. That was only the second unbeaten, untied team in Ohio State history. The school turned down a Rose Bowl invitation and finished second to Army in the final Associated Press poll.

Known as Deacon or Deke, Willis went on to an outstanding career with the Cleveland Browns and is credited with reintegrating professional football. Although African Americans had played professional football in the 1920s, they were then barred in 1933. But Willis and three other African Americans signed with teams in 1946, a year before Jackie Robinson integrated baseball. Paul Brown, who had coached Willis at Ohio State, brought him on at Cleveland, then a member of the All-American Football Conference.

"I never looked upon a player as black or white, just whether or not he could do the same job that I asked of every player," Brown later said.

Willis could do that and more. He played both ways professionally as well, but he made his name as a lightning-quick middle guard who many centers found almost unblockable. Coaches moved him off the line to take advantage of his speed to run down ball-carriers, and he is considered the first middle linebacker. He was named first team All-League seven times with the Browns, who joined the NFL in 1950, and was inducted into the Hall of Fame in 1977. Brown presented Willis into the Hall, and Willis, in his induction speech, gave special thanks to longtime Ohio State assistant Ernie Godfrey, who was Willis' line coach.

In an interview with the NFL Network in 2006 regarding the 60th anniversary of professional football's reintegration, Willis reflected on his legacy. He said that despite the racism he and other early African American players endured, he harbored no bitterness.

"There's too much good that's happening in today's world," he said, in reference to the numbers of black players, coaches, and executives in football. "You know how it was then, and you did the best you could in order to rectify the situation. Now that things have improved, you think…I had something to do with it."

Willis, who had been an excellent student while at Ohio State, returned to Columbus following his playing days and served as director of the Columbus Youth Commission of Ohio. He has the distinction of being in the Ohio High School, College Football, Pro Football, and Ohio State Varsity O halls of fame.

Ohio State retired Willis' No. 99 on November 3, 2007, and Willis attended the ceremony, sitting in a golf cart at midfield surrounded by family and waving to the crowd. He died less than four weeks later at the age of 86.

"I don't know that I've ever had a more popular football player nor a better one at his position," Brown once said of Willis.

Bill Willis, shown here in September 1944, was a two-time All-American at Ohio State and Hall of Famer with the Cleveland Browns who helped break down football's color barrier in the 1940s.

Vic Janowicz

Considering the dramatic changes football has undergone over the years and the size and speed of today's players, Buckeyes fans trying to choose the greatest athlete in the history of Ohio State football would probably limit the discussion to the last few decades. That would be short-sighted, however, because it would leave out Vic Janowicz.

Many football historians bestowed Janowicz with that "greatest athlete" title following his playing days, and a case could be made for it even today. While the game has indeed undergone amazing changes and the players are indisputably bigger and faster than ever, Janowicz did things on the field for Ohio State that no one has done before or since.

While his statistics are modest compared to the numbers put up today—802 career rushing yards with six touchdowns, 685 yards passing for 14 touchdowns, and nine receptions for 167 yards—they don't tell half the story. Janowicz was a dynamo who never left the field. He was a running back and quarterback who frequently worked out of the single-wing, was a ball-hawking safety on defense, and handled all of the kicking duties. This sequence of events was not unusual: Janowicz recovers the fumble... Janowicz throws for a touchdown... Janowicz kicks the extra point... Janowicz kicks off. Repeat.

After leaving Ohio State he played two years of professional baseball, although he hadn't picked up a ball and bat in six years. He returned to football in 1954 and immediately established himself as one of the best running backs in the NFL with the Washington Redskins. It seems there was little he couldn't do on a playing field.

"Vic excelled in every phase of the game," said his coach at Ohio State, Wes Fesler. "He not only was a great runner, passer, and blocker, he also did all of our kicking, including punting, field goals, quick kicks, kickoffs, and extra points. He was one of the finest, most versatile athletes I have ever seen."

Consider the Iowa game in 1950. Janowicz ran for one touchdown, threw for another, and returned a punt for a touchdown. He recovered two fumbles on defense, and on kick-offs he booted the ball out of the end zone three times in a row to deny Iowa any chance for a return. And all of that was in the game's first five minutes. Ohio State went on to win 83–21, and Janowicz was responsible for six touchdowns and kicked 10 extra points, which was a Big Ten record.

Ohio State closed out that season by hosting Michigan in the famous Snow Bowl game. Neither team could get any offense going, and Janowicz punted a school-record 21 times for 685 yards. He did account for Ohio State's only points of the day when he kicked a 38-yard field goal through driving snow that rendered the goal posts barely visible. The Ohio State athletics office called the kick "one of the greatest individual accomplishments in Ohio State sports history."

On the season, Janowicz ran for four touchdowns and threw for 12 more, was an All-American, and won the Heisman Trophy, although he was just a junior. The Buckeyes finished a modest 6–3.

Janowicz's NFL career was cut short when he was involved in a near-fatal automobile accident in 1956. The Elyria, Ohio, native was inducted into the Ohio State Varsity O Hall of Fame and the College Football Hall of Fame, and his jersey No. 31 was retired in 2000, four years after he passed away.

18 The 2002 National Champions

Ohio State was performing a high-wire act all season in 2002, but for sheer drama there was nothing like the November 9 game at Purdue University. It was a frustrating afternoon for the Buckeyes' offense, and with 1:36 to play in the game, they trailed the Boilermakers 6–3 and were staring at a fourth-and-one at the Purdue 37-yard line.

Rather than take a timeout to talk things over or quickly try to ram it over for a first down, Ohio State came to the line looking to pass. Quarterback Craig Krenzel faded back, looking for tight end Ben Hartsock underneath, but Hartsock was covered. With the pocket quickly collapsing around him, Krenzel stepped up and let fly with a pass to a streaking Michael Jenkins, who had a step on the defender but no more. As the ball floated in the air, here's what hung in the balance: Ohio State's perfect season and a shot at a Big Ten and national title. It's a wonder that ball was able to travel so far with all of that weighing it down.

But travel it did, coming down in Jenkins' arms as he crossed the goal line. "I think they thought maybe we'd run the ball since it was fourth-and-one, so they went straight man-to-man, with no deep safety," Krenzel said. "They brought the blitz off the edge, but the line did a great job of picking it up and Mike ran a great route. He got a step on his man, and I just got him the ball."

It was a perfect pass and a gutsy play that is one of the most significant in the history of Buckeyes football. "We called the play at the line of scrimmage," Krenzel said. "No one was thinking about our season hanging on one play."

Ohio State had two timeouts, but Jim Tressel kept them in his pocket. "I'm glad we didn't [call a timeout] because then maybe we start thinking, 'Okay, this is it,'" Hartsock said. "We just went out, called the play, and it worked. If you do take a timeout there, you might seize up."

The 10–6 win over Purdue lifted Ohio State to 11–0 and into first place in the Bowl Championship Series rankings. With two

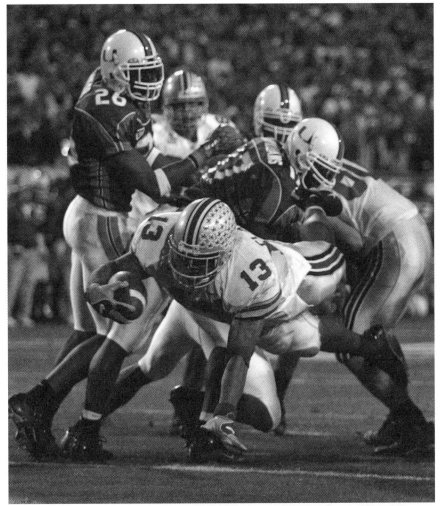

Maurice Clarett bursts through for a five-yard touchdown in the second overtime of the Fiesta Bowl against Miami in Tempe, Arizona, on January 3, 2003. His touchdown provided the Buckeyes with their first national championship since the 1968 season.

games remaining in the regular season—they played a record 13 regular-season games that year—the Bucks were perfectly aligned for a date in the national championship game.

Of course nothing came that easy in 2002. The week after the miracle in West Lafayette, Indiana, Ohio State traveled to the University of Illinois and needed overtime to defeat a mediocre Illini team, 23–16. It was the first overtime game in Ohio State history. That set up the traditional season finale with Michigan, which was ranked ninth in the nation and three times in the past 10 years had beaten Ohio State to spoil undefeated seasons. Again, the Buckeyes trailed late before coming back to win 14–9 before a delirious Ohio Stadium crowd. These Bucks never seized up, and they'd prove their superiority again in the Fiesta Bowl against favored Miami University. It took two overtimes, but Ohio State downed the Hurricanes 31–24 to capture its first national championship in more than 30 years.

The 14–0 Bucks had the most wins in school history, and seven of them came by seven points or fewer. It was a team that reflected its focused and calm-under-fire coach.

"Our guys wouldn't fold; they kept slugging away," Tressel said after the thriller at Purdue. "We always talk about if you keep banging away, something good is going to happen."

It was all good in the end for this Buckeyes team, which put together one of the most memorable seasons in Ohio State's long history. More than 50,000 fans came out on a bitterly cold day two weeks after the Fiesta Bowl for an emotional rally at Ohio Stadium honoring the team.

"This is the last page in our book," safety Donnie Nickey said that day. "It's over for us. We went out on the highest of highs."

19 Coach John Wilce

John Wilce was a man of many firsts at Ohio State. He coached Ohio State's first All-American (Boyd Cherry) and led the Buckeyes to their first conference win (58–0 over Northwestern University in 1913). He was the coach of the first unbeaten, untied team in school history in 1916, which also represented Ohio State's first conference title. He was on the sideline for Ohio State's first win over the University of Michigan in 1919 and the Buckeyes' first bowl appearance, a 28–0 loss to the University of California in the 1921 Rose Bowl. He led the team to its first win at Ohio Stadium, 5–0 over Ohio Wesleyan University, in the inaugural game there in 1922. And when he resigned, he was first in number of wins until surpassed by Woody Hayes decades later.

And all of this from a man who found the time to graduate from medical school while he led the Buckeyes. Wilce was a three-sport star at the University of Wisconsin, an all-conference fullback for the Badgers, and later an assistant coach there before getting the call from Ohio State. He took over as head coach in 1913 as the Buckeyes began play in the Western Conference, which would become the Big Ten.

After posting three winning seasons, the Buckeyes took off in 1916. Led by Wilce and All-American running back Chic Harley, Ohio State went 7–0 that season and 8–0–1 in 1917. In 1918 the team was depleted by the influenza epidemic and World War I—Harley and others missed the season because of military service—and fell to 3–3. The Buckeyes were back among the national elite the following season, winning their first six games before dropping the season finale to Illinois on a last-second field goal.

Ohio State then went 7–0 in 1920 to win the Western Conference and accepted an invitation to the Rose Bowl, where it was overwhelmed by California on New Year's Day. It was the school's first game against a team from west of the Mississippi River. It was also the Buckeyes' first bowl appearance and would be their only appearance for the next 29 years.

Wilce put together a string of mediocre seasons in the 1920s, with the exception of a 7–1 mark in 1926, and pressure started to build on him from fans, alumni, and so-called "downtown coaches." He announced his resignation prior to the 1928 campaign but stayed on to lead the team to a 5–2–1 record that year. He finished his career with a 78–33–9 record and is a member of the Ohio State Varsity O Hall of Fame and the College Football Hall of Fame.

While Harley gets most of the credit for turning Ohio State into a national power and creating unprecedented interest in the team, Wilce was the guiding force throughout these important years. He provided much-needed stability for a program that had had 11 different head coaches in its first 23 seasons, and he found as yet unseen success on the field.

In addition to his coaching firsts, Wilce was also on hand for the origin of some traditions that still exist. Wilce initiated the senior tackle ceremony and was on hand when the fight song was first performed on October 16, 1915, during a game against Illinois. It was dedicated to the coach.

Wilce, who received his medical degree from Ohio State in 1919, entered private practice following his resignation and remained at the school for the next three decades as an instructor at the college of medicine.

20 Lynn St. John: Longtime Athletics Director

Lynn W. St. John was a halfback on the Ohio State football team in 1900, before a death in the family forced him to withdraw from school. He wouldn't return for more than a decade. By then he had started studying medicine and was a coach and director of athletics at Ohio Wesleyan University.

St. John wanted to be a doctor, but he also had a strong interest in athletics. So when Ohio State came calling in the fall of 1912, the pull of sports was too hard to resist. He was hired by Ohio State to be the business manager of athletics, and he also worked as head coach of the basketball and baseball teams and an assistant football coach. When the director of athletics suddenly resigned a few months after St. John's arrival, he was elevated to that post. The formal title at the time was manager of competitive and recreative athletics.

The promotion came as a surprise to St. John, but he seemed to settle in nicely—he stayed there for the next 34 years. "Saint" would lead a program that would become one of the largest and most successful in the nation and was one of the driving forces behind the construction of Ohio Stadium, and he would be a skilled administrator who became a national leader in intercollegiate athletics.

One of St. John's first tasks was to hire a new head football coach for the 1913 season. His selection of John Wilce provided the program with stability and led to unprecedented success on the field, although it must be said that the position was offered to two others before Wilce was hired. Regardless, Saint eventually got it right.

Together Wilce and St. John, the latter as athletics director and still an assistant football coach, guided Ohio State into the Western Conference, which would later become the Big Ten, and to national prominence. Besides coaching the line on the football team, St. John was also head baseball coach for 16 years and head basketball coach for eight years.

In his administrative duties he oversaw the development of the Scarlet and Gray golf courses and the construction of a huge new headquarters for the athletics department, which opened in 1931. And he also played an integral role in development of plans for the new Ohio Stadium and in the subscription campaign that raised the private funds to pay for its construction.

That was no modest project. Many on campus questioned the need for such a large stadium and wondered if too great an emphasis was being placed on athletics. But St. John and other key administrators forged ahead, arguing that athletics were a key part of the educational experience and kept students and alumni invested in the school. The new stadium's backers argued that the stadium would put Ohio State and Columbus on the map. Almost nine decades later it appears they were right.

St. John retired in 1947. He died on September 30, 1950, at the age of 73 as he prepared to attend a football game at Ohio Stadium. St. John Arena, home to Buckeyes basketball for years and which today hosts the band's Skull Session and various other events, is named in his honor. St. John is in the Ohio State Varsity *O* Hall of Fame, where he is described as "the greatest single force in building the tradition of excellence in athletics at the Ohio State University."

Give a Shout

Ohio State head coach Jim Tressel made a significant effort to high-light the great traditions surrounding Buckeyes football upon his arrival on campus and also added a few of his own. One of these is the walk the team makes to Ohio Stadium the morning of games. It's a chance for the players to soak up some game-day atmosphere before getting serious and for fans to experience a more personal connection to the team.

For years the Buckeyes stayed at a downtown hotel and made their way to the stadium in buses, drawing cheers from fans as they moved through campus and got closer to the Horseshoe. Now they spend the night before games at the Blackwell Hotel on campus and walk to the stadium, stopping in at the Skull Session at St. John Arena along the way to hear the band. Tressel wanted his players to gain an appreciation of Buckeyes history and traditions and to experience the band because they're kind of busy once the game starts.

This walk also provides an opportunity for fans to get an up-close look at the team. After a brief stop at the Skull Session about two hours before kickoff, the players walk from the arena across Woody Hayes Drive to the stadium. Fans line the route and create a tunnel for the players to pass through as they shout words of encouragement and snap pictures. Many players have described this as their favorite game-day tradition.

As kickoff approaches, the band follows the same route to make its popular ramp entrance at Ohio Stadium's north end. Fans line the walkway for this as well to see and hear the Best Damn Band in the Land. Script Ohio may get most of the publicity, but there's no more hair-raising tradition than the ramp entrance with the drummers beating out a cadence and the band taking the field to the "Buckeye Battle Cry." Most fans are in their seats 10 to 15 minutes before kickoff in anticipation of this tradition, although they're quickly out of them and clapping along when they first hear those drums.

In the book *"Then Tress Said to Troy..."* Rex Kern recalled his first visit to Ohio Stadium after his playing days were over and how he was overcome with emotion at that moment. "I saw that band come down the ramp, march onto the field, and the drum major touching his head to the ground behind him (as) the stands were erupting," Kern said. "The next thing I know, tears are rolling down my face."

In another new tradition initiated by Tressel that gets many fans choked up, the entire team gathers in front of the band in the south stands at the end of every home game, win or lose, to sing the alma mater, the beautiful "Carmen Ohio." The team and fans, thousands of whom stick around to take part, raise their arms to sign the final "O-HI-O" before the players head to the locker room.

22 Don Sutherin's Punt Return

After a season-opening loss to Texas Christian University at Ohio Stadium, the 1957 Buckeyes traveled to Seattle and were locked in a 7–7 tie with the University of Washington in the second half. Then came what Woody Hayes would later describe as "the play that turned our '57 season around."

Ohio State had forced a punt by the Huskies that Buckeyes halfback Don Sutherin gathered in at his own 19-yard line. He proceeded to weave his way through the Washington coverage and returned the punt 81 yards for the go-ahead score. The Bucks never looked back, rolling to a 35–7 win that day. Eight more wins gave them a number-one ranking in the final United Press International poll. It was Woody's second mythical national championship in three years and the third overall for the school.

"We just seemed to jell from this point forward," Hayes said of Sutherin's return.

That they did, although even the most ardent Buckeye supporter probably didn't predict as much before the season. Ohio State had lost several key players from the previous year, and only 18 lettermen returned. The media picked the Bucks to finish fifth in the Big Ten.

But Ohio State had leading rusher Don Clark back, and several other players stepped up, including All-American guard Aurealius Thomas. There was a pair of sophomore linemen, Jim Houston and Jim Marshall, who would also go on to All-American honors in their careers. Behind a balanced rushing attack that used 17 different ball carriers in one game and a defense that gave up just six points in the fourth quarter all season, Ohio State started piling up the wins and climbing in the polls.

The biggest game of the year wasn't the traditional season finale against the University of Michigan but the November 16 contest with the number-five-ranked University of Iowa at Ohio Stadium. Iowa was favored by nearly a touchdown, and a then-record crowd of 82,935 that included Vice President Richard Nixon was on hand.

The Buckeyes trailed 13–10 midway through the fourth quarter when they got the ball back on their own 32–yard line. The strategy was simple: give the ball to Bob White. The sophomore fullback carried on seven of the next eight plays, concluding with a 5-yard touchdown run. He accounted for 66 of the drive's 68 yards. Bill Jobko intercepted an Iowa pass to end the Hawkeyes' final threat, and Ohio State had a 17–13 win.

"We knew what was happening, but we were just powerless to stop it," Iowa coach Forest Evashevski said of Ohio State's final drive. "It was fantastic."

Ohio State had to travel the following Saturday to Ann Arbor, Michigan, to take on 19th-ranked Michigan, and the Buckeyes fell behind 14–10 at the half before charging back to a 31–14 win. The Buckeyes were Big Ten champions and headed to Pasadena, California, to take on the underdog University of Oregon in the Rose Bowl.

The underdog Ducks were not about to lie down, though. The teams were tied 7–7 early in the fourth quarter when Sutherin kicked a 34-yard field goal that would provide the final margin in the 10–7 win. Oregon quarterback Jack Crabtree had kept the Buckeyes off balance all day and was named game MVP. But Ohio State got the win and, with a 9–1 record, was voted number one in the final United Press International poll. They finished second to Auburn University in the Associated Press poll. Interestingly, this team is the only one in Ohio State history to lose the opener and then win all of their remaining games.

The 1954 National Champions

As the 1953 season came to a close with a shutout loss to the University of Michigan and a second consecutive 6–3 record, many Buckeyes fans had seen enough of their new young coach, Woody Hayes. Ohio State was 16–9–2 in Hayes' first three seasons, and fans, as demanding and impatient as ever, were calling for change. At one game at Ohio Stadium that fall, fans began to chant, "Good-bye Woody! Good-bye Woody!"

It's all a little difficult to imagine now, but Hayes was definitely on the hot seat as the 1954 season opened. His Buckeyes were picked by pundits for fifth place in the Big Ten. But Ohio State opened with a 28–0 pounding of Indiana University and a 21–13 victory over California. After a blowout win at the University of Illinois, the Buckeyes returned to Ohio Stadium to face the Hawkeyes of the University of Iowa.

Ohio State led 20–14 late in the fourth quarter when the Hawkeyes drove inside the Buckeyes' 5-yard line, but Ohio State stuffed them to preserve the win. It wasn't the last time the Buckeyes would need a late-game, goal-line stand to save a game and their season.

After reeling off four more wins, Ohio State welcomed Michigan to Ohio Stadium on November 20, with the Big Ten title and a Rose Bowl berth—and for the Bucks a possible national title—on the line. Michigan, ranked 12th and with just one loss in conference, took the opening kick and marched 68 yards to jump ahead 7–0 before a packed Ohio Stadium and a national television audience.

The score remained unchanged until just before halftime, when little-used reserve Ohio State linebacker Jack Gibbs intercepted a pass and returned it to the Michigan 10. Buckeyes quarterback Dave Leggett then hit Fred Kriss with a touchdown pass, and the game was tied.

The turning point of the game came early in the fourth quarter after Michigan drove to the Ohio State goal line looking for the go-ahead score. With a first down at the Bucks' four, Michigan repeatedly tried to ram the ball into the end zone but was stifled by the Ohio State defense, led by linemen Jim Parker, Jim Reichenbach, and Frank Machinsky. The Wolverines turned the ball over on downs six inches from the goal line.

The Ohio State offense then took over and marched nearly 100 yards in the other direction, taking the lead on a Leggett-to–Dick Brubaker pass. Halfback Howard "Hopalong" Cassady scored another touchdown as the game neared an end, and Ohio State had a 21–7 win and a perfect regular season.

A possible dream match-up with 9–0 UCLA didn't happen because the Rose Bowl at the time didn't allow consecutive appearances by the same team, and UCLA had gone the year before. So, Ohio State faced an 8–3 University of Southern California team… and the rain. The teams played through a downpour that turned the field muddy, but Ohio State was able to build a 14–0 lead on a Leggett three-yard run and a 21-yard pass from Leggett to Bobby Watkins.

USC closed to within 14–7 before the half on an 86-yard punt return by Aramis Dandoy, but the Trojans would get no closer. Halfback Jerry Harkrader scored the clincher on an eight-yard run in the fourth quarter, and Ohio State had a 20–7 win. The Buckeyes finished at number one in the final Associated Press poll for Woody Hayes' first national title. (United Press International had ranked UCLA number one and the Bucks number two.)

It was sweet redemption for Hayes. He would later relate a story of sitting on his porch the summer before the 1954 season and overhearing a neighbor at a barbeque talking about Buckeyes football and saying, "This is the year we get Woody!"

Hayes said he used it as motivation. "I even got up an hour earlier each day so I could prepare all the more for our season," he said. The reward for Hayes and skeptical Buckeyes fans was a perfect season and a national title.

The 10-Year War

Bo Schembechler knew. Having spent six years on the staff at Ohio State under the tutelage of Woody Hayes, Schembechler understood as well as anyone what the game against the University of Michigan meant to Hayes, how a day didn't go by that the Ohio coach didn't think of the Wolverines and how to beat them. So when Schembechler took over as head coach at Michigan in the spring of 1969, after a successful stint at Miami of Ohio, right away he started talking about beating the Buckeyes.

The coming fall he would do just that, stunning undefeated and number-one ranked Ohio State in Ann Arbor, 24–12, earning a share of the Big Ten title and snapping the Buckeyes' 22-game winning streak. The victory launched the so-called 10-Year War, a decade of games between Hayes and Schembechler that took this already heated rivalry to a new level of intensity.

Hayes considered the 1969 team his best ever, and he was devastated by the loss. The coach reportedly went straight to his office upon the team's return to campus that Saturday night and began preparing for the next year's game. And in case his players weren't thinking about Michigan every day, Hayes had a large rug made that had the score from the game embroidered on it in big block letters and numbers. It was placed right outside the locker room so the players had to cross it every day.

To say passions ran strong before the 1970 game would be a massive understatement. Both teams came in undefeated, the game was on national television, and an Ohio Stadium record crowd of 87,331 was on hand. Ohio State was ranked fifth and Michigan fourth. Behind an opportunistic offense and a tough defense that limited the ground-oriented Wolverines to 37 yards rushing, Ohio State won 20–9.

Hayes called it the greatest game in Ohio State history, while the players involved said it was by far their most emotional moment as Buckeyes. And that was just game two of 10 between Hayes and Schembechler. Over the next four years, Michigan won one, Ohio State two, and they tied once. Each game was decided by a field goal or less.

Bo Schembechler laughs with Woody Hayes before a game. The Buckeyes or Wolverines were in the Rose Bowl each year the two legendary coaches dueled for a win in one of college football's greatest rivalries from 1969–78.

One of the teams finished first in the Big Ten every year over the course of the 10-Year War, 1969–78, and six times they shared the conference title. The Big Ten had become the "Big 2 and Little 8." Adding greatly to the magnitude of the games was the fact the Big Ten didn't allow its teams to play in any other bowl but the Rose Bowl until 1975. Hayes held an early edge in the series, 4–2–1, but then Schembechler won the final three, including the most lopsided game, 22–0, in 1976.

"It was a very personal rivalry. And for the first and only time, it was as much about the coaches as it was about the game," says Earle Bruce, an Ohio State assistant under Hayes in the late '60s and early '70s. "Bo and Woody were very close…but their friendship was put on hold when Bo took the Michigan job because it was the protégé against mentor."

There were some bitter moments along the way. In the 1971 game, Hayes, incensed after a Michigan interception that he felt should have been pass interference, stormed the field to berate the referees and ripped up some yard markers. Two years later Ohio State players infuriated Michigan fans in Ann Arbor when they took the field and tore down the "Go Blue" banner the Michigan team always runs under. That game ended in a 10–10 tie as Michigan missed two long field goals late in the game that could have won it.

That left the two teams tied for the conference crown, and Big Ten athletics directors gathered in Chicago the next day to decide who would go to the Rose Bowl. The vote went to Ohio State even though the Buckeyes had been there the year before, and Schembechler and everyone else affiliated with Wolverines football was infuriated again. Supposedly weighing on the decision was the fact that Michigan quarterback Dennis Franklin had broken his collarbone in the Ohio State game and would likely miss the Rose Bowl.

There was controversy the following year, too, when Ohio State won 12–10 after a last-second field goal by Michigan was just wide and went high over the left upright. Schembechler and Michigan fans saw it differently. "I would say without reservation, if that kick had been in Ann Arbor we win the game," Schembechler said years later. "But in Columbus we didn't win the game."

The two again tied for the league title and again the athletics directors voted Ohio State into the Rose Bowl, although it was less controversial this time around, as the Buckeyes had won the head-to-head match-up. In three years (1972–74) Michigan had compiled a record of 30–2–1, beating everybody on the schedule except Ohio State, and the Wolverines never went to a bowl.

Hayes' Paranoia

Woody Hayes was notoriously paranoid when it came to the University of Michigan rivalry and Wolverines coach Bo Schembechler, worrying about spies who might steal his game plan or little tricks that could affect his players. He used to whisper when talking strategy inside the visitor's locker room at Michigan Stadium.

Archie Griffin recalls one such story from the morning of the Michigan game his senior year, which was played in Ann Arbor. The team was having breakfast that day at the hotel, and several attractive young women were serving them food.

"I'll never forget, Woody went into the kitchen and got the guys working back there to come out and serve us," Griffin says. "He said Bo planted those girls there to distract us. It really broke everybody up. He had a little smile on his face when he did it."

The focused Buckeyes then went on to beat Michigan 21–14 that afternoon.

The heartbreak continued the next fall for Michigan. The Wolverines thoroughly outplayed undefeated and top-ranked Ohio State in Ann Arbor, holding Archie Griffin to just 46 yards rushing to snap his streak of 100-yard games at 31. Michigan led 14–7 until two late scores by Ohio State, the second of which was set up by a Ray Griffin interception that was returned to the Michigan 3 and led to a 21–14 Buckeyes win.

Hayes had an overall mark of 16–11–1 against Michigan, but his toughest stretch was those 10 years against Schembechler. "We respected one another so damn much," Hayes once said. "Now that doesn't mean I didn't get so mad at him that I wanted to kick him in the, uh, groin."

At a banquet years after the 1969 upset, Hayes shared a dais with Schembechler. Hayes made reference to that team and then glanced down at Schembechler. "Damn you, Bo!" Hayes said. "You will never win a bigger game than that."

Urban Meyer

Following the painful departure of coach Jim Tressel in the spring of 2011, Ohio State limped through a 6–7 season that fall under interim coach Luke Fickell, closing with four straight losses. When it was over, administrators wasted little time and energy in choosing a permanent successor to Tressel.

On November 28, 2011, Urban Meyer was named the new coach of the Buckeyes after signing a hefty six-year contract. School officials knew exactly who they wanted to lead the Bucks into this next phase of the program's history, and they got their man.

"In Urban Meyer we have found an exemplary person and remarkable coach to lead the university's football program into the future," then–Ohio State president Dr. Gordon Gee said at the time. "As an alumnus, he understands and believes in the core academic mission of the University. As an Ohioan, he shares our common values and sense of purpose."

Gee could be known to lay it on kind of thick, but there was no denying this: Meyer sure as heck knows how to win. The Buckeyes went 12–0 in his first season but were on probation from the tattoos-for-memorabilia scheme, so were shut out of the bowls and denied a national title shot. Amazingly, they went 12–0 in 2013, too—24 straight wins to start the Meyer era! Even Gee, who was gone by the 2013 season after sticking his foot in his mouth one too many times, couldn't have seen that coming.

Then came a couple bumps in the road (Buckeye fans might have a more profane description for what happened next). The Bucks came out flat in the Big Ten Championship game against a tough Michigan State team, falling behind 17–0. They did storm back to take the lead but eventually fell 34–24. The loss ended Meyer's winning streak and killed the dream of another national title, but an Orange Bowl date with Clemson was a nice consolation prize. The Bucks, however, again didn't look particularly sharp, and ended up losing 40–35.

A record of 24–2 after two seasons is excellent by anyone's standards, but the two straight losses created some grumbling around Columbus. Had the Buckeyes been exposed as frauds after finally facing some tough teams? And wasn't Meyer hired for just these types of games? Was he relying too much on quarterback Braxton Miller? And what's up with the defense?

"The honeymoon is over," shouted a Yahoo! Sports column shortly after the Orange Bowl loss.

"What honeymoon?" Meyer might reply. This is a man who, though fit and seemingly in the prime of life, left Florida after suffering apparently stress-induced health problems. A man who walked into his very first meeting with Ohio State players following his hiring and snapped at players to sit up straight in their chairs. If Meyer was on a honeymoon he didn't act like it.

"The stakes are extremely high," he told John U. Bacon, author of *Fourth and Long: The Fight for the Soul of College Football.* "It's Ohio State. Do you build up to next year? No, we simply try to win every game we play, every year."

That's pretty much what he's done at every stop along the way, from Bowling Green to Utah, Florida, and, after a one-year hiatus to get his health right and spend more time with his family, Ohio State. He took Utah to national prominence and won two national titles at Florida, including a thrashing of Ohio State and Tressel in one title game.

Like Tressel, Meyer understands the traditions of Buckeye football. He's from Ashtabula, Ohio, and attended the University of Cincinnati, where he played football. He got a graduate degree from Ohio State and was an assistant for the Bucks for a couple of seasons in the 1980s. He gets the winning tradition thing, too.

"There will never be a time at Ohio State that we're worried about next year," he told Bacon. "We always want to win now."

Urban Meyer was hired in 2011 to become the 24th head coach in Ohio State football history.

Chris Spielman

Chris Spielman was slowed by an ankle injury in his first training camp at Ohio State and so didn't get the start when the Buckeyes opened the 1984 season against Oregon State University at Ohio Stadium. The hyper-intense Spielman felt he was ready to play, and although just a freshman, he made his feelings known to coach Earle Bruce and anybody else within earshot. He was like a "caged animal walking back and forth" on the sideline, former teammate Jim Lachey says.

"Finally, Coach gave up and put him in," says Jim Karsatos, who was a quarterback on that team. "And he never came out."

Spielman tallied 10 tackles in that game and would go on to a career total of 546, third on the all-time list. He also had 283 solo tackles, which is still a school record. He was a three-time All–Big Ten player, a two-time All-American, and won the Rotary Lombardi Award his senior season in 1987.

Spielman wasn't exceptionally big or fast, but he played with a ferocity that was unmatched. "I always kind of played with a chip on my shoulder," he once said. More like a block of granite, especially when the opponent was Michigan. Spielman understood and appreciated the rivalry as much as anyone. Against Michigan his junior year he had 29 tackles, tied for the most ever in a single game. The following season, in the final game of his career, he had 16 tackles, including 14 solos, in a 23–20 upset of the Wolverines that was also coach Earle Bruce's last game at Ohio State.

Spielman points to the win over number-one-ranked Iowa in his sophomore season and the 1987 Cotton Bowl following his junior year as the top games in his career. "[Texas A&M

University] had three or four number-one draft picks on that team, and everybody in Texas thought they were going to blow us out," Spielman says. "I remember sitting at the press conference before the Cotton Bowl and asking, 'What are we? I mean, hey, we're Ohio State.'"

Aggies fans should have known right then their team was in trouble. The Buckeyes beat Texas A&M 28–12, and Spielman was named defensive MVP.

Spielman was known more for his work ethic and intensity than for his athleticism, but that wasn't entirely fair because he was always around the ball and making plays. He picked off two passes in that Cotton Bowl win, returning one for a touchdown, and he finished his career with 11 interceptions.

Spielman was actually a legend even before he got to Columbus. He grew up in football-mad northeast Ohio, was a star at the legendary Massillon Washington High School, and was featured on a Wheaties box as a high school senior. His dad was a high school football coach, and all Spielman ever wanted to do was play football—and play linebacker.

"Chris was born a linebacker. I think he popped out and tackled the doctor," Karsatos says. "[He was] just relentless."

Spielman played in the National Football League for 11 years for Detroit, Buffalo, and Cleveland, and he made the Pro Bowl four times. He is now a college football analyst and lives in Columbus, where he also can be heard on sports talk radio. He has also dedicated considerable time to the Stefanie Spielman Fund for Breast Cancer Research after his wife died from the disease in 2009.

27 Braxton Miller

Ohio State has had some excellent running quarterbacks, including Cornelius Greene and Rod Gerald, and more classic drop-back passers, such as Bobby Hoying and Joe Germaine. And they've had several who did both, going back to Rex Kern and including Art Schlichter, Troy Smith, and Terrelle Pryor. But none did it as well as Braxton Miller.

The 2000s saw the rise of the hyper-athletic quarterback who could run and pass equally well, and Ohio State got one of college football's best in Miller. The 6'2", 215-pounder out of Huber Heights, Ohio, was elusive and fast, leading the team in rushing his freshman and sophomore seasons; he rushed for more than 1,000 yards as a junior despite missing three games due to an injured knee but trailed running back Carlos Hyde. At the same time he was maturing as a passer, his accuracy and confidence improving by the game as he threw for more than 2,000 yards as both a sophomore and junior.

Heading into his senior year, Miller was in the top 10 all time in both rushing and passing yards at Ohio State—no one else is even close to pulling this double—and several significant career records were in reach. When he announced following his junior year that he would be returning for one more season rather than take an early shot at the NFL, a collective sigh of relief could be heard across Buckeye Nation.

"I want to improve as a quarterback in all aspects of my game," Miller said in a statement at the time. Defensive coordinators all over the Big Ten probably shuddered at the thought. He also said he wanted to fulfill his goal to graduate from Ohio State and lead the team to a Big Ten title, which had so far eluded him. He led the team to a 12–0 mark as a sophomore but the Bucks were on probation, and another 12–0 season as a junior ended with a loss to Michigan State in the Big Ten Championship Game (and to Clemson in the Orange Bowl).

Miller was named Big Ten MVP after both his sophomore and junior seasons, and finished in the top 10 in the Heisman vote each season—fifth as a sophomore and ninth as a junior, when he missed those three games. School records within his reach include all-time passing yards and passing touchdowns, and total offense.

There was a learning curve along the way, though, and occasional criticism, which isn't surprising considering the high-profile position. Miller could look unpolished as a freshman and it took some time to establish himself, unlike red-shirt freshman quarterbacks Johnny Manziel (Texas A&M) and Jameis Winston (Florida State), who won Heismans in 2012 and 2013, respectively.

When Miller went down with an injury his junior year and backup Kenny Guiton played wonderfully and kept winning, there was talk around town that maybe the team would be better off with the senior Guiton at the helm. Coach Urban Meyer would have none of it, though, and Miller returned as starter when healthy and continued on his record-setting pace.

Miller compares favorably to Troy Smith, the Heisman-winning quarterback who was pegged as an "athlete" but transformed himself into a true quarterback who was among the best passers in the nation. Miller attributes that to hard work and the right attitude.

"Sometimes you just have to remember it is just football, it's supposed to be fun," he once said. "My dad taught me when things go wrong, because at some point they will, you just have to smile and be calm because it could be worse. When you have achievements, especially when you do good things on the field, you have to act like you've been there before."

28 Tailgating at the 'Shoe

Ohio State football fans are as passionate and knowledgeable about their team as college football fans anywhere. They pack Ohio Stadium on fall Saturdays, and it's not a casual pursuit. Glance around the Horseshoe, and you'll see 100,000-plus people, most decked out in some combination of scarlet and gray, riveted to the action on the field.

So while the outcome of the game is the focal point of the day, to many fans there is a close second in importance: the tailgate. Thousands of fans arrive hours before the game, cramming into every parking spot around Ohio Stadium, as well as the many lots spread throughout campus and its vicinity, to set up for their own pregame fun. A typical spread might have burgers and chicken on the grill, with chips and dip, cheese and crackers, and other snacks spread out on a card table topped with a scarlet table cloth. Coolers are stocked with a variety of beverages, from soda to beer and wine, and the ingredients for Bloody Marys and other mixed drinks are often on hand. The Ohio State marching band blares from the cars' sound systems or a portable CD player, and an Ohio State flag flies above. And fans can be found playing games of cornhole with Buckeyes-themed boards or tossing footballs. It's a scene every Buckeyes football fan, and even fans of other teams, should experience.

The lots directly adjacent to the stadium are always full of tailgaters, and fans tailgate in the nearby parking garages, although grilling isn't permitted there, even on the roof. The bus and RV lots over near the Jerome Schottenstein Center are festive with elaborate spreads, and many of the vehicles are decorated in Buckeyes scarlet and gray.

The Ohio State website emphasizes that city ordinances prohibiting open containers of alcohol apply on campus and around the stadium, and Columbus and campus police have been known to give tickets and make fans pour out their drinks. "We will not overlook behavior on game days that would not be tolerated at

Eat a Buckeye

Every child who grows up in Ohio is taught that the buckeye is poisonous and should not be eaten, but that doesn't stop them from clamoring for them and consuming as many as possible when the buckeyes appear at tailgates or football parties. We're talking, of course, about the chocolate-and-peanut-butter confection, not the nut, which is formally described as "mildly toxic."

The buckeye treat is a peanut butter ball dipped in chocolate that resembles the nut but probably tastes a lot better. You can buy boxes of them at the store, but not surprisingly, the homemade version is usually much better. No Ohio State tailgate is complete without them. Here's a recipe:

Buckeyes
1 lb. creamy peanut butter
1 cup butter
1½ lbs. confectioners' sugar
1 pkg. (12 oz.) chocolate chips
2 squares (2 oz.) semisweet chocolate
¼ bar paraffin

Mix the peanut butter, butter, and sugar until a smooth texture develops. Roll the dough into small balls the size of buckeyes, and place them in the refrigerator. Slowly melt the chocolate chips, semisweet chocolate, and paraffin together in the top of a double boiler. Using a toothpick, dip the chilled balls of peanut butter into the chocolate until they are about two-thirds covered (until they resemble buckeyes). Smooth over the toothpick holes, and let the chocolate cool and harden on wax paper. Makes about 65 buckeyes.

Note: the paraffin helps the chocolate keep its shape but is optional. There are variations on this recipe that call for nuts or rice krispies or chunky peanut butter rather than smooth peanut butter.

other times," the school says. "The laws are the same on football Saturdays as any other day of the year." But many fans simply pour their drinks into plastic cups, and the police mostly look the other way.

Although the origins of tailgating aren't precise, there were reports of spectators at the very first football game in 1869 between Princeton University and Rutgers University who traveled to the game in their carriages and brought along food to eat while taking in the contest. Other eastern schools such as Yale University lay claim to establishing the tradition. Now it seems schools in the South believe they've perfected the practice, and everything else pales in comparison. They do have the weather on their side, but those cold, drab, late fall Midwest afternoons only prove the extreme devotion of the Buckeyes tailgater.

Andrew Smullen and a few friends host a huge tailgate party every game day in a private lot right up the alley from the Varsity Club. Their party has gotten so big that they have their own sponsor, City Barbeque, which provides the food. "It's about tradition. We have the same morning routine," he says. "We call it the early bird crew: who sets up the TV and the stereo and the tent, who goes and gets the beer and ice and the food.... Typically we go over to the Varsity Club and do a morning shot."

Before the University of Illinois game in 2007, Smullen took a different route to the tailgate and stopped at a different place to buy beer. "The guys in the car were like, 'You can't be doing this,'" Smullen says. "Ohio State lost that day, and people were mad at me."

The website ESPN.com did a campus tailgate tour a couple of years back, with a series of stories from around the country. "I've been to a lot of football games. I've seen a lot of devotional behavior, a lot of fans swept up in the pageantry and the promise of rooting for the home team. But I've never seen anything quite like home-game Saturday in Columbus, Ohio," columnist Eric Neel wrote. "The tailgating goes on for miles…the cars, tent-tops, and smoking grills seem to stretch on forever. It looks like the pilgrims come to Mecca; it looks like mass at St. Peter's."

No, it's just another Saturday at the 'Shoe.

Jim Parker

Although Ohio State integrated its teams decades before many schools in the South did, the campus was not exactly welcoming to African Americans when Jim Parker arrived there in the late summer of 1953. There were only a handful of African Americans on the football team at that time, and few black students lived on campus. So, faced with what he may have seen as an inhospitable environment, Parker did what would be unthinkable for most players: he moved in with his coach.

Woody Hayes probably had his own motivations (it's doubtful he wanted to lose such a prized recruit), and the arrangement worked out for player, coach, and team. Parker would go on to star for the 1954 national champions and earn praise from Hayes as "the greatest offensive linemen I ever coached…. He was everything an offensive lineman should be."

Parker grew up in Georgia and worked on the family farm picking peaches and cotton. According to his obituary in the *Baltimore Sun*, he started playing football when he was 13 years old but weighed just 105 pounds. "I got the living hell beat out of me the first day of practice," he said. "So my daddy bought a case of oatmeal and a case of grits and had me eat it three times a day."

Four years and approximately 100 pounds later he was at Ohio State after having finished out his high school years in Toledo.

Woody Hayes chats with some of the players he hopes will lead the Buckeyes to another Big Ten Conference championship in September 1956. From left to right: Hubert Bobo; co-captain Bill Michael; Hayes; co-captain and quarterback Frank Ellwood; and guard Jim Parker.

He told an interviewer a few years before his death that his goals weren't modest when he arrived on campus. "When I'm gone, I'd like to be known as the best offensive lineman that ever lived," Parker said. "I set that goal as a college freshman, but I didn't get bodacious about it until later."

Parker played both ways for the Buckeyes but made his name as an offensive guard, where he was a two-time All-American. He helped lead the Buckeyes to Big Ten titles in 1954 and '55, and a national title in '54. He also opened holes for Howard "Hopalong" Cassady as Cassady won the Heisman Trophy in 1955. Parker won the Outland Trophy as the nation's best lineman as a senior and was the team MVP that year.

Parker went on to a Pro Football Hall of Fame career with the Baltimore Colts, protecting Johnny Unitas and opening holes for Lenny Moore. Parker and Hayes later came full circle when Hayes presented Parker at his induction into the Pro Football Hall of Fame. "Physically, Jim was in a class by himself," Hayes said. "Attitude-wise, he was even greater."

Parker also was inducted into the College Football Hall of Fame and was a charter member of the Ohio State Varsity *O* Hall of Fame. He passed away in 2005 at the age of 71.

30 John Hicks and Orlando Pace

Ohio State has a justly deserved reputation for producing outstanding running backs, linebackers, and even defensive backs over the years. But one pair of Buckeyes offensive tackles, the guys who mostly toil in anonymity doing the important dirty work that moves the offense, became superstars in their own right and earned unprecedented accolades for their position.

John Hicks in the early 1970s and Orlando Pace in the mid-'90s turned offensive tackle into a glamour position. Both were exceedingly talented athletes and dominant at their positions, so much so that they received national attention usually reserved for the so-called "skill positions." Hicks finished second in the Heisman Trophy voting in 1973, and Pace was fourth for the award in 1996.

To understand the effect Pace had on the game of football you only need to know one thing: he was the inspiration for a new statistic, the *pancake block*. Statisticians trying to illustrate Pace's greatness started keeping track of how many times he knocked an opponent to the ground, or *pancaked* him. In his dominant junior year, he recorded 80 pancakes and won both the Outland Trophy and Rotary Lombardi Award, becoming the first player to repeat as the Lombardi winner.

A massive man, 6'6" and 330 pounds, Pace also was an incredible athlete who was quick and light on his feet. The combination was deadly for opposing defensive linemen. "Every day I'm a little more amazed at his ability than I was the day before," Coach John Cooper once said about Pace.

Pace played left tackle and did not allow one sack his sophomore and junior seasons, and his fourth-place finish in the Heisman voting in 1996 was the highest by an offensive lineman since Hicks had finished second. "He's a bigger version of me," Hicks said when Pace was still at Ohio State. "I told him I was passing the baton to him." Pace was an All-American in 1995 and '96 and was both the team and Big Ten MVP in '96.

Pace, out of Sandusky, Ohio, skipped his senior season at Ohio State to enter the NFL draft in 1997, and he became a perennial All-Pro after being selected by the St. Louis Rams with the first pick. He was a member of the 1999 Super Bowl champions Rams.

Hicks, Pace's precursor, started as a sophomore in 1970—freshman weren't eligible then—and helped to lead Ohio State to an undefeated season and a Rose Bowl berth, where they were upset by Stanford University. He injured his knee before the start of the 1971 season and sat out the entire year before returning for two more seasons. The 6'3", 258-pounder from Cleveland was named to consecutive All-American teams and was the emotional leader of Buckeyes teams that returned to the Rose Bowl following the 1972 and '73 seasons.

In 1973 Hicks won the Rotary Lombardi Award and the Outland Trophy and was second to Penn State running back John

Cappelletti in the Heisman voting. Hicks was drafted in the first round by the New York Giants, but his career was cut short by a knee injury. He lives in Columbus and is in private business, and he was elected to the College Football Hall of Fame in 2001. He also is in the Ohio State Varsity *O* Hall of Fame.

Paul Brown

If there was a Mount Rushmore of professional football icons, certainly Paul Brown would be one of the four faces carved in stone. Brown's name is synonymous with the NFL and, of course, with the teams in Cleveland and Cincinnati that he coached and helped found.

So, casual fans of college football and Ohio State may not know the brief but important impact he had on Buckeyes football. Brown coached Ohio State for three seasons, 1941–43, before being called into military service, and he led Ohio State to its first national championship.

Brown came to Ohio State after a phenomenally successful run at Massillon Washington High School, the same high school Chris Spielman would attend decades later. Brown coached teams that went 80–8–2 during his nine seasons there, including a 58–1–1 record in his last six seasons, and his teams won six state championships.

He was 33 years old when he took over at Ohio State in the fall of 1941. "I never even discussed money. I never asked them what the Ohio State job paid," Brown once said. "I didn't care. I just wanted to go there and have the job." Known for his meticulous preparation and innovation, Brown as head coach paid dividends right away as the Buckeyes went 6–1–1 that season. It was in 1942 that he'd make history, though.

Ohio State had an inexperienced squad heading into the 1942 season, which was not unusual for the time as many young men were being called into the military to serve in World War II. He pulled them together quickly, though, and the Bucks ran out to five straight wins, the closest a 32–21 victory over Indiana University. The Ohio team then traveled to the University of Wisconsin for a showdown with the number-six ranked Badgers, who were 5–0–1. But several Buckeyes players became ill on the train ride from Columbus because of bad drinking water, and Wisconsin won 17–7.

Ohio State recovered to win the final four games of the season, including a 21–7 defeat of fourth-ranked Michigan at Ohio Stadium that drew 71,896 fans, an impressive turnout considering everything else going on in the country and world at the time. Wisconsin was upset by the University of Iowa, and a couple of other teams ahead of the Bucks in the polls lost, too, giving Ohio State a Big Ten title and its first national championship.

Brown returned to coach in 1943, but the team was decimated by losses to graduation and military enlistments. His team struggled to a 3–6 record. His final record at Ohio State was 18–8–1. Brown himself was then appointed a lieutenant in the U.S. Navy and became head coach of the Great Lakes Naval Training Center team. He would bring his Great Lakes team to Ohio Stadium in the fall of 1944, where they would lose to the Buckeyes, 26–6.

After Brown left, Carroll Widdoes was named acting coach in the belief that Brown would return following his military commitment. But in 1945 Brown signed a then-lucrative contract to coach and be part owner of the Cleveland entry in the new All-American Football Conference, leaving many Buckeyes fans disillusioned.

There are different theories as to why Brown didn't return: he didn't want to supplant Widdoes, who was his friend; the Ohio

State administration let him know they were happy with the way Widdoes was running things. However it played out, Brown's brief and successful career on the Buckeyes sideline was over, despite the fact that in his autobiography he described the Ohio State position as "the only job I ever wanted."

Brown reportedly expressed an interest in returning to Columbus when Wes Fesler resigned following the 1950 season. There was some lingering bitterness at Ohio State, though, and that may have contributed to a decision to go instead with Woody Hayes.

Brown, who passed away in 1991, is in the Pro Football, College Football, and Ohio State halls of fame.

The Stadium Expansion

Ohio Stadium made the leap into the new millennium with a turn-of-the-century renovation that expanded capacity, added new club seats and suites, and increased various amenities such as restrooms and concessions stands. The three-year renovation was designed to improve the spectator experience by enhancing sight lines and bringing fans closer to the action with the removal of the track that had circled the field. The goal also was to generate more revenue for the athletics department through the construction of the suites and club seats and to modernize the nearly 80-year-old stadium while retaining the classic horseshoe design.

Designers accomplished that, but just barely. Architect Howard Dwight Smith might have to squint to see his original vision of the place, at least from the outside. A new concrete shell now encapsulates the stadium, except for the south towers and an opening at the north end that reveals the original ornate rotunda. This allowed for the addition of 17 rows of seats to the top of the upper deck. Also, the south stands were greatly expanded (they now seat more than 17,000 fans) and are a permanent concrete structure, meaning the Horseshoe is nearly enclosed.

The renovation, which was completed for the start of the 2001 season, cost $194 million (the stadium was built for $1.5 million) and was financed mostly through the sale of the 81 new suites and 2,625 club seats located on the west side of the stadium. That accounted for about 80 percent of the total cost, with the rest coming from naming-rights gifts, monies from additional ticket availability, increased concessions, and merchandise revenues and bonds. The school proudly notes that no university or student monies were used during the renovation process.

Besides the additional seats in C deck and the south stands, the field was lowered 14 feet, allowing rows of seats in the new AA section. Capacity increased by several thousand to 102,329, although 105,708 squeezed in for the 2006 Michigan game, which was a new Ohio Stadium record. The scoreboard and press box were expanded, and aisles were widened. "All the seats are good," Ohio State says on its website. Perhaps whoever wrote that hasn't sat in the top corner of the south stands or in the last row of C deck.

The truth is, the inside of the stadium does retain its original character, just on a grander scale. And the renovation has improved the view for most of the fans, although like everywhere else, they're paying more for the experience. But that's the reality of big-time college athletics in the 21st century. Most Ohio State fans are probably just happy the Buckeyes still call the old Horseshoe home.

That was director of athletics Andy Geiger's ultimate point when plans for the renovation were revealed. "Perhaps most importantly, the renovation project will add at least 50 years to the life of a monument that symbolizes the Ohio State University," he said.

Ohio Stadium was rededicated on September 8, 2001, with a 28–14 Buckeyes win over the University of Akron, which also happened to be Jim Tressel's first game as coach.

Les Horvath

When Carroll Widdoes took over as head coach at Ohio State before the 1944 season he faced a dilemma similar to that of coaches all over the country. World War II was raging, and thousands of young men were serving in the armed forces, making it a challenge to simply field a team. With his roster mostly made up of freshman who hadn't yet been called to service, a desperate Widdoes turned to a student enrolled in Ohio State's school of dentistry for help.

Les Horvath had helped to lead the Buckeyes to their first national title in 1942, when they finished 9–1, and then he enrolled in Ohio State's school of dentistry the following year. Players were granted an extra year of eligibility by special wartime rules, so Widdoes went to Horvath before the start of he 1944 season to try to convince him to return to the team. But Horvath wasn't easily swayed.

Besides dental school, Horvath was serving in the school's Army Specialized Training Program, which did not allow participation in varsity athletics. The program was disbanded before the start of 1944 season, however, and Widdoes made his pitch. The 23-year-old Horvath finally agreed to return, but only after winning some concessions from Widdoes.

"At first I wasn't sure I wanted to play. Dental school was quite taxing," Horvath said years later. "But Coach Widdoes said I wouldn't have to practice all the time and agreed to fly me to the games, both of which gave me more time to study."

What a prima donna. The move paid off for Widdoes, the Buckeyes, and Horvath, who led Ohio State to a 9–0 mark and won the Heisman Trophy. In doing so he became Ohio State's first Heisman winner and the only one in the history of the award who did not play the previous season.

Playing quarterback and halfback, and safety on defense, Horvath earned the title of playing coach for his leadership and smarts. He was also pretty talented, rushing for 924 yards and 12 touchdowns that season, with a 5.7 yards-per-carry average. He also threw for 344 yards and six scores. He set a new Big Ten rushing record (669 yards) and was named conference MVP as well as the Heisman winner. Ohio State finished second nationally to Army.

Horvath, of Parma, Ohio, served in the navy after graduating from dental school, and then he played professionally for the Los Angeles Rams and Cleveland Browns. He later practiced dentistry in Los Angeles and is a member of the College Football and Ohio State halls of fame. He died in 1995.

34 Rex Kern

Even taking into account Woody Hayes' disdain for the forward pass and the difficulty of comparing different years, Rex Kern's statistics as a Buckeye quarterback were modest. He finished his career with 2,444 passing yards, 19 touchdowns, and 24 interceptions. In his best year, 1969, he threw for 1,002 yards with nine touchdowns and 10 interceptions, and was named an All-American. He did set a school record for total offense that season with 1,585 yards, but it's since been passed many times.

But what Kern brought to the game was immeasurable. Despite what the statistics might say, he was a great athlete who kept defenses off balance with his running and passing, and he was known to come up with the big play when the Bucks needed it most. And maybe most importantly, he was a tremendous leader and a fiery competitor whose passion on the field belied his choir-boy looks. As just a sophomore, Kern beat out the incumbent quarterback, a returning senior, and took control of a team that would go 10–0 and win the national championship.

"Woody Hayes had tremendous confidence in Rex," says his former teammate Jim Stillwagon. "He was a great athlete. Everybody counted on him to make it work. And he made it work a lot of times."

During Kern's three seasons, Ohio State went 27–2, won the 1968 national title, won three Big Ten titles, and played in two Rose Bowls. Kern closed out the perfect season of '68 by rushing for 96 yards and two touchdowns against the University of Michigan and then threw a pair of fourth-quarter touchdown passes against USC in the Rose Bowl as the Buckeyes came back to win, 27–16. He was named Rose Bowl MVP.

Woody Hayes called the 1969 team his greatest ever, and they were perfect up until a devastating 24–12 loss at Michigan, during which Kern threw four interceptions. In 1970 Kern was captain, and the Buckeyes again went undefeated, gaining revenge against Michigan in the season finale. They were then upset by Stanford University and Jim Plunkett in the Rose Bowl.

Kern battled injuries throughout his career, and his back-ups, Bill Long and Ron Maciejowski, made significant contributions to those teams. Still, he finished third in the balloting for the 1969 Heisman Trophy and fifth the following year, when he passed for a total of just 470 yards on the season. There is also

Hall of Fame Players

Orlando Pace was inducted into the College Football Hall of Fame in 2013, meaning 24 Buckeyes have been so honored. Additionally, five former head coaches are enshrined, although they are honored for their entire body of work and not just their time at Ohio State.

Players

Player	Position	Years at Ohio State University
Chic Harley	halfback	1916–17, 1919
Gaylord Stinchcomb	halfback	1917, 1919-1920
Wes Fesler	end	1928–30
Gomer Jones	center	1934–35
Gust Zarnas	guard	1935–37
Jim Daniell	tackle	1939–41
Les Horvath	quarterback	1940–42, 1944
Bill Willis	tackle	1942–44
Warren Amling	guard/tackle	1944–46
Vic Janowicz	halfback	1949–51
Howard Cassady	halfback	1952–55
Jim Parker	guard	1954–56
Aurealius Thomas	guard	1955–57
Jim Houston	lineman	1957–59
Bob Ferguson	fullback	1959–61
Jim Stillwagon	middle guard	1968–70
Jack Tatum	defensive back	1968–70
Rex Kern	quarterback	1968–70
John Hicks	tackle	1970, 1972–73
Randy Gradishar	linebacker	1971–73
Archie Griffin	tailback	1972–75
Chris Spielman	linebacker	1984–87
Eddie George	running back	1992–95
Orlando Pace	left tackle	1994–96

Coaches

Coach	Years at Ohio State University
Howard Jones	1910
John Wilce	1913–28
Francis Schmidt	1934–40
Woody Hayes	1951–78
Earle Bruce	1979–87

this sign of respect: Despite not appearing near the top of the list in any major statistical category for Ohio State football, he was made an offensive captain by the Touchdown Club of Columbus, along with Archie Griffin, when it named an all-20th-century team in 2000.

Kern was a three-sport star in high school in Lancaster, Ohio, was selected in the Major League Baseball draft and planned to play basketball for Fred Taylor at Ohio State. He did play on the freshman team but injured his back and decided to dedicate himself solely to football. Kern was probably closer to Coach Hayes than any other player—his teammates used to joke about Hayes being Kern's father because they were together so much—and it was a relationship that lasted until Hayes' death.

Kern briefly played defensive back in the NFL before he retired because of an injury. He is in the Ohio State Varsity O Hall of Fame and was inducted into the College Football Hall of Fame in 2007. Kern is modest and often deflects praise to his ex-teammates, and after being inducted into the College Football Hall of Fame, told the *Columbus Dispatch* he found it hard to put his finger on what exactly made him such a success on the football field. "[I had] a passion for doing my best, I guess, which was instilled in me by all my coaches through the years," he said.

He then described a story that he's told other times about his very first game in 1968, against Southern Methodist University at Ohio Stadium. It was fourth-and-long at midfield, and Woody was sending in the punt team. Kern, just a sophomore and in his first start, waved them off. The pass play Kern called broke down, and he had to improvise with a defender bearing down on him.

"I did a pirouette, landed on my feet, and gained 16 or 17 yards," he said. "I guess that sort of set the tone for my personality."

The Punch

It has to be the saddest moment in the history of Ohio State football and certainly one that reverberated throughout the college football world. The punch Woody Hayes landed on a Clemson University player near the end of the 1978 Gator Bowl would cost Hayes his job and forever brand him in some circles as an out-of-control tyrant whose time had passed. It was the ignominious end to an incredible career, a moment that in hindsight may not have been inevitable, but was, at least, unsurprising.

The Buckeyes came into the Gator Bowl after an up-and-down 7–3–1 season. They had lost to the University of Michigan for the third straight year, and there was growing talk around Columbus and elsewhere that the game had passed Hayes by. More and more he seemed to be from a different era, both personally and in his run-first football philosophy.

He seemed to challenge that view when he started dynamic freshman quarterback Art Schlichter in the opening game, but Hayes was rewarded with a 19–0 pasting at the hands of a strong Penn State team. Schlichter would throw five interceptions that day and a record 21 on the year. The regular season culminated with a 14–3 loss to the Wolverines, who were on their way to their third straight Rose Bowl.

And then there was the infamous play itself.

The Buckeyes trailed Clemson 17–15 near the end of the game but were driving and were within field goal range at the Tigers' 24-yard line. An upset of seventh-ranked Clemson would be a positive end to an up-and-down season. Ohio State coaches decided to take a final shot at the end zone on third down, and if that failed, they would bring on the field-goal unit.

According to players who were there, Schlichter was given strict instructions to throw the ball away or sit on it if the touchdown wasn't possible. Instead, he looked to hit a secondary receiver, running back Ron Springs, with a short pass. Clemson nose guard Charlie Bauman stepped in front of the pass, picked it off, and was brought down in front of the Buckeyes bench.

Bauman got up off the ground facing Hayes and the Ohio State bench. There's no indication that he said anything, but apparently it was just all too much for Woody. He was just steps away and went at Bauman and threw a punch at his throat. A big scrum ensued, Hayes was pulled away, and then he actually went at one of his own players who was trying to restrain him. Bauman wasn't hurt and it was over in moments, but so was Hayes' career.

The Ohio State administration acted quickly—some fans felt Hayes was on thin ice already, and this was the perfect excuse to let him go. Athletics director Hugh Hindman and assistant athletics director Jim Jones met with Hayes, and Hindman announced the next morning that Hayes had been relieved of his duties.

In typical Hayes fashion, he would not go down without a fight. The meeting with Hindman and Jones reportedly was tense, with Hayes arguing that one incident should not overshadow all he had done for the university. "Should I apologize for all the good things that I've done?" he reportedly asked at the suggestion that he issue a formal apology. He then told *Columbus Dispatch* sports editor Paul Hornung, a friend, that he was resigning, which led to confusion over whether he was pushed out or jumped on his own. Either way, Hayes was not going to be back as coach of the Buckeyes after throwing that punch.

Besides the unhappy buildup to that moment, some who knew Hayes said the outburst may have been related to his poor health. Hayes was a diabetic, a fact he hid from all but those closest to him, and several former players and associates say he had not been taking his medication and watching his diet that week. They claim Hayes was out of sorts the night of the game, and that that may have been the tipping point.

Or maybe it was simply a combination of everything: a frustrating season, the hounding of critics who questioned his football and personal philosophies, his health, a volatile personality that had gotten him in plenty of trouble before, and the single final play (a pass!) that lost the game. Hayes snapped, as he'd done so many times before, but this time the damage wasn't to a yard marker or the psyche of a fumbling running back, it was his career. And it was irrevocable.

Eddie George

Talk about an inauspicious start. As a freshman running back, Eddie George received significant playing time in an early Big Ten matchup with the University of Illinois and fumbled twice inside the Illini 5-yard line. The first fumble was returned 96 yards for a touchdown, and George's play was met with boos from the Buckeyes faithful as Illinois went on to win 18–16.

George came to Ohio State from Philadelphia because Coach John Cooper promised to give him the football, as opposed to other schools, which saw his 6'3" frame and wanted to stick him at linebacker. But in one afternoon he had essentially blown his shot to be the featured back, and over his first two seasons he rushed for fewer than 400 yards.

He continued to work hard, however, and as the starting tailback in 1994 he piled up 1,442 yards and scored 12 touchdowns. Still, he was relatively unknown nationally as his senior year opened, and he received little of the preseason Heisman hype that surrounded other top players. That was about to change.

In the second game of 1995, George ran for 212 yards and two touchdowns against the University of Washington, and he followed that performance two weeks later with 207 yards and two more touchdowns in a much-hyped contest with Notre Dame. College football fans and Heisman voters alike knew who he was now.

George continued to run up impressive numbers—141 yards and three touchdowns at Wisconsin and 178 yards and three scores at Minnesota—before a historic afternoon against, ironically, Illinois. George would rush for a school-record 314 yards and two touchdowns, and he'd catch four passes, one for a score, in a 41–3 Ohio State win. The Heisman Trophy was all but his.

"Reflecting back, the game against Illinois [freshman year] was pivotal," George would say later. "I was known for the longest time as the guy who fumbled twice inside the 5. People said I couldn't make it here, and I should transfer out. I believed in myself and continued to work hard."

It paid off for George and the Buckeyes. He finished the season with a school single-season record 1,927 yards, scored 25 touchdowns, and also caught 47 passes, a record for a running back. He was the runaway winner of the 1995 Heisman Trophy. He also won the Doak Walker Award as the top running back in the nation and the Maxwell Award, given to the top collegiate football player. In addition, he was awarded the Walter Camp Player of the Year Award and was the Big Ten MVP.

Cooper said it was no secret how George got there. "His work ethic was the best. I can't imagine another college football player in history having a better work ethic," Cooper said. "He is a great athlete with tremendous focus, and that is why he did so well at Ohio State and as a professional."

George closed his career with 3,768 yards, second on the all-time list to Archie Griffin, and 44 rushing touchdowns, third on

Eddie George runs for a touchdown against Notre Dame in October 1995.

the all-time list. George was drafted by the Houston Oilers, now the Tennessee Titans, with the 14th overall pick, won rookie of the year, and was one of the top running backs in the NFL over the course of his career. But George says his NFL experience, even playing in a Super Bowl paled in comparison to his time as a Buckeye. He is in the Ohio State Varsity *O* Hall of Fame, and the school has retired his No. 27. George remains a presence at Ohio State and opened a restaurant not far from Ohio Stadium called Eddie George's Grille 27, a popular spot on game days for Buckeye fans.

Buckeyes Shrines

Hayes' Headstone

Woody Hayes passed away in 1987, but he didn't go far. Hayes is buried in Union Cemetery, about a mile and a half north of Ohio Stadium on the other side of the Olentangy River. Hayes and his wife, Anne, who died in 1998, rest beneath a black granite marker with *HAYES* etched on the front in big block letters. There is an inscription at the bottom of the stone: "And in the night of death, hope sees a star, and listening love hears the rustle of a wing." There is no mention of his beloved Buckeyes.

That's not surprising for the man who was known to ask a football recruit what book he was reading, and who appeared at rotary club meetings and school assemblies and talked for an hour about U.S. history without mentioning the game he loved.

The gravesite draws occasional visits from fans, who sometimes have their pictures taken next to it or leave mementos. Cemetery assistant superintendent Joe Glandon says the visits mostly come in the fall on football Saturdays, and fans have left everything from pennies to miniature Ohio State footballs, buckeye necklaces, and scarlet and gray beads. Before the 2003 Tostitos Fiesta Bowl national title game, someone left a bag of Tostitos chips.

"Every once in a while we have to go clean it off," Glandon says.

Chic Harley is also buried at Union Cemetery, and fans occasionally ask to see his grave or notice it as they drive in. "He's on the main road coming in, and it's taller than most, with a bust of Harley with his helmet on," Glandon says.

Union Cemetery is but one site to visit for Buckeye fans looking to pay homage to Ohio State's past.

Harley's Rock

A parking garage stands on the site of the old Ohio Field, where Ohio State played before moving into Ohio Stadium, but nearby there is a rock commemorating what went on there: Harley's Rock. The large rock lies just a few feet off the sidewalk on the west side of High Street, just south of Woodruff Avenue, and it has a plaque explaining its significance. The inscription tells about Ohio Field and the great "Charles W. 'Chic' Harley."

Buckeye Grove

Just outside Ohio Stadium is the Buckeye Grove, where more than 100 buckeye trees have been planted for each of Ohio State's first-team All-Americans. There is a tree and a plaque for each player to have earned that honor. The first trees were planted in 1934. The grove was originally located east of Ohio Stadium but was moved near the southwest corner as part of the 2001 renovation.

The North Rotunda

The new concrete exterior added to the stadium in 2001 hides the original facade of Ohio Stadium, except for the ornate rotunda at the north entrance. It's often said that football is religion in Columbus, and if that is true, this is the cathedral. The rotunda contains the original decorative stonework and three stained-glass collages, which were added prior to the 2001 season. The windows, approximately 18 feet tall and 13 feet wide, depict two scenes of Buckeyes football on either side of a block *O*.

The Ohio State Athletics Hall of Fame

The Ohio State Hall of Fame, or Varsity *O* Hall of Fame, is located on the east side of the Jerome Schottenstein Center, the home to Buckeyes basketball and hockey, and a short walk from Ohio Stadium. In the Hall there are dozens of former Buckeyes football players honored with plaques, as well as athletes from a variety of other sports and memorabilia from championship teams of the past.

The Buckeye Hall of Fame Café

This might be a better bet than the official hall of fame because it's loaded with Buckeyes memorabilia, including one of Archie Griffin's Heisman Trophies, and you can sip your beverage of choice while perusing the displays. Located about a mile south of Ohio Stadium on Olentangy River Road, it'll be packed on game day and is a popular spot for Buckeyes fans year 'round.

38 Notre Dame versus Ohio State: The Game of the Century

Ohio State returned a talented and veteran squad in 1935, and through the season's first month the Buckeyes didn't disappoint. Led by coach Francis Schmidt, quarterback Stan Pincura, and All-American center and captain Gomer Jones, the Buckeyes opened with four straight wins, including an 85–7 destruction of Drake University. At midseason the Bucks were riding a 10-game winning streak overall.

But that was all preliminary to the November 2 showdown at the Horseshoe with undefeated Notre Dame, coached by Elmer Layden, one of the Four Horseman from his Irish playing days.

The game generated unprecedented interest locally—at a time when sellouts were rare, the ticket demand far outstripped the supply—and among the national media, with luminaries such as Grantland Rice and Damon Runyon on hand. CBS radio broadcast it nationwide. "The game of the century," it was called, in a display of hyperbole that obviously isn't limited to the modern media.

Through the game's first two quarters it looked to be just that for Ohio State. The Buckeyes jumped ahead 7–0 and thrilled the home crowd when Frank Antenucci intercepted a pass and, in mid-run back, lateraled to teammate Frank Boucher, who took it the remaining 65 yards for the score. Joe Williams scored the next touchdown for the Bucks in a drive set up by a Pincura interception. The extra point failed, but Ohio State led 13–0 at the half.

The game remained 13–0 through the third quarter, but Notre Dame scored a touchdown early in the fourth to make it 13–6. The momentum had clearly swung to the Irish, and Schmidt didn't help things when he removed some Buckeyes starters. Under the rules of the day they couldn't return in the same quarter, so they were done for the game. Still, Ohio State received a couple of late breaks that seemed to seal the win for the Bucks.

First, Notre Dame was at the goal line and going for a possible tying score when they fumbled into the end zone. Ohio State recovered for the touchback. Then, after Notre Dame scored with less than two minutes to play, the Irish again missed the extra point, preserving a 13–12 Buckeyes lead.

An on-side kick by Notre Dame failed, so all Ohio State had to do was run out the clock. But on second down the Bucks fumbled out of bounds, and a Notre Dame player touched the ball last before it went out. So what? Well, 1935 rules said that meant that the ball belonged to the Irish, even though they hadn't technically regained possession.

They promptly marched down the field, and a backup quarterback named Bill Shakespeare hit Wayne Millner with the winning touchdown pass. Final score: Notre Dame 18, Ohio State 13. A Shakespearean tragedy for the Buckeyes, indeed.

Notre Dame fans were ecstatic and rushed the field, tore down one of the goal posts, and carried it to their downtown hotel. The media got swept up in the euphoria, and for years to come they called it the greatest game ever played. For Ohio State it was a bitter, if historic, loss. They did, however, recover to win their final three games and a share of the Big Ten title.

The Snow Bowl

The Ohio State–Michigan rivalry has featured some of the greatest teams and players in the history of college football, and the games frequently had national title implications. With all of this history, though, one of the most memorable games in the series occurred when the winning team didn't get a first down or complete a pass.

That game occurred on November 25, 1950, at Ohio Stadium in a driving snow storm in what came to be known as the Snow Bowl. Columbus and much of the Midwest were socked with a blizzard that day, and by game time playing conditions were brutal, with freezing temperatures and swirling winds adding to the misery. There was talk of postponing the game because much of Columbus was paralyzed by the storm. The decision was made to go ahead with the game, although it started more than two hours late as the grounds crew and volunteers worked to clear the field of snow.

Once the game started, it quickly became apparent it was better *not* to have the ball. The teams combined for 10 lost fumbles and an incredible 45 punts, and as the game wore on, they sometimes punted on first down in a battle for field position. Michigan won 9–3 despite not completing a pass or earning a first down.

Vic Janowicz, who would win the Heisman Trophy that year, kicked a field goal to account for the Buckeyes' only points. Considering the playing conditions, the Ohio State athletics office

The Graveyard of Coaches

Miami of Ohio became known as the cradle of coaches after Woody Hayes, Bo Schembechler, and several other prominent coaches moved through there early in their careers. Ohio State, on the other hand, earned a less complimentary moniker in the first half of the 20th century: graveyard of coaches.

A string of coaches in the 1930s and '40s were either fired or resigned and complained of the intense pressure of coaching at Ohio State. Francis Schmidt had some success at Ohio State but then left after going 4–4 in the 1940 season, his seventh. Paul Brown replaced him but lasted just three seasons before being called into the military service. His replacement, Carroll Widdoes, would coach two seasons before asking to become an assistant, and then Paul Bixler was elevated to the head job but lasted just one season. Both reportedly complained about the intense scrutiny of the job and the pressure to win. Ohio State legend Wes Fesler then took over and coached four seasons before departing, saying the stress was too much for him and his family. His deal breaker was the Snow Bowl loss to Michigan in 1950, after which he received intense criticism. He promptly took the head job at the University of Minnesota.

That made for four coaches in a decade and six in 21 years, including Schmidt and Sam Willaman, who coached from 1929 to 1933. But Fesler's departure led to the hiring of one Woody Hayes, and Hayes was firmly planted at Ohio State for almost three decades.

So, the graveyard title was gone, right? Not completely. Hayes was let go after his outburst at the 1978 Gator Bowl, and Earle Bruce and John Cooper were both fired as well. That means every head coach who came along after Brown, who coached from 1941 to 1943, was either fired or resigned under—or due to—the pressure of the job.

called the kick "one of the greatest individual accomplishments in Ohio State sports history." The kick was set up by a blocked punt, which was kind of the theme of the day. Michigan blocked a punt out of the end zone in the first quarter for a safety and then scored a touchdown just before halftime on another block.

That was the difference in the game, and it would have ramifications for Ohio State well beyond this one contest. Here's how it happened: The Buckeyes had the ball deep in their own territory when Coach Wes Fesler decided to punt on third down rather than run another play that some fans argued could have drained the remaining time off the clock before halftime. The punt was blocked and recovered by Michigan in the end zone—apparently. Officials had to dig down through the snow to confirm the call.

Fesler's strategy was criticized, and he resigned a few weeks after the season, saying the pressure of coaching at Ohio State was too much. A coach from Miami University named Wayne Woodrow Hayes replaced him, so Buckeye football would recover.

Attendance at the Snow Bowl was announced at 50,503—over the years probably twice that many fans claimed to have been in the stadium that day—but many had headed for the exits long before the end of the game. Although it's one of the most written- and talked-about games in Ohio State history, the players and coaches on that team likely aren't nostalgic about it. They not only lost to their archrivals but saw their Big Ten championship hopes buried in the snow as well.

"There is no doubt that on a normal day in November we would have whipped Michigan," said Thor Ronemus, a junior guard for the Buckeyes that day. "We had a better team."

40 Krenzel to Jenkins— Again: Top Plays of All Time

Underdog Ohio State had battled defending national champion University of Miami all night in the 2003 Fiesta Bowl. The Buckeyes seemed primed for the upset and their first consensus national title in 34 years. Ohio State led 17–7 when a touchdown run by the Hurricanes' Willis McGahee late in the third quarter cut into the lead, and a 40-yard field goal by Miami on the final play of regulation tied it up.

The Hurricanes got the ball first in overtime, and a Ken Dorsey–to–Kellen Winslow Jr. touchdown pass put them ahead, 24–17. Now it was Ohio State's national championship hopes that were on the ropes. The Buckeyes got the ball at the 25-yard line and promptly went backward four yards in three plays. That made it fourth-and-14 from the 29. Buckeye Nation was holding its collective breath.

Craig Krenzel took the snap in the shotgun, stepped up in the pocket, and fired just as a Miami player closed in on him, hitting Michael Jenkins near the right sideline. Jenkins gathered it in, turned, and was knocked out of bounds at the 12. First down. Exhale.

Ohio State would score several plays later, following an interference call in the end zone against Miami on another fourth down, and the game would go into a second overtime. The Buckeyes scored first on a 5-yard touchdown run by Maurice Clarett, and then the defense held. Ohio State was the national champion.

There have been more spectacular plays in Ohio State history as far as displays of sheer athleticism and execution—Clarett's strip of Sean Taylor after a Miami interception in this same game, and a fourth down Krenzel-to-Jenkins touchdown pass against

Purdue University earlier in the season are two. But none could match the drama and significance of this one. Simply put, the season, the national title, and this team's place in history were on the line in one play. And, as they had all season, the Bucks came through.

"It's no different than what we've done all year," Krenzel said afterward. "We make plays in the big games when we have to."

Clarett's strip and Krenzel's game-winning touchdown pass to Jenkins against Purdue would also make any short list of greatest plays in Buckeyes history. Here are a handful of others (drawing heavily from the era when television and videotape allowed more than just those in attendance to witness what happened):

November 23, 2002—Safety Will Allen intercepts a pass at the goal line on the final play of the game against the University of Michigan, clinching a 14–9 win and a berth in the Fiesta Bowl against Miami.

October 13, 1984—Keith Byars loses his shoe but doesn't slow down on his way to a 67-yard touchdown run in a thrilling home win over the University of Illinois.

November 17, 1979—Ohio State trails Michigan 15–12 late in the game, and the Bucks' perfect season is in jeopardy. But then Jim Laughlin blocks a Michigan punt, and Todd Bell scoops it up for the touchdown and an 18–15 win.

November 22, 1975—Ohio State and Michigan are tied at 14 points apiece with fewer than three minutes to play when Ray Griffin intercepts a Rick Leach pass and returns it to the 3-yard line. The Bucks score on the next play to win 21–14.

October 12, 1968—Ted Provost returns an interception 35 yards for a touchdown in a scoreless game against top-ranked Purdue, and Ohio State is on its way to a 13–0 win.

October 5, 1957—Don Sutherin fields a punt in a tie game with the University of Washington and returns it 81 yards for a score in a play that Woody Hayes says "turned our '57 season around." Ohio State would later win the national title.

October 23, 1954—Ohio State trails the University of Wisconsin 7–3, and the Badgers are threatening late in the third quarter when Hopalong Cassady intercepts a pass and weaves his way 88 yards for a touchdown. The Bucks would go on to win 31–14 and to capture a national title.

November 25, 1950—Vic Janowicz kicks a 38-yard field goal in the Snow Bowl loss to Michigan in a feat the Ohio State athletics office calls "one of the greatest individual accomplishments in Ohio State sports history."

41 Football Inc.

The pistol squad—yes, Ohio State has a pistol squad—arrives at matches in new Buckeyes sportswear from Nike. The synchronized swimmers compete at a facility dubbed the Taj Majal that has seven pools as well as two whirlpools. And the cheerleaders travel to road games on the football team's chartered jets rather than packed into vans.

All of this is possible in large part because of the revenues generated by the Ohio State football team. Ohio State's athletics budget is well over $100 million and the school fields 37 varsity teams. But unlike most state schools, the athletics department doesn't depend on state funding for these extracurricular activities. The department is separate from the rest of the school and is self-supporting, with football and, to a lesser degree, men's basketball generating profits that support themselves as well as the other sports.

In 2006 the football program generated about $57 million in revenue and supplied nearly $36 million to the athletics department. So while many schools are cutting nonrevenue sports such as lacrosse or swimming, these profits mean Ohio State can support them all. And the athletics department also has contributed to renovations at the library, spends millions on scholarships, and pays for its own operating costs at its facilities.

Of course Ohio State also depends on the generosity of outside donors. Limited Brands chief executive Leslie Wexner, an Ohio State graduate, helped fund a renovation of the football team's practice facility with a large donation. Yes, the football team benefits, too, with some of the finest facilities in the country.

The sheer size of the athletics department and the dollar figures tossed around have drawn criticism from some quarters about supposedly skewed priorities. According to an analysis by *The Wall Street Journal*, the school spends approximately $110,000 on each of its nearly 1,000 athletes, or triple the amount spent per undergraduate on education. And in response to cutbacks in state funding, Ohio State raised tuition nearly 60 percent from 2002 to 2006.

But to the school, such criticism is off the mark for the simple fact that the athletics department is self-sustaining. Money is not being shifted from the biology department to buy eye black for the football players or new sticks for the hockey team. And sports aren't being cut to pay for a new flat-screen TV for the football players' lounge.

So when an Ohio State fan buys a scarlet foam figure and takes his seat in the Horseshoe or purchases a Buckeyes jersey for her nephew, he or she can do so knowing that the money is supporting the entire Ohio State Athletics Department—flat-screens and eye black for the football team, yes, but also a new swimming pool and soccer equipment and shiny diamonds for the baseball and softball teams to play on.

Some Buckeye fans were nervous when the school rehired E. Gordon Gee as president in 2007 (he had also been president from 1990 to 1997). Gee has been a frequent critic of some dimensions of big-time college athletics, and he made national headlines when at Vanderbilt University he dissolved the athletics department and placed it under the office of student life. The controversial move seemed to work for Vanderbilt, however, as the school experienced success both on and off the field. Gee said Buckeyes fans needn't worry.

"It is the largest, most complex, and best-run athletics department [in the country] in many ways," he said, shortly after his reintroduction as Ohio State president. "[Vanderbilt] was the most radical restructuring of college athletics in this country. But the premise that we have is right for Ohio State University—a fully integrated program of athletics and academics. It is that [which] I will strive for."

John Cooper

Is there a more polarizing, star-crossed figure in the history of Ohio State football than John Cooper? Cooper coached the Buckeyes for 13 seasons, won Big Ten titles, won a Rose Bowl, and returned the program to national prominence in the mid-'90s, coming within a whisper of a couple of national championships.

But Coop was never widely loved in Columbus, and to many Buckeyes fans his legacy is defined not by the numerous accomplishments, but by this: 2–10–1. That's his record against the University of Michigan, and to some fans, it should be his epitaph.

Cooper was hired following the dismissal of Earle Bruce, and while not much was known about Cooper in Columbus, he was considered a rising star in the ranks of college football coaches. In 1986 his Arizona State University team won the Pac-10 and beat Michigan and Bo Schembechler in the Rose Bowl. What more did a Buckeyes fan need to know?

Cooper's arrival in Columbus was a bit rocky. His slight southern twang was not exactly endearing to midwesterners (Cooper was from Tennessee), especially when it was heard in the many television commercials he started shooting. And an early comment about the dearth of talent on the Buckeyes roster didn't go over too well, either. His third game in Columbus was a stunning come-from-behind victory over Louisiana State University, but that was one of the few highlights in a season that would end 4–6–1, the first losing season at Ohio State in more than 20 years.

But Cooper started to turn things around in the next few years and was an incredible recruiter. When that talent arrived on campus the Buckeyes were on their way. They went 10–1–1 in 1993 and shared the Big Ten title, dropped to 9–4 the following season (but beat Michigan), and then went on an incredible 4-year run. For those four years they were 11–2, 11–1, 10–3, and 11–1. The 1995 team featured Rotary Lombardi Award–winner Orlando Pace, Biletnikoff Award–winner Terry Glenn, and Heisman Trophy–winner Eddie George. Cooper and his players ran up a school record 475 points. The 1996 squad came from behind to beat Arizona State and Jake Plummer 20–17 in the Rose Bowl, Ohio State's first win in Pasadena in 23 years.

That team finished ranked second in the country, as did the 1998 team, which suffered an upset loss to Michigan State at home but beat Michigan in the regular season finale and Texas A&M in the Sugar Bowl. Both the 1995 and '96 teams beat Notre Dame in much-hyped matchups.

John Cooper was a solid if not beloved coach in Columbus.

Unfortunately for Cooper, that's not nearly the whole story. His teams couldn't beat Michigan, especially when the stakes were highest, and critics said he never fully grasped what the game meant to Ohio State fans. In 1993 the Buckeyes were 9–0–1 and lost to

Michigan 28–0. In 1995 they were 11–0 and lost to the Wolverines 31–23, a score that is deceivingly close because Michigan's Tim Biakabutuka ran wild on the Bucks that day, racking up 313 yards on the ground. Another perfect season was ruined the following year when the 10–0 Bucks lost 13–9 at home to number 21 Michigan. On top of that was a 3–8 record in bowl games. Cooper wasn't a closer.

After seasons of 6–6 in 1999 and 8–4 in 2000, including an embarrassing 24–7 loss to South Carolina in the 2001 Outback Bowl, the Ohio State administration had seen enough, and Cooper was let go. Athletics director Andy Geiger also cited a "deteriorating climate" within the football program that included academic and disciplinary problems, something Cooper disputed.

"If I had beaten [Michigan] more, I'm sure I'd still be there," Cooper said a few years later. "But everybody has an Achilles' heel, and I guess that was mine."

While many Buckeyes fans were likely happy to see him go, Cooper's overall record places him among the best Buckeyes coaches of all time. He went 111–43–4 for a .715 winning percentage and ranks second behind Woody Hayes in most wins. His teams shared three Big Ten titles and finished in the top 25 in 12 of his 13 seasons, and he coached 21 All-Americans. It's a mixed legacy, not unlike what Cooper once said about the blessing and curse of coaching in Ohio Stadium.

"One of the best things about this place is that it's Ohio State University," said Cooper, who after leaving Ohio State maintained a home in Columbus and worked as a college football analyst. "But you know at the same time one of the worst things about it is it's *the* Ohio State University."

43 The Sweetest Victories

A rivalry, by its very definition, requires competitiveness, and there was very little of that in the early games between Ohio State and the University of Michigan. Ohio State mustered two ties over the first 15 games, but otherwise Michigan won each contest, usually in convincing fashion. The Wolverines outscored the Buckeyes 371–21 over the course of those games and administered the worst beating in the history of Ohio State football, 86–0, in 1902. It easily could have been a triple-digit loss had the game not been called midway through the second half.

So when Chic Harley and other players returned from the service in 1919 and the team opened with three blowout wins, there was much excitement that the Bucks might finally beat that team from up north. An estimated 5,000 fans made the trip to Ann Arbor for the October 25 game, and Harley electrified them with a 42-yard touchdown run in the second half.

The two teams hadn't played in the previous few seasons, so this was Harley's first and only shot at the Wolverines, and he made it count. In addition to his touchdown run he also intercepted four Michigan passes, and as the punter, he repeatedly pinned Michigan back in its territory. Ohio State came away with a 13–3 win, and legendary Michigan coach Fielding Yost was so impressed that he visited the Buckeyes locker room afterward to offer congratulations.

The win not only thrilled the Buckeyes backers on hand in Ann Arbor, but it set off "the biggest celebration Columbus has ever seen," according to a magazine at the time, the *Ohio State University Monthly*. That victory also injected the series with the competitiveness it lacked. Since 1919 the rivalry is almost even, with Michigan holding a 44–41–4 edge.

Besides 1919, the top wins for the Buckeyes in the rivalry are 2002, 1970, and 2006.

Ohio State entered the 2002 Michigan game with a 12–0 record, a number-two national ranking, and needing a win to earn an invitation to the Fiesta Bowl national championship game. It was a cold, gray day, but a then–Ohio Stadium record crowd of 105,539 had the Horseshoe buzzing maybe like never before. Buckeyes fans could be forgiven some jitters, too, as three times in the previous 10 years Michigan had ruined undefeated seasons for Ohio State.

With the Wolverines leading 9–7 midway through the fourth quarter, it looked like a horrible repeat. But then quarterback Craig Krenzel and running back Maurice Clarett led a 57-yard scoring march that included a gutsy Krenzel sneak on fourth-and-1 and that was capped by a Maurice Hall touchdown run. The Buckeyes led 14–9 and then thwarted two late drives by Michigan by forcing a fumble and intercepting a pass at the goal line on the game's final play.

That pick-off ignited a huge celebration because Ohio State had come through against its bitter rival when it counted most, and was on its way to a national championship showdown with Miami University. The Buckeyes would win that in dramatic fashion, too, to capture Ohio State's first consensus national title in 34 years.

Both number-five-ranked Ohio State and number-four-ranked Michigan entered the 1970 game undefeated, so a Big Ten title and possibly a national title were on the line when the teams met at Ohio Stadium. And Woody Hayes and Ohio State had been pointing to this day literally since the final gun had sounded on the 1969 contest, which had been a 24–12 upset by Michigan and its first-year coach Bo Schembechler of the unbeaten and top-ranked Bucks. Hayes had called it his worst loss and had plastered the score on rugs at the athletics complex and almost everything else to give his players a daily reminder.

Thirty-Four Titles and Counting

Ohio State had won 34 Big Ten football championships heading into 2014, which ranked the Buckeyes second to Michigan, which had 42. Ohio State also won five straight titles (2005–09) for the first time since capturing six consecutive from 1972 to 1977. Only one of those titles was outright (1975), which demonstrates how difficult it is to be sitting alone atop the Big Ten at season's end. And it makes the two straight outright titles under coach Jim Tressel in 2006–07 all the more impressive because it's only been done by Ohio State two other times, in 1916–17 and 1954–55. Technically, all five of those titles in the 2000s are now considered outright because Penn State vacated their share of the 2005 and 2008 championships. Ohio State also won the title in 2010 but vacated that, too, due to NCAA sanctions. Michigan has more Big Ten victories because it's been in the league longer, but Ohio State's winning percentage is higher.

The pre-ESPN buildup was incredible, and many of then-record crowd of 87,331 were in their seats an hour before kickoff. Ohio State came away with a 20–9 victory, which Hayes called the greatest in Ohio State history. His team, maybe still emotionally drained from the contest or overconfident, was then upset by Stanford University in the Rose Bowl.

Fans who witnessed the hype surrounding the 2006 game and the subsequent 42–39 Ohio State win had their own "greatest" moment. Again, both teams came in undefeated, and this time they were ranked number one (Ohio) and number two in the nation, the first time that had ever happened in the series. It was the game of the young century, and it lived up to the hype.

Michigan jumped out to a 7–0 lead, but Ohio State, led by Heisman Trophy–winning quarterback Troy Smith, responded with 21 unanswered points and never trailed again. Michigan scored a late touchdown to get within three points, but the Buckeyes recovered the onside kick and ran out the clock.

The win might be remembered as the greatest ever except for what happened next: heavily favored Ohio State was blown out in the national title game by Florida. It was 1970 all over again.

Four other games in the rivalry were also remarkable, including:

1954—Ohio State used a dramatic goal-line stand early in the fourth quarter to stifle Michigan on its way to a 21–7 win and a Big Ten and national title.

1972—This time the Buckeyes used two goal-line stands to hold off Michigan, one right before the half and the other early in the fourth quarter, on the way to a 14–11 win.

1975—Number-one ranked Ohio State was outplayed most of the day in Ann Arbor and trailed 14–7 late in the game. But a pair of Pete Johnson touchdowns, the second set up by a Ray Griffin interception that was returned to the Michigan 3, led to a 21–14 Ohio State win. Hayes called it "our greatest comeback, and the greatest game I've ever coached."

1987—Not much was on the line in this one, except for pride and the legacy of Coach Earle Bruce. Bruce had been told he was being let go that week, and his players donned headbands with Earle written on them in a show of solidarity. The Buckeyes fell behind before coming back for an emotional 23–20 win.

The Most Bitter Defeats

Ohio State entered the 1996 Michigan game as the heavy favorite, and it was with good reason. The Buckeyes were 10–0, ranked second in the nation, had already clinched at least a share of the Big

Ten title and a Rose Bowl berth, and had a lineup stocked with All-Americans and All–Big Ten players. The 21ˢᵗ-ranked Wolverines, meanwhile, were 7–3 and coming off two straight losses. The game was in Columbus, and the Buckeyes had the revenge factor on their side, too, as Michigan had spoiled their perfect season the year before with a 31–23 win in Ann Arbor.

The Wolverines would do it again that day, and it was one of the worst losses for the Bucks in the history of the storied rivalry. Ohio State dominated much of the first half but three times had to settle for field goals, and the Buckeyes led just 9–0 at the half. Still, they seemed to be in control—at least until Shawn Springs slipped.

On the second play after halftime, Michigan wide receiver Tai Streets caught a quick slant as Springs, an All-American cornerback, slipped, giving Streets a clear path to the end zone. Any momentum Ohio State had evaporated with the 69-yard scoring play.

Michigan added two field goals to take the lead, while the Buckeyes failed to get anything going. "This can't be happening again" was the general sentiment pervading Ohio Stadium, and maybe the headset of Coach John Cooper, as the seconds ticked away. But it did happen, a stunning 13–9 Michigan win that again ruined a perfect Buckeye season and forced Ohio State to share the Big Ten title with Northwestern University.

The 1996 Bucks recovered to beat Arizona State in the Rose Bowl and finish at number two in the nation, but this was a bitter, bitter pill to swallow, more so because Ohio State and its fans hadn't yet lost the taste from recent Michigan defeats. The year before, the Buckeyes were 11–0 and also ranked number two and had a load of talent that included Heisman Trophy–winner Eddie George. But 8–3 and 18ᵗʰ-ranked Michigan rolled over them, with Tim Biakabutuka rushing for 313 yards in a 31–23 win that denied the Bucks the Big Ten title and a shot at a national championship. In 1993, 9–0–1 Ohio State was trounced by an unranked Michigan team in Ann Arbor, 28–0. Losing meant a share of the Big Ten title rather than an outright crown, and a berth in the Holiday Bowl instead of the Rose Bowl.

In an interview a few years after his dismissal, Cooper seemed to acknowledge that those teams felt pressure heading into the big game. "If we had losing teams or hadn't been very good, there wouldn't have been much pressure against Michigan," he said. "Who would care? Pressure comes when you're playing for a national championship."

But Cooper, who still lives in Columbus, bristled at suggestions that he didn't appreciate the intensity of the rivalry. "That isn't true. When I first came here, for goodness sakes, we had ex-players come talk to the squad, motivational speakers," he said. "If you win the game, whatever you did leading up to the game was right.… But in the ballgame, players are the ones who win or lose, not some great call made on the sideline, not because some speaker comes in and talks to your team."

The Michigan losses came in a bunch in the 1990s, and there were other tough defeats in the series: a missed extra point in 1926 that led to a 17–16 loss and cost the Bucks a perfect season and Big Ten title, the Snow Bowl, and the 22–0 defeat at home in 1976 are near the top of the list. But the single-most devastating loss was in 1969.

Rookie Michigan coach Bo Schembechler was facing his mentor Woody Hayes that day, and he had his charges ready to play. Ohio State came in undefeated, ranked first in the nation, and riding a 22-game winning streak. Although his Buckeyes didn't win a national title, Hayes would later call it his best team ever.

But on that day in Ann Arbor they weren't the best team on the field. Michigan fell behind 12–7 in the first half but then scored 17 unanswered points in the second quarter to jump ahead 24–12. The Michigan defense repeatedly stymied Ohio State in the second half, and that's how it would end. The Buckeyes had to share the

Big Ten title with their rivals, and their national championship hopes were dust.

Years later, Hayes told Schembechler he would never win a bigger game. "And he was right. I don't think I ever did," Schembechler said.

Earle Bruce

Taking over for Woody Hayes at Ohio State was kind of like being asked to replace Mick Jagger as frontman of the Rolling Stones or Moses at the head of the Israelites. You weren't supplanting a coach so much as trying to fill the shoes of a man who was the face of Buckeye football for almost three decades.

So when it was announced that Earle Bruce of Iowa State University would be the new coach, the response wasn't exactly overwhelming. Bruce was a former assistant coach under Hayes at Ohio State and had racked up a nice record with the Cyclones, but he wasn't exactly the high-profile choice some fans were pining for.

While some coaches may have been intimidated by the assignment—Lou Holtz reportedly said he didn't want to follow Hayes but wanted to follow the guy who followed Hayes—Bruce relished the opportunity. He focused on rebuilding a program that had stumbled to 7–4–1 the year before, including the Gator Bowl loss to Clemson University that featured Hayes' undoing.

And Bruce had the Buckeyes back on track faster than you could say Wayne Woodrow Hayes. Behind sophomore quarterback Art Schlichter and a tough defense, Ohio State ran up a 10–0 mark before winning the season finale at Michigan, 18–15. It was a

The Pregame Flick

One Buckeyes tradition that dates back decades occurs the Friday night before games, when the entire team watches a movie. It was a routine started by Woody Hayes as a way to keep the players loose, but Hayes, of course, took it very seriously. He usually skipped the flick to spend time studying game film, but he insisted on a few criteria: no chick flicks, no comedies, nothing controversial, and nothing liberal. War and action movies were fine.

Hayes assigned an assistant coach to pick the movie, and it wasn't a job anyone wanted or enjoyed. If Hayes didn't like the movie the assistant coach would hear about it, especially if the team played poorly the next day.

When he was an assistant, Earle Bruce allowed the team to view Easy Rider, not knowing the content beforehand. Hayes fired him from the job when the team didn't play well the next day, which probably was a relief to Bruce.

perfect regular season and Big Ten championship for Bruce, as well as a number-one ranking, as he headed to the Rose Bowl to face the University of Southern California.

The Buckeyes may have been the top team in the land, but they were underdogs to the third-ranked Trojans, who were led by Heisman Trophy–winning running back Charles White. Ohio State held a 16–10 lead with just minutes to play and seemed on the verge of its first national title in a decade. That was when White took over.

He got the ball on almost every play of the final drive, rushing for 71 yards including the final 1-yard dive into the end zone. The extra point ruined the perfect season for Bruce and the Bucks, although they ended up fourth in the country, and it is still remembered as one of the most surprising seasons in Ohio State history.

Bruce won National Coach of the Year honors, but how could he ever match that phenomenal rookie campaign? Although he won or shared three more Big Ten titles and returned to the Rose

Bowl following the 1984 season—another close loss to USC, this one 20–17—he never achieved as much as he had in his first season coaching the Buckeyes.

Instead, he became known as "9-and-3 Earle." And while a string of 9–3 seasons may get you a statue at most schools, at Ohio State it can get you fired. After that initial 11–1, the Bucks went 9–3 for six straight seasons and then 10–3 in 1986. The following year Ohio State dropped three straight Big Ten games late in the season, and Bruce was done.

The school took the unusual step of informing him he was fired before the finale against Michigan, but it allowed him to coach in the game. An inspired Buckeyes team, with the players wearing headbands with *Earle* written on them and the coach sporting a classic fedora, upset Michigan, 23–20, in Ann Arbor. The team then carried their fired coach from the field.

The 1987 team finished 6–4–1, and Bruce was 81–26–1 over nine seasons. That left him second all-time behind Hayes in wins, although he's since been displaced by John Cooper and Jim Tressel is bearing down. Bruce was 5–4 against Michigan and 5–3 in bowl games, marks that Buckeyes fans would soon be very sentimental about. He went on to coach at the University of Northern Iowa and Colorado State University, and he is in both the Ohio State and College Football halls of fame.

46 Jim Stillwagon

Ohio State put together the finest three-year run in school history from 1968 to 1970, behind a typically punishing ground game and a tough-as-nails defense. In the middle of that defense, both literally and figuratively, was one of the most accomplished, and maybe most overlooked, Buckeyes players ever: Jim Stillwagon.

Stillwagon was from Mt. Vernon, Ohio, but attended high school at the Augusta Military Academy in Virginia and wasn't well known in Ohio. Besides that, he was a Notre Dame fan. "I hated Ohio State," he says. "My dad went to Notre Dame. I had the Notre Dame helmet growing up and all that stuff and always loved it. I was going to Notre Dame."

But a visit to South Bend, Indiana, didn't go well, and Stillwagon came to Ohio State and met Woody Hayes. "He just liked me because I had a short haircut and went to military school and said 'yes sir,'" he said.

Stillwagon said he was given the last scholarship. Even Hayes couldn't have known he'd turn into maybe the best player in what would be the greatest recruiting class in school history.

The "Wagon" was one of the Super Sophs who led Ohio State to an undefeated season and the national championship in 1968. Playing middle guard, he was simply the best defensive lineman in the nation over his three-year career. The 6'1", 220-pounder wasn't big but was probably the strongest player on the team, and he was known for his aggressive, relentless play.

The defenses he anchored were virtually impenetrable. The Buckeyes surrendered just 93 points in 1969 for a per-game average of just over 10 points (it would have been in single digits if not for the 24–12 season-ending upset to the University of Michigan). Stillwagon was an All-American that season and repeated the feat the following season as the Buckeyes defense was stifling yet again, giving up more than 13 points just twice and holding seven opponents to 10 points or fewer.

In 1970 Stillwagon won both the Outland Trophy as the nation's best lineman and was the first winner of the Rotary Lombardi Award, given to the best lineman or linebacker in the country. He was also named as the team's Most Valuable Player.

Former Buckeyes quarterback Rex Kern, another leader on those teams, recalls the final game that class played at Ohio Stadium in 1970, a 20–9 win over Michigan. It meant that those seniors never lost a game at the Horseshoe.

"Our defense played a perfect game that afternoon," Kern said. "Jim Stillwagon was outstanding. He was so great that often we took his greatness and effort for granted."

Stillwagon was drafted by the Green Bay Packers but decided to play in the Canadian Football League instead, where he became one of the CFL's top defenders. A member of both the Ohio State and College Football halls of fame, he is in private business in Columbus.

47 Bucks in the Rose Bowl

When Arizona State University's Jake Plummer slithered his way through the Ohio State defense and dove over for a touchdown with fewer than two minutes to play in the 1997 Rose Bowl, it appeared that the Buckeyes' 23-year victory drought in the "Granddaddy of Them All" would be extended at least one more year. Ohio State trailed 17–14, had just one timeout left, and was in serious jeopardy of losing in Pasadena for the fifth-straight time, dating back to the 1974 game. Also, it appeared the Buckeyes would match their ignominious feat of the previous season: going undefeated until dropping their final two games, to the University of Michigan and their bowl opponent.

The Sun Devil defense and this daunting history stood in the way when Ohio State sophomore Joe Germaine, who shared time at quarterback with Stanley Jackson, and the offense took over at the Bucks' own 35-yard line with 1:33 to play. The drive Germaine engineered was a thing of beauty only to Buckeyes fans. He opened with two incompletions before hitting Dimitrious Stanley for a first down. There were more incompletions, a couple of big receptions by Stanley, and two interference penalties on Arizona State that moved the ball to the Sun Devil 5.

Germaine then found wide receiver David Boston with a touchdown pass with 19 seconds to play, sending the tens of thousands of Buckeyes fans who filled the Rose Bowl into a frenzy. The Sun Devils were done and Ohio State's demons exorcised. The Buckeyes were Rose Bowl champions for the sixth time, and to fans recalling the pre-BCS days, all was right in the universe again. Because of the Big Ten's longtime contract with the Rose Bowl, for decades a trip to Pasadena was *the* goal every season.

"It was all about winning the Big Ten by beating Michigan and getting to play in the Rose Bowl," says Archie Griffin. His former teammate, Brian Baschnagel, agrees. "We never even talked 'national championship' because there wasn't the emphasis on it that there is now," Baschnagel says. "We just said, 'We have to win the Big Ten.'"

Ohio State has appeared in 14 Rose Bowls, going 7–7. It is the only team to appear in four straight Rose Bowls (1972–75), and Archie Griffin is the only player to start in four in a row. Griffin, Woody Hayes, Rex Kern, and Curly Morrison are in the Rose Bowl Hall of Fame.

The first Rose Bowl was held in 1902 as a side event to the Tournament of Roses parade and celebration. When Michigan trounced Stanford University 49–0, the experiment was called off after one year, with polo and then Roman-style chariot races taking the place of football. The game returned for good in 1916, and Ohio State's first appearance was in 1921, in a battle of unbeatens against California, Ohio State's first ever game against an opponent west of the Mississippi River. It didn't go well for the boys from the Midwest, as California won easily, 28–0.

Ohio State wouldn't return to Pasadena for almost 30 years because many mediocre seasons followed, and the Big Ten's contract with the Rose Bowl wouldn't come about until 1946. Ohio State finally made the trip again at the end of the 1949 season, when it shared the Big Ten title with Michigan; the rivals had tied that year, but the Buckeyes got the invitation because Michigan had just gone two years prior.

Again Ohio State would face an undefeated California team, but the outcome would be different. Ohio State got 127 yards rushing and one touchdown from fullback Curly Morrison, and Jimmy Hague kicked a field goal with just under two minutes to play to provide the winning margin in the 17–14 victory. "This is the biggest thrill I've ever had in football," Buckeyes coach Wes Fesler said. "Every boy dreams of playing in the Rose Bowl and winning."

With Woody Hayes at the helm, Ohio State would return in 1955 (20–7 over USC) and 1958 (10–7 over Oregon) to cap off national championship seasons with Rose Bowl wins. The Buckeyes wouldn't appear in the game for another 11 seasons, but then, starting in 1969, they would play in six of the next eight. There was a 27–16 win in 1969 by the Super Sophs that ensured an unbeaten season and national title; an upset loss to Stanford two years later, 27–17, that spoiled another perfect season and a shot at a consensus national championship; three straight games against USC (1973: USC 42–17, 1974: OSU 42–21, 1975: USC 18–17); and finally a devastating upset loss to UCLA, 23–10 in 1976, that cost the Bucks another unbeaten season and national title.

The story was the same in 1980 when rookie coach Earle Bruce and the undefeated and number-one Bucks faced USC and led late until Trojan running back Charles White took over. The result was another one-point loss to USC, this time 17–16. Five years later the national title wasn't on the line, but Southern Cal again got the better of Bruce and the Bucks, winning 20–17.

It would be a dozen years before Ohio State would be back in Pasadena, and that too looked like it would end in frustration for the Buckeyes. Then Germaine found Boston with seconds to play, and the scarlet and gray could again come home Rose Bowl champions.

48 Sing Along

The year was 1902, and Ohio State had just suffered a humiliating 86–0 loss to the University of Michigan. The Buckeyes were traveling home from Ann Arbor on the train when one of the freshman players, Fred Cornell, had an inspiration. Cornell thought a song capturing what Ohio State meant to him and others would lift the spirits of his teammates and the entire school. So he got out an envelope and started scribbling lyrics on the back.

So was born "Carmen Ohio," Ohio State's alma mater and oldest school song, the playing of which on Saturday afternoons turns thousands of rabid Buckeyes fans to mush. "Carmen Ohio" (*Carmen* means *song* in Latin) is set to a Christian hymn and is performed before every home game, with 100,000-plus fans on their feet singing along. It's also sung after the game, when the team and Coach Jim Tressel gather in front of the band in the south stands. Only the first stanza, however, is sung:

Oh come let's sing Ohio's praise
And songs to alma mater raise
While our hearts rebounding thrill

With joy which death alone can still
Summer's heat or winter's cold
The seasons pass, the years will roll
Time and change will surely (truly) show
How firm thy friendship...Ohio!

Ohio State also has two fight songs, the "Buckeye Battle Cry" and "Fight the Team across the Field." The latter was written in 1915 by Ohio State student William Dougherty Jr., who felt the school needed something more up-tempo than "Carmen Ohio." Basically he wanted a song that would get fans juiced, and it's been doing just that since it was introduced at a pep rally before the University of Illinois game that year.

The "Buckeye Battle Cry" was written by Frank Crumit in 1919 in response to a contest for new school fight songs. The contest was held as planning began for the new Ohio Stadium. Crumit actually went to Ohio University and not Ohio State, but

Cie Grant Sings

Ohio State linebacker Cie Grant pressured Miami University quarterback Ken Dorsey into an errant throw on the final play of the 2003 Fiesta Bowl as Ohio State captured its first national title in more than three decades. So after helping author one of the most thrilling plays in the history of Ohio State football, what did Grant do for an encore? Two weeks later he gave Buckeyes fans another moment to remember by singing the alma mater at the championship celebration at Ohio Stadium. It was a goosebump-inducing moment that had nothing to do with the freezing temperatures that day.

Grant had sung "Carmen Ohio" in front of the team way back in August as punishment for being late for a team meeting. So a couple of coaches asked if he'd do it again at the rally following the Fiesta Bowl. Grant was hesitant but took the microphone in front of the tens of thousands of fans at the 'Shoe, and he hit every note. It was a moment none of them will likely ever forget.

he was a big Buckeyes fan and his entry won. "Buckeye Battle Cry" is played by the band after its ramp entrance and throughout the game.

Another song the band is certain to play during the game that will have fans swaying and clapping along is "Hang on Sloopy." "Sloopy" was recorded by the rock group the McCoys in 1965, and shortly thereafter it was picked up by the Buckeyes band. There was no connection to Ohio State football beyond the fact that the McCoys were from Ohio, but fans liked it so much that it's been in the game-day mix ever since.

Finally, there are songs that are bound to emanate from tailgates, the Ohio Stadium stands, and anywhere groups of Buckeyes fans gather, such as "I Wanna Go Back to Ohio State" and the derisive "We Don't Give a Damn about the Whole State of Michigan." Columbus homeboy James Thurber used the latter song in a play he wrote, *The Male Animal*, which was later turned into a movie (although producers changed *damn* to *darn*). The lyrics are pretty easy to pick up:

Oh, we don't give a damn for the whole state of Michigan
The whole state of Michigan, the whole state of Michigan
We don't give a damn for the whole state of Michigan,
we're from Ohio
We're from Ohio...O-H
We're from Ohio...I-O
Oh, we don't give a damn for the whole state of Michigan
The whole state of Michigan, the whole state of Michigan
We don't give a damn for the whole state of Michigan,
we're from Ohio.

The website www.scarletandgray.info/ contains an archive of Ohio State songs with lyrics, as well as the known history and origin of the pieces. There are also audio files of the songs.

Art Schlichter

If Art Schlichter wasn't real, a Hollywood screenwriter would have made him up. A farmboy from the small Ohio town of Washington Court House, self-assured and with a cannon for a right arm, Schlichter stepped in as the starting quarterback at Ohio State in 1978 as a true freshman and remained there every game over the next four seasons. By the time he was a sophomore he was leading Ohio State to an 11–0 record and appearing on the cover of *Sports Illustrated*. He would go on to set every significant passing record at Ohio State, lead the Buckeyes to a record of 36–11–1, and be a number-one draft pick.

But the story had holes. The incredible expectations that arrived with him at Ohio State were never quite realized. There was no national title, although he came close one season. He never won the Heisman Trophy, although he finished in the top 10 in the voting three straight years. And along with the record passing yards came a record number of interceptions, including 21 in his up-and-down freshman season that ended with one of the worst moments in Ohio State history: Schlichter throwing an interception near the end of the Gator Bowl and Coach Woody Hayes slugging the Clemson University player who picked it off.

Then there was the gambling. Schlichter liked to gamble and, in fact, couldn't stop. While there was never evidence that it affected his play at Ohio State, it consumed him after he left, ruining his shot at the NFL and eventually landing him in prison for several years for stealing from and scamming people to support his habit. One of the greatest players in Ohio State history had become a pariah, unwelcome at Ohio Stadium and mostly erased from history by the school.

Schlichter arrived at Ohio State at a moment of transition for Hayes and the program. Hayes' run-dominated style seemed a thing of the past, and his decision to start the freshman Schlichter over returning quarterback Rod Gerald, a better runner, was big news. But the immediate results weren't positive. Schlichter threw five interceptions in the season opener against Penn State, a 19–0 Ohio State loss. He found some consistency over the course of the year, though, and ironically played maybe his best game in the fateful Gator Bowl.

Under new coach Earle Bruce in 1979, Schlichter and the Buckeyes were the story of the college football season. They were undefeated in the regular season and ranked number one in the nation before dropping the Rose Bowl by a single point to the University of Southern California. Schlichter was an All-American and finished fourth in the Heisman vote. His passes were frequently wobbly but almost always accurate, and Schlichter could keep defenses off balance with his running ability. He was an excellent athlete who briefly played basketball at Ohio State, too.

Although he continued to put up impressive numbers it wouldn't get any better for Schlichter or the Buckeyes after that 1979 season, as they would finish 9–3 the next two seasons. Schlichter did close out his career by beating the University of Michigan and earning a share of a Big Ten title, then winning in the Liberty Bowl over Navy. He still holds the career records for passing yards (7,547) and total offense (8,850 yards), and for passing yards in a game, when he went 31-of-52 for 458 yards in a 1981 loss to Florida State University. He had 50 career touchdown passes (fourth of all time) and holds the mark for interceptions in a season with 21 and a career with 46.

Schlichter was drafted fourth overall by the Baltimore Colts in the 1982 NFL draft, but shortly thereafter gambling began to dominate his life. He would bet on the horses and sports in a habit that started in high school. It continued at Ohio State with

Art Schlichter is carried off the field after an 18–15, come-from-behind win over Michigan in November 1979 in Ann Arbor.

frequent trips to Scioto Downs in Columbus, where he was reportedly sometimes seen in the company of Bruce. The former coach vehemently denies that he ever went to the track with Schlichter or that he was aware his player had a problem.

After signing an NFL contract, Schlichter began to pile up gambling losses. He was suspended by the NFL, and by his mid-twenties he was out of the game for good. There were many low points. He scammed friends and family members out of thousands of dollars, stole from his wife, and pawned his and her wedding rings. His dad Max died in 2002 of an apparent suicide, and his son couldn't attend the funeral because he was in prison. Schlichter was placed in solitary confinement after he convinced his attorney to smuggle him a cell phone in prison and began placing bets. He was divorced from his wife, and his two daughters grew up as he spent approximately 10 years behind bars in various locations. "This addiction has taken everything I've ever loved or owned in my life," Schlichter said in a jailhouse interview with the New York *Daily News*. "I don't have anybody to blame but myself."

Schlichter was released from prison in 2006 and said he was making amends. He established the organization Gambling Prevention Awareness, and traveled around the country giving talks about compulsive gambling, using his life story as exhibit A. And he returned to Ohio State and saw some games at Ohio Stadium for the first time in years. Before the 2006 Michigan game, he was allowed on the field with other ex-players.

But trouble eventually caught up with him again when he was sentenced to 11 years in prison in 2012 after being convicted of participating in a million-dollar ticket scheme that scammed sports fans for tickets they never saw. At his sentencing, a tearful Schlichter apologized to his victims and his mother, who was in court.

50 Other Great Buckeyes Quarterbacks

Joe Germaine split time at quarterback with Stanley Jackson during his sophomore and junior seasons, when Germaine put up some fine statistics and was the hero of the 1997 Rose Bowl after leading the game-winning drive in the final minute. But when Jackson graduated, the job was all Germaine's, as he returned for his final year at Ohio State. Germaine became a baby-faced assassin for the Buckeyes. Finally free of the awkward quarterback rotation that had many fans questioning the methods of Coach John Cooper, Germaine turned in maybe the finest season ever for an Ohio State signal-caller.

ANDREW BUCHANAN

Germaine threw for 3,330 yards, still a school record, and 25 touchdowns that 1998 season, and he was named Big Ten Most Valuable Player. He set 11 Ohio State records and was cocaptain of a team that held the number-one ranking most of the season, until an upset loss to Michigan State University. The Buckeyes and Germaine recovered to defeat the University of Michigan and then beat Texas A&M University in the Sugar Bowl, finishing the season 11–1 and ranked second in the nation.

For his career, Germaine threw for 6,370 yards (third all time) and 56 touchdowns (second all time), and he is first in both average passing yards per game for a season (277.5 in 1998) and a career (172.2). His 378 yards passing against Penn State in 1997 is the second highest single-game total ever, and he has six of the top 12 games in Ohio State history. Ohio State was 32–5 in Germaine's three seasons.

Germaine is a native of Arizona who bypassed Arizona State because that school wanted to make him a defensive back, ironic because that was the team he beat as the Buckeyes quarterback in the Rose Bowl. He was drafted by the St. Louis Rams in the fourth round but saw little action, and so he moved on to the Arena Football League. He set a new AFL passing mark in 2007 by throwing for more than 5,000 yards for the Utah Blaze.

The Germaine-Jackson combo came on the heels of another record-setting Buckeyes quarterback: Bobby Hoying. Hoying was a three-year starter for Ohio State and set records his senior year for passing yards (3,269, later passed by Germaine) and touchdowns (29, eclipsed by Troy Smith's 30 in 2006). Hoying's 57 career touchdown passes remain first all time, and Hoying is second to Germaine in average passing yards per game for a season (251.5) and career (160.7).

Like Germaine, Hoying was the leader of Cooper-coached teams that Woody Hayes would hardly recognize. They went to the air early and often, racking up the yards and points and victories.

Also like Germaine, Hoying led some excellent teams that fell just short of Buckeyes immortality. Hoying was 30–7–1 as a starter (1993–95) but was 1–2 against Michigan, both losses ruining undefeated seasons for Ohio State.

51 Experience the Traditions

College football traditions vary from the sentimental to the silly, and fans can experience the entire range from a program as old and storied as Ohio State's.

Jump in a Lake

The Thursday night before the game against the University of Michigan each year, thousands of students jump into Mirror Lake on campus to get pumped up for the game and to bring some luck to the Buckeyes. The November temperatures may be at or below freezing, but that does little to discourage the revelers.

Senior Tackle

This one dates all the way back to 1913, when Coach John Wilce started the tradition of giving every senior a final whack at a tackling dummy or blocking sled in the last practice of the season. Often former Ohio State players or coaches are invited to speak at the ceremony, and it's an emotional moment for all those involved.

The tradition was opened to the general public in the 1990s and became hugely popular, drawing close to 30,000 people to Ohio Stadium one year. That was thought to be a bit much, especially after a couple of devastating losses to Michigan, so the event was scaled back again to include just family and friends.

Bruce Hits the Dummy

The Senior Tackle ceremony is always emotional for Buckeyes players and coaches, who take some time to reflect on their careers and enjoy one of their final moments together after a long four or five years.

The 1987 Senior Tackle was particularly moving for Coach Earle Bruce. It was Michigan Week, and Bruce had been informed by the school just days prior that he was being let go.

So the players decided to give Bruce a shot at the blocking sled. He had never participated in the ceremony as a player because his career was cut short by injury, and when given his chance, the coach didn't hold anything back.

"He tried to kill the thing," says Chris Spielman, who was a senior that year. "To see how he felt about that was pretty awesome."

Bruce has another connection to Senior Tackle, and this one isn't necessarily positive—not that it was his fault. Coach John Cooper asked Bruce to speak to the team at Senior Tackle before the Michigan game in 1996. The ceremony was open to the public and was broadcast on local television, including into the hotel rooms of the Michigan players. Apparently more than a few Wolverines watched Bruce's stirring address, and it got them fired up. Michigan pulled off a 13–9 upset the next day to ruin Ohio State's perfect season and shot at a national championship.

Buckeye Leaves

One of the traditions most unique to Ohio State football involves the buckeye-leaf stickers on the players' helmets. While many other schools use stickers as rewards for good play, it's usually pretty subtle, like the tiny dog bones on the back of Georgia's helmets. At Ohio State, it's one of the defining features of the uniform.

Woody Hayes and longtime trainer Ernie Biggs started the tradition in 1968. It came as part of a general uniform redesign that Hayes hoped would reenergize the program, and apparently it worked. The Bucks went undefeated that season and captured the national championship. Forty years later the buckeye leaves remain a distinctive part of the uniform.

Victory Bell

The Victory Bell chimes after a Buckeyes victory, in a tradition started in 1954, another national championship year for the Bucks. The 2,420-pound bell is located in Ohio Stadium's southeast tower and, according to the school, can be heard up to five miles away. It also rings on commencement days.

Tunnel of Pride

In a sign of Buckeyes pride across the generations, former Ohio State players form a long tunnel for the players to run through as they take the field for the Michigan game.

Former director of athletics Andy Geiger and ex-quarterback Rex Kern came up with the idea, and it was actually first done during the 1995 game against Notre Dame. Archie Griffin says this is his favorite tradition.

Gold Pants

When Coach Francis Schmidt took over in 1934, he was asked about playing Michigan. He responded by saying that the Wolverines "put their pants on one leg at a time, just like everyone else." So was born the gold-pants tradition.

If Ohio State beats Michigan, all the players and coaches receive a golden charm in the shape of football pants with the game's score inscribed on it. Schmidt's calming influence was effective—Ohio State defeated Michigan four straight years, starting in 1934.

The Best Team Ever

Seven Ohio State teams have won at least a share of a national championship, but many football historians, and no less an authority than Woody Hayes himself, have pointed to another team as the best in Buckeyes history. This squad didn't go undefeated or win a national title, and it even failed to beat the University of Michigan and capture an outright Big Ten championship.

The 1969 Ohio State team was "probably the best team that ever played college football," Hayes once said. The Buckeyes had gone 10–0 and captured a consensus national title the year before, and the core of that team returned. The Super Sophs—Rex Kern, John Brockington, Jim Stillwagon, Jack Tatum, Mike Sensibaugh, and others—were now juniors, and they quickly showed that the 1968 season was no fluke.

Kern hit split end Bruce Jankowski with a 58-yard touchdown pass on the first offensive play of the season, and the Buckeyes demolished Texas Christian University, 62–0, at Ohio Stadium. The Buckeyes followed that with a 41–14 win at the University of Washington before returning home for the Big Ten opener against 19th-ranked Michigan State University. Mark Debevc returned an interception for a touchdown, Kern scored on a 1-yard plunge in a play set up by a fumble recovery, and then Larry Zelina returned a punt 73 yards for a touchdown. It was 20–0 Bucks after just six minutes, and Ohio State was on its way to a 54–21 romp.

The University of Minnesota actually out-gained the Buckeyes the following week but repeatedly turned the ball over and fell, 34–7. That was the closest any team would come to Ohio State over the season's first eight weeks. There were scores of 41–0 over the University of Illinois, 62–7 against the University of Wisconsin, and a 42–14 win over 10th-ranked Purdue University. The Bucks then traveled to Ann Arbor on November 22 for the season finale unbeaten and ranked first in the nation, riding a 22-game winning streak.

The Wolverines, 7–2 and ranked 12th, had stumbled to a 3–2 mark in the first half of the season but then won four straight games, and none of them was close. They had revenge on their minds after a 50–14 shellacking at the hands of Ohio State the year before and also had a not-so-secret weapon: Bo Schembechler. Schembechler, who had served as an assistant under Hayes at Ohio State and was in his first season in Ann Arbor, had been preparing for the Bucks since his arrival, and it showed.

"That team probably was the greatest football team that Woody ever had," Schembechler said later. "Geez, it had no weakness."

The crowd of 103,588 was at the time the largest ever to see a regular-season college football game, and by some estimates about a quarter of those spectators were Ohio State fans. Although the Buckeyes had secured at least a share of the Big Ten title, because of the Big Ten's no-repeat policy, they would not be going to Rose Bowl no matter what happened at Michigan Stadium. So this was the final game for this team, and those fans who made the trip to see them were in for an unpleasant surprise.

Michigan built a 24–12 halftime lead and then completely stifled the Bucks in the second half, shutting down their running game and forcing them to pass. The result was six interceptions on the day for Ohio State and one of the worst losses in the program's history. Neither team scored in the second half, and Michigan had its upset.

"They beat the greatest team that ever stepped on a college football field," Hayes said years later. "I don't think there's any question…and I don't say that with bias."

Ohio State finished at number four in the final Associated Press poll. The team had five All-Americans—Kern, Stillwagon, Tatum, Ted Provost, and Jim Otis—and an astounding 11 All–Big Ten players. The Bucks that season outscored their opponents 383–93, and their 42.6 per-game average is the highest in the history of Ohio State football. So while the ultimate prize eluded the 1969 Buckeyes, they're still remembered by some as the greatest Ohio State team of all time.

53 The 1961 & 1970 National Champions

Ohio State lays claim to seven football national championships, but as befitting the only college sport without a season-ending tournament or playoff, the picture is somewhat muddled. Only three are consensus or undisputed titles: 1942, 1968, and 2002. Two others were shared titles: 1954, when the Buckeyes finished first in the Associated Press poll but second in the United Press International; and 1957, when they were first according to the UPI and Football Writers Association of America but second in the AP.

Then there was 1961 and '70. In both years the Buckeyes had outstanding teams that finished at number one in minor polls but out of the top spot in the final AP and UPI polls. While these titles aren't generally recognized outside Columbus, it does nothing to take away from the fact that these were two of the finest teams in Ohio State history.

The 1961 Buckeyes followed a script that was almost identical to the one written by the 1957 team. That year, Ohio State lost the season opener to Texas Christian University at Ohio Stadium before reeling off nine straight wins and capturing a share of a national title. In 1961 the Bucks again hosted Texas Christian to start the season, and this time the result was a 7–7 tie, after which Ohio won eight straight.

After the tie with Texas Christian, Ohio State defeated eventual Pac 8 champion UCLA, 13–3, and rolled through the rest of the season with no team coming closer than nine points. The '61 Bucks had a powerful offense and a backfield for the ages: Matt Snell, Bob Ferguson, and Paul Warfield. Ohio State closed out the season by clobbering Michigan in Ann Arbor, 50–20, as Ferguson ran for 152 yards and four touchdowns, and Warfield added 122 yards and one score.

Then the trouble started. The Ohio State Faculty Council rejected an invitation from the Rose Bowl in a close vote, with some of its members expressing concern that football was starting to overshadow academics at the school. Woody Hayes was livid and for years complained about the decision, saying it damaged his recruiting. Ohio State was home for the holidays and finished second in both the final AP and UPI polls. It finished first in the Football Writers Association of America poll.

In 1970 the Super Sophs, who had captured a consensus national title two years prior, were now seniors. This was long before it was common practice for star underclassmen to leave school early, so this team was loaded. There was the steady hand of Rex Kern and occasionally Ron Maciejowski at quarterback, in addition to All-Americans Jack Tatum, Jim Stillwagon, John Brockington, and Mike Sensibaugh. This was the greatest class in Ohio State history, and they didn't disappoint. The Buckeyes won their first eight games before capturing a grudge match against Michigan to close out the season. The Wolverines had upset the unbeaten Bucks the previous year, and Hayes had been waiting for this day ever since. It was an emotional 20–9 win—maybe too emotional.

When the unbeaten and number-two-ranked Buckeyes traveled to Pasadena, California, to take on underdog Stanford University, it seemed some of the players had left their intensity back on the Ohio Stadium turf. At one point during the trip, some seniors got together and wrote a letter to Hayes, asking him to ease up on the rigid practice schedule. The team was in California two weeks before the game, and players wanted to enjoy themselves.

Presumably Stanford and Heisman Trophy–winning quarterback Jim Plunkett weren't taking the same approach. The Cardinal jumped out to a 10–0 lead early, before a pair of Brockington touchdown runs put Ohio State up 14–10 at the half. Ohio State led 17–13 at the start of the fourth quarter and had marched to the Stanford 19 when Brockington was stuffed on fourth-and-1. Plunkett then took over, leading Stanford to two touchdowns and a 27–17 win.

The 1970 team was named national champs by the National Football Foundation but finished second in the final UPI poll and fifth in the AP survey.

54 In the Beginning...

Ohio State students had been playing informal games of the new sport of football for several years when, in 1890, it was decided to create a team to represent the school. The first challenge was one faced by schoolyard and sandlot players everywhere: they needed a ball.

The pickup games that had become popular on campus often used a homemade football, so student George Cole took up a collection to purchase a real ball. Cole also got his hands on a football rule book and convinced his friend Alexander Lilley to be coach. It had been more than two decades since the first college football game between Princeton University and Rutgers University in 1869, but Ohio State finally had itself a squad.

The first official game was against Ohio Wesleyan University on their home turf in Delaware, Ohio, on May 3, 1890, and Ohio State won 20–14 before a crowd of several hundred spectators. Joseph Large scored the first touchdown in school history, which then counted for just four points. Another game wasn't scheduled until the following fall, when the College of Wooster came to

Columbus for a November 1 contest at Recreation Park, located on the south side of the city at the intersection of High and Whittier Streets. Wooster was the first school in Ohio with an organized team, and it showed: Ohio State fell 64–0. The *Columbus Dispatch* described the carnage: "A number of ladies were present and attempted to cheer the O.S.U. boys to victory, but it was of no avail, as there was not the remotest possibility of their winning." The paper also reported "several accidents" during the game, including one to "Kennedy of the O.S.U. team. He was kicked in the chest, and the calling of a physician was found necessary."

Ohio State followed with losses to Denison and Kenyon to finish its first season 1–3. There is a plaque honoring this first team

A Dark Day for Ohio State Football

Ohio State has had one player fatally injured in its nearly 120-year history, and that tragedy left the school reconsidering its commitment to football. Center John Sigrist, a 27-year-old senior, injured his neck during a 1901 game against Case Western Reserve University and died the following Monday at Grant Hospital. The next game, with Ohio Wesleyan University, was canceled, and there was talk of getting rid of football entirely, echoing a wider discussion that was occurring around the country about the sport.

The school and athletic board left the decision up to the team, and they decided to play on after the one cancellation. Sigrist's brother, Charles, was a tackle on the team, and he argued for the resumption of play. Ohio State lost its next three games before beating Kenyon College to close the season, 5–3–1.

John Sigrist is the only player who died from injuries suffered playing for Ohio State, but there have been other frightening moments, including one in April 2006. During a spring scrimmage, walk-on wide receiver and punter Tyson Gentry was working with the scout team when he was tackled and broke his neck, leaving him paralyzed. Gentry has undergone intensive therapy and regained some feeling and movement in his body. And he has high praise for the support he has received from the university and Buckeyes fans.

and listing all of its members at the entrance to the Buckeye Grove outside Ohio Stadium.

The next fall the team was 2–2, with wins over Denison University and the University of Akron, then called Buchtel College, and the sport was gaining in popularity. In 1892 there was an eight-game schedule, and a small set of stands was constructed for spectators at a new field located west of Neil Avenue. Ohio State went 5–3 for its first winning record. Two of the losses were by scores of 40–4 and 50–0, both to Oberlin College, which was coached by John Heisman, the college football legend for whom the famous trophy is named.

Lilley and Jack Ryder had taken turns coaching the squad over the first couple of seasons, but Ryder was on the sideline for the 1892 season and would stay three more years. A semiformal schedule developed with other Ohio colleges, including an annual Thanksgiving Day contest with Kenyon College. The Ohio State program was gaining some stability and growing in popularity.

Ohio State played Akron at the state fair in 1894 in an effort to raise the sport's profile, and the school beat the University of Kentucky, 8–6, the following season in the first out-of-state contest.

The first sustained success came when John Eckstrom took over as coach in 1899 and ran up a 22–4–3 record in three seasons, including a 9–0–1 mark and championship of the Ohio colleges in his initial year. That team shut out every opponent except for one, a 5–5 tie with Case Western Reserve University, and five points allowed remains an Ohio State single-season record.

Coach A.E. Herrnstein also found success, leading Ohio State for four seasons starting in 1906 and compiling a 28–10–1 mark. In 1913 came one of the program's important early milestones as Ohio State began play in the Western Conference, which would morph into the Big Ten. Almost 100 years later the Buckeyes and the Big Ten are still around.

Linebacker U.

Penn State is called Linebacker U., but to Buckeyes fans that's a misnomer. If there's been a Linebacker U. over the past four decades or so, it's in Columbus.

Ohio State has produced a stable of linebacking studs, starting with two-time All-American Ike Kelley in the mid-1960s, through Randy Gradishar, Tom Cousineau, Marcus Marek, Chris Spielman, Pepper Johnson, Andy Katzenmoyer, A.J. Hawk, and Ryan Shazier, all of whom were All-Americans. Or how about Steve Tovar, Na'il Diggs, or Matt Wilhelm, also first-team All-Americans? Bobby Carpenter? James Laurinaitis? Where do you stop?

It's been amazing, really. One All-American would leave and another would step in his place. It's a legacy that's unmatched by Penn State or any other school in the nation. It's difficult even to pick a starting three from this group. Marek and Cousineau were tackling machines, one and two, respectively, in career stops; Johnson and Tovar put up big numbers, too, and made plays all over the field; Hawk and Laurinaitis were both two-time All-Americans, and Laurinaitis won the Butkus Award in 2007. But for sheer impact on Buckeye football, here are the starters.

Randy Gradishar

Woody Hayes said Gradishar was the "best linebacker I ever coached at Ohio State." Gradishar was a three-year starter and two-time All-American ('72–'73) who could stuff the middle and run down a toss sweep. His senior year, he was the leader of a defense that gave up just 64 points and recorded four shutouts. He finished sixth in the Heisman Trophy voting that season, went on to an

All-Pro career with the Denver Broncos, and was inducted into the College Football Hall of Fame in 1998.

Chris Spielman

Thanks to his appearance on a Wheaties box his senior year in high school, Spielman had a national reputation before he even arrived on campus. That's a lot of pressure on an 18-year-old freshman, but Spielman simply responded the only way he knew how: by playing harder than anyone on the field. The Massillon, Ohio, native is the school's all-time leader in solo tackles, was a three-time All–Big Ten selection, and a two-time All-American ('86–'87). And his work ethic and incredible on-field intensity made him the unquestioned leader of the Buckeyes when he was there.

Andy Katzenmoyer

Other Ohio State linebackers racked up many more tackles and were steadier over the course of their careers, but no one arrived at Ohio State with a bigger bang than Katzenmoyer. Wearing Archie Griffin's No. 45, Katzenmoyer started his first game at Ohio State and went on to earn All–Big Ten and Big Ten Freshman of the Year honors, and he was a second-team All-American. He was a devastating tackler who had a knack for the big play, recording 12 sacks and intercepting four passes as a freshman. His sack total and 23 tackles for loss that season are both second of all time for a single season and tops among linebackers. He capped off his first season by recording three sacks and intercepting a pass in the Rose Bowl win over Arizona State. He followed that by being named All-American as a sophomore and winning the Butkus Award as the top linebacker in the country. Katzenmoyer also was an All-American as a junior, although some observers felt he underachieved that season, possibly because of distractions from unfavorable press coverage of his less-than-stellar academic record at the school. He finished with 18 sacks and six interceptions, and he returned two interceptions for touchdowns, which is tied for a school record. He left for the NFL after that season and was a late first-round pick of the New England Patriots, but his career was cut short by a neck injury.

James Laurinaitis is just one of the great linebackers who played his college football at Ohio State.

56 Varsity Club and Other Buckeyes Bars

When Ohio State earned an invitation to the 2003 Fiesta Bowl and a shot at its first national title in more than three decades, Buckeyes fans turned the Valley of the Sun into Columbus Southwest. By some estimates, Ohio State fans outnumbered University of Miami backers 5-to-1. There was so much scarlet and gray in the Phoenix area in the days leading up to the game that the local media did stories on the phenomenon.

So, where did these fans go to have a beer and talk Buckeyes football? The Varsity Club, of course. Owners of the Varsity Club in Columbus rented out a bar about a block from Sun Devil Stadium in Tempe and took it over. It was packed before, during, and after Ohio State's scintillating victory.

The move by the Varsity Club was unusual but not all that surprising. The bar, located on Lane Avenue just a short walk from Ohio Stadium, has been the spiritual home to so many Ohio State fans for almost 50 years. A scarlet-and-gray striped awning adorns the outside, while inside the walls are covered with photos and memorabilia from Buckeyes sports. On nongame days it attracts patrons who come for a drink and to catch a game or to sample from a menu that offers fairly typical but above-par bar fare.

On game days, it's Buckeyes central. Actually, the Varsity Club has pregame parties the night before and then shuts down for a few hours before opening back up, sometimes as early as 8:00 AM. If it's a noon kickoff, there'll be plenty of fans having beer for breakfast. The club takes over a side street on game days, and it becomes one giant tailgate party that draws students, older alums, and everyone in between.

The Varsity Club may be home base for many Buckeyes backers, but it's far from the only spot to bond with fellow fans pre- or post-game. There are dozens of bars and restaurants within walking distance of the stadium, particularly along the High Street corridor, and almost all will be sporting a Buckeyes theme on game day. High Street for decades was the traditional party spot for Ohio State students, alums, and others who crowded into the bars for cheap drafts and buckets of beer.

While still a destination, High Street's rowdier days are behind it, and today there is more of a mix of bars, restaurants, and specialty shops. The South Campus Gateway project is one such recent development on High that includes restaurants, retail and office space, and a movie theater. Eddie George's Grille 27, a restaurant owned by the former Buckeyes star, is part of the complex. And not a bucket of beer in sight.

About a mile or so south of Ohio Stadium, and just on the other side of the Olentangy River, is the Buckeye Hall of Fame Café. This place offers more of an upscale experience than the Varsity Club, with a menu that includes steaks and seafood as well as burgers and sandwiches. But fans come as much for the impressive displays of Buckeyes memorabilia, including one of Archie Griffin's Heisman Trophies and the 2002 national championship trophy. It has rooms to host wedding receptions and other private parties, but on game days it's all about the Buckeyes.

57 Jack Tatum

Leroy Keyes was a fast and elusive running back for Purdue University, an All-American and Heisman Trophy candidate who was the driving force for the number-one team in the nation in the fall of 1968. When the Boilermakers came to Ohio Stadium for an early season matchup with the Buckeyes, there were serious concerns among the Buckeyes faithful about how the young Ohio State defense would handle Keyes and his quarterback, Mike Phipps.

But the Buckeyes had a strategy for containing Keyes, and it didn't involve complex Xs and Os or a fancy new formation. The strategy was simple, and its name was Jack Tatum.

The Ohio State coaches gave the defensive back more freedom that week to roam the field and shadow Keyes, which in reference to Tatum is a nice way of saying "knock his block off." Ohio State fans were finding out that the sophomore specialized in that, and Keyes, too, would find it out on that October day.

Tatum, along with the entire Ohio State defense, completely neutralized Keyes, holding him to 19 yards rushing. They also harassed Phipps all day. Ohio State held the Boilermakers to just 186 yards in total offense and kept them off the scoreboard for the only time that season. The defense also scored a touchdown on a Ted Provost interception as the Buckeyes won, 13–0. It was a huge early-season win for Ohio State, which would go on to a 10–0 record and the national championship.

And it showed what Tatum would mean to the Buckeyes over the next three seasons. The 6'1", 208-pound defensive back was more like an extra linebacker, covering the entire field to deliver his teeth-rattling hits. After the Purdue game and the 1968 season, the national press started to take notice. Tatum was named All-American his junior and senior years and was the national Defensive Player of the Year following his final season.

Tatum, a native of Passaic, New Jersey, actually came to Ohio State as a running back, before being moved to the defensive side of the ball before his sophomore season. It paid off as a dominant Ohio State defense led the Buckeyes to an incredible three-year record of 27–2, including two Rose Bowls and the one national title.

Tatum was selected in the first round of the 1971 NFL draft by the Oakland Raiders and went on to a productive and controversial career. He made three Pro Bowls and won a Super Bowl with the Raiders in 1976, but his hard-hitting ways and seemingly callous disregard for the running backs and receivers he laid out also made him a poster-boy for the violent nature of the sport.

In a preseason game in 1978, Tatum put a devastating hit on New England receiver Darryl Stingley on a pass that went over Stingley's head. The hit left the Purdue alumnus paralyzed until his death in 2007. But it was Tatum's reputation that took the hit when it was revealed that he never apologized to Stingley, although Tatum said he tried to visit Stingley in the hospital and wasn't allowed in.

Tatum seemed to revel in his violent image, penning a best-selling book titled *They Call Me Assassin*, as well as two similarly named follow-up books.

Reputation aside, Tatum, who passed away in 2010, is remembered by Buckeyes fans as a dominating force during the most successful three-year run in Ohio State history. He was inducted into the Ohio State Hall of Fame in 1981 and the College Football Hall of Fame in 2004.

Craig Krenzel

Among the pantheon of Buckeyes greats, is there a more unlikely member than Craig Krenzel? An unheralded quarterback from the state of Michigan of all places, he was known more for his smarts than for his arm strength or athleticism. And his all-time statistics, while impressive, don't place him near the top of the list of Ohio

Craig Krenzel is carried across the field by teammates and fans after the Buckeyes beat Michigan 14–9 in November 2002.

State signal-callers in passing yards or touchdowns. Instead, he's grouped with the likes of Mike Tomczak, Jim Karsatos, and Greg Frey, good but not great Buckeyes quarterbacks from the recent past.

What Krenzel did better than those three, and almost all other Buckeyes quarterbacks, was win. As a junior he led Ohio State to a 14–0 record and its first national championship in more than three decades, and he followed that up with an 11–2 mark his senior year, that included a repeat win in the Fiesta Bowl and a second consecutive Offensive MVP award.

The molecular genetics major was a first-team Academic All-American as a senior and received several other awards and honors for his work in the classroom, including being one of 13 seniors nationwide to receive a National Football Foundation and Hall of Fame Draddy Award—sometimes called the "academic Heisman."

But the bookish demeanor and boyish face on the 6'4" Krenzel hid a fire within. His first start came as a sophomore against 11th-ranked Michigan when subbing for suspended quarterback Steve Bellisari. This was coach Jim Tressel's first game against the Wolverines, and the Michigan media was playing up Tressel's remarks upon his arrival at Ohio State that Buckeyes fans would be proud of his team the next fall in Ann Arbor. To Michigan fans, that was as good as a guarantee of an OSU victory.

So, into this firestorm stepped the inexperienced Krenzel, and all he did was lead underdog Ohio State to a 23–0 halftime lead. Krenzel and the Buckeyes cooled off considerably in the second half before hanging on for the 26–20 win. Krenzel struggled in that year's Outback Bowl and was replaced by Bellisari in the second half, but Krenzel came into the 2002 season as the starter.

The Buckeyes opened the 2002 season with a 45–21 rout of Texas Tech University, during which Krenzel completed a steady but unspectacular 11 of 14 passes for 118 yards. That would be the theme of the season for him, with a few exceptions. Half of Ohio State's wins would come by seven points or fewer in 2002, and one of those exceptions came in a 10–6 win over Purdue University.

During that game, the Buckeyes trailed 6–3, with fewer than two minutes to play, and faced a fourth-and-1 from the Boilermakers' 37, with the Buckeyes' perfect season on the line. Krenzel, under pressure, stepped up in the pocket and launched one of the prettiest passes in the history of Ohio State football. Receiver Michael Jenkins gathered it in as he crossed the goal line, and Ohio State's national championship hopes remained alive.

Krenzel was spectacular when he needed to be in the Fiesta Bowl national title game against the heavily favored University of Miami. He led all rushers with 81 yards and scored twice, including a one-yard run that tied it up in the first overtime. That score was set up by a fourth-and-14 completion to Jenkins. Krenzel completed just seven of 21 passes with two interceptions, but his running kept the Hurricanes off balance all night. He was named offensive MVP.

"Craig Krenzel stepped up. He did for us what we needed done," Tressel said. "He led the team and fought like crazy and made the plays when he had to. He was tough."

Krenzel and the Buckeyes would roll to an 11–2 mark the following season, including a 35–28 Fiesta Bowl win over eighth-ranked Kansas State in which Krenzel threw four touchdown passes and was again Offensive MVP. The Buckeyes would finish the season fourth in both major polls, and Krenzel would close his career with a 24–3 mark as a starter.

He was drafted by the Chicago Bears in the fifth round and found himself starting as a rookie because of injuries, and he promptly led the Bears to three straight wins despite less-than-stellar statistics (sound familiar?). He then lost the next couple, was injured, and later was cut by the Bears. He hung on with the Cincinnati Bengals for another season before retiring, and he is now a radio voice for the Buckeyes.

Keith Byars

When talk turns to the greatest running backs in Ohio State history, Keith Byars likely doesn't come immediately to mind for many Buckeyes fans. He never won the Heisman Trophy, the school hasn't retired his number, and none of the teams he played on won a national title or came close.

Byars, however, should be in that discussion. He is one of the school's all-time leading rushers and scorers despite missing more than half his senior season because of a foot injury, and in his junior year he put together what is arguably the greatest season for a running back in Ohio State history.

A native of Dayton, Ohio, Byars led the nation in rushing (1,764 yards), scoring (144 points), and all-purpose yards (2,441) in 1984. And in a nationally televised shoot-out with the University of Illinois at Ohio Stadium in October, he rushed for 274 yards and five touchdowns, including a 67—yard run in which his shoe came flying off about halfway through.

Looking back, it's easy to wonder why he didn't win the Heisman Trophy that season. The award instead went to Boston College quarterback Doug Flutie, with Byars a distant second. Popular sentiment says Flutie clinched it with his nationally televised Hail Mary pass that beat Miami the day after Thanksgiving. But according to the folks who hand out the award, all the votes were in prior to that day.

Regardless, Byars was a first-team All-American and Big Ten MVP that season. Besides his then-school record 1,764 rushing yards and 22 touchdowns on the ground, he also caught 42 passes for another 479 yards and two scores. Byars was fast and elusive in the open field and had great hands, and he was a big back who could also run defenders over.

He rushed for 1,199 yards his sophomore year and scored 22 touchdowns, but he appeared in just four games his senior season after fracturing a bone in his foot. Additionally, he reinjured it twice trying to come back. He remains fifth on the all-time rushing list (3,200 yards), second to Eddie George in single-season rushing, and second to Pete Johnson in career touchdowns (50).

Byars was also a team leader who, even when hurt, had an impact. Chris Spielman, who played with him, said his favorite memory of playing with Byars is when Byars gave a stirring pregame speech before a 1985 showdown with number-one-ranked University of Iowa at Ohio Stadium. Byars, then a senior, was hurt and wouldn't play. "You could just see the pain and sorrow and feel it and hear it in his voice that he wasn't able to play," Spielman says. "But you knew for him to give that kind of speech, heartfelt like he gave, 'I wish I could play but I can't, but I'm gonna be there with you'...that's the best memory I have of Keith Byars."

The Buckeyes, by the way, went out and knocked off Iowa 22–13.

Byars went on to a long and productive NFL career with Philadelphia, Miami, New England, and the New York Jets, although he became known more for his pass-catching abilities than his running. He is a football analyst for the YES Network, which is based in New York City.

60 "We're Coming Back"

Ohio State hosted defending Big Ten champion the University of Illinois on October 13, 1984, before a packed Horseshoe and a national television audience, and the game couldn't have gotten off to a worse start for the Buckeyes. They turned the ball over twice early and couldn't stop an Illini offense led by quarterback Jack Trudeau. Illinois jumped out to a 24–0 lead before Keith Byars finally got the Bucks on the board with a 16-yard touchdown run with just over four minutes to play before the half.

The two teams got into a scrum in the end zone, and Illinois safety Craig Swoope decked Buckeyes center Kirk Lowdermilk, earning himself a personal foul penalty and ejection. It may have been the wake-up call the Bucks needed. When Byars returned

Count the Victories

Ohio State had won 849 games through the end of the 2013 season (12 wins from the 2010 season were vacated) to place it fifth among Division I-A (Football Bowl Subdivision) teams. Ahead of the Buckeyes were, in order: Michigan, Texas, Notre Dame, and Nebraska. The Buckeyes are 849–318–53 all time, for a winning percentage of .718, which places them sixth (the NCAA computes a tie as half win, half loss).

According to Ohio State's media guide, the Buckeyes have a record of 411–109–20 at Ohio Stadium though the 2013 season.

to the sideline, he looked directly into a camera and said, "We're coming back."

That they did, in one of the greatest games old Ohio Stadium has ever seen. They scored twice more before the half when wide receiver Cris Carter made a spectacular catch of a Mike Tomczak pass and Byars ran in for his second touchdown. The Illinois lead was down to 24–21.

Ohio State recovered a fumble on the opening kickoff of the second half, and several plays later Byars had his third score, giving the Buckeyes their first lead at 28–24. Illinois responded with a field goal to cut the margin to one, and then came one of the most memorable plays in Ohio State history.

The Buckeyes had the ball on their own 33-yard line when Byars took a handoff and ripped off a 67-yard touchdown run, about half of which he accomplished after his left shoe came flying off. The Bucks were up 35–27, and Ohio Stadium was rocking.

The teams continued battling back and forth, and an Illinois field goal tied the game at 38 with a little more than three minutes left to play. Using Byars and backup tailback John Wooldridge, the Buckeyes pounded the ball down the field, and Byars scored from the 3 with 36 seconds left. It was his fifth touchdown on the day to go with 274 yards rushing, both Ohio State records at the time.

Ohio State then stopped a last-gasp drive by Illinois and had the win, 45–38. It was one of the most dramatic victories in school history and hugely important: Ohio State would go on to win an outright Big Ten title, finishing one game ahead of Illinois and Purdue.

Here are some other incredible games in Buckeye history:

September 24, 1977—Number-four ranked Ohio State falls behind number-three ranked Oklahoma 20–0 before scoring 28 unanswered points to take the lead. Oklahoma scores a late touchdown, though, and then recovers an on-side kick to set up a 41-yard field goal attempt by Uwe von Schamann with three seconds left. Ohio State calls a timeout to ice von Schamann, a native of Germany, and the kicker mockingly 'conducts' the Ohio Stadium crowd as they chant "Block that kick!" He drills it, and the Sooners have a historic 29–28 victory.

September 25, 1982—Ohio State has Stanford University on the ropes with a little more than a minute to play, the Cardinal trailing and pinned back on their own 20. But Stanford has this guy named Elway at quarterback. John Elway gives the Ohio Stadium crowd a glimpse of things to come as he calmly leads Stanford down the field before hitting Emile Harry with the 18-yard, game-winning touchdown pass with 30 seconds remaining. Stanford wins 23–20.

September 24, 1988—The Buckeyes fall behind seventh-ranked Louisiana State University 33–20 following a Tigers touchdown with four and a half minutes to play, and some fans at Ohio Stadium head for the exits. The ones that stay are rewarded. The Bucks quickly march down the field and score on a Carlos Snow five-yard run to make it 33–27. Ohio State then stuffs LSU, which has its punter take a safety, making the score 33–29. Bobby Olive returns the free kick to the LSU 39 and then makes a diving catch of a pass from Greg Frey for the winning score. Ohio State stops LSU one final time, and delirious Buckeyes fans storm the field prematurely. The refs get it sorted out, and Ohio State has an unbelievable 36–33 win.

September 13, 2003—North Carolina State University, led by quarterback Philip Rivers, scores 17 unanswered points over the final nine minutes to send the game into overtime. The teams then trade touchdowns until the N.C. State running back T.A. McLendon is stopped just short of the end zone on fourth down in the third overtime. He reaches the ball over the goal line, but the officials, after conferring about 30 seconds, decide he didn't make it. The final score: Ohio State 44, N.C. State 38 in triple overtime.

October 28, 1989—Ohio State falls behind the University of Minnesota 31–0 in the first half at the Metrodome before mounting the comeback of all comebacks. The Bucks slowly climb their way back into the game before Frey hits Jeff Graham with a touchdown pass with less than one minute to play. It was the first time Ohio led all game, and the resulting score was 41–37 Ohio State.

November 20, 1920—Playing Illinois in the season finale with an outright conference title on the line, quarterback Harry "Hoge" Workman hits Cyril Myers with a 37-yard touchdown pass on the final play of the game for a 7–0 win. The undefeated Buckeyes earn the first Rose Bowl trip in school history.

61 Skull Session

For many Buckeyes fans, the only place to start game day at Ohio State is in the old basketball arena on campus. It's there that the marching band hosts the Skull Session, a rousing rehearsal and pep rally that gets the Buckeyes faithful, as well as the players, pumped for the game.

The Skull Session was started in 1932 by band director Eugene J. Weigel and originally was held in the old Rehearsal Hall. And it was designed as just that—a final rehearsal so band members could nail down the music so that they could focus on marching during halftime. But the sessions became so popular with family members of the band and its fans that in 1957, the Skull Session was moved to St. John Arena, the then-home of Ohio State basketball.

It remained mainly a rehearsal session for several years until Dr. Paul Droste, who took over as director in 1970, gave it more of a pep rally feel. That's what it is today as fans pack the arena the morning of games. Admission is free, and more than 10,000 fans often attend, lining up early to get good seats (it's general admission). Chants of "O-H, I-O" and "Let's Go Bucks" go back and forth as fans eagerly await the arrival of the band, the pride of the buckeyes.

Each Skull Session starts a couple of hours before kickoff, sometimes with visiting college and high school bands as the warm-up acts. The main attraction, though, is the Ohio State University Marching Band, and the Best Damn Band in the Land performs for about an hour, rocking the old barn in the perfect prelude to the game.

In a tradition created by former coach Jim Tressel, the football team makes a brief appearance at the beginning of the show.

Fans of Ohio State will also enjoy soaking up some of the atmosphere in St. John Arena, which opened in 1956 and was named for former athletics director, basketball coach, and assistant football coach Lynn St. John. It was home to the history-making Ohio State basketball teams of the early 1960s that included John Havlicek and Jerry Lucas, and which captured one national championship and were runners-up two other years. The men's and women's basketball teams have moved into the Jerome Schottenstein Center, but St. John Arena is still home to men's and women's volleyball, men's and women's gymnastics, and wrestling.

The Skull Session leads in to another Ohio State tradition that fans should experience. After the practice, the fans line the walkway from St. John Arena to Ohio Stadium to see the players and band. After the team's appearance at the Skull Session, Tressel leads his charges on the short walk across Woody Hayes Drive to the stadium. Fans line the route to give the Bucks some shouts of encouragement. Fans then do the same for the band as, closer to game time, the musicians leave the Skull Session and make the march to the stadium for their traditional ramp entrance.

The Linemen

Les Horvath had Bill Willis. Vic Janowicz had Robert Momsen. Howard Cassady had Jim Parker. Archie Griffin had Kurt Schumacher. Eddie George had Orlando Pace. And Troy Smith had Nick Mangold.

For every Heisman Trophy–winning back in Ohio State history, there was at least one All-American lineman in front of him during his career, clearing a path and protecting his backside. Often there was more than one such lineman. Griffin also played behind John Hicks, Steve Myers, and Ted Smith. Robert McCullough was an All-American center the year Janowicz won his Heisman, and guard William Hackett blocked alongside Willis for Horvath. One could even go as far back as Ohio State's first superstar, Chic Harley, who enjoyed the services of All-Americans Robert Karch and Kelley Van Dyne when he was thrilling fans at Ohio Field. The foundation of Ohio State's football success was built on the running game, epitomized best by Woody Hayes and his "three yards and a cloud of dust" offense. It was off-tackle and up the middle, with the occasional option and pitch sweep thrown in to keep the defense honest.

"I will pound you and pound you until you quit," Hayes would say.

He liked big backs, but it was mostly the linemen who were doing the pounding. Pace, Hicks, Parker, and Willis are generally considered the greatest linemen in Ohio State history, but there were many more along the way whose importance can't be overstated. A lineman can be great without an outstanding back following him, but the reverse simply doesn't happen. Without a good offensive line, the greatest running back in history isn't going far.

Iolas Huffman was a two-time All-American (1920–21) at guard and tackle, and he was one of the first great linemen for Ohio State, helping to lead the Buckeyes to a conference title in 1920 and their first Rose Bowl. Dozens of Ohio State linemen have been named first-team All-American since, although many of the names would be lost on even an avid Buckeyes fan.

There were two-time All-Americans Edwin Hess (1925–26), Leo Raskowski (1926–27), and Joseph Gailus (1932–33). Center Gomer Jones and guard Gust Zarnas were All-Americans who played together in the mid-1930s and who are both in the College Football Hall of Fame. Also in the Hall is "Big" Jim Daniell, a tackle who played in the late 1930s and early '40s. Warren Amling was an All-American at guard (1945) and then tackle ('46), while

Aurealius Thomas earned the honor for the 1957 national champions and is also in the College Football Hall of Fame.

David Foley and Rufus Mayes both made All-American for the 1968 national championship teams, and Chris Ward was a massive tackle who was twice an All-American (1976–77). When Keith Byars was setting records in 1984, he had All-American guard Jim Lachey opening holes for him. Korey Stringer was a two-time All-American (1993–94) who helped power the potent Buckeyes offense of the early 1990s and set the stage for Pace. Rob Murphy made All-American at guard twice (1997–98) for John Cooper–led teams that were some of the best in the country, while LeCharles Bentley was an All-American in 2001 and won the Rimington Award as the nation's top center.

It's an impressive list, and that's not nearly all of the great linemen over the nearly 120 years of Buckeyes football. When Troy Smith took the podium to accept the 2006 Heisman Trophy, he had a list of his own. "Kirk Barton, Doug Datish, Steve Rehring, T.J. Downing, Alex Boone, my guys up front," Smith said. "Those are my offensive linemen who made this possible today."

The Other Running Backs

If Tim Spencer had played just about anywhere else he'd be a legend. His number would likely hang from the stadium façade, and his name would come up when fans reminisced about the greatest of all time. But when you have a running back tradition like Ohio State's, with multiple Heisman Trophy winners and All-Americans, some names get lost to history. Spencer's is among them.

He was neither a Heisman winner nor an All-American, although he was All–Big Ten his junior and senior years (1981–82). Besides that, he only rushed for more yards than any player in Ohio State history but two: Archie Griffin and Eddie George. "It feels good to be in the company of two great running backs like Archie and Eddie," Spencer said upon his induction into the Ohio State Hall of Fame in 1997. "In company like that you don't mind being third."

Spencer played fullback his sophomore year at Ohio State, before making the move to tailback his junior season. It didn't take him long to settle in. On the very first play from scrimmage that season Spencer busted off an 82-yard touchdown run against Duke University at Ohio Stadium. Fans quickly realized the tailback position was in good hands. Spencer led the Buckeyes that season with 1,217 yards rushing and the next with 1,538, which at the time was the best season ever besides a couple from that guy named Griffin. Spencer closed out his career with 124 yards and two touchdowns in a 24–14 win over the University of Michigan, and then he was named the Most Valuable Player of the Holiday Bowl after rushing for 167 yards and two scores in a 47–17 win against Brigham Young University.

Spencer finished his career with 3,553 yards and 36 rushing touchdowns, which is tied for fourth all time. He played three seasons in the United States Football League before signing on with the San Diego Chargers and playing there for six years. Spencer returned to Ohio State following his playing career and was the running backs' coach from 1994 to 2003, including the national championship season of 2002. He also held the same position with the Chicago Bears in the NFL.

Spencer is far from alone as an overlooked ex-Buckeye running back. A year after Les Horvath won Ohio State's first Heisman in 1944, fullback Ollie Cline out-gained him on the ground (with 936 yards) and was named All-American and Big Ten MVP.

Don Clark took over with the departure of Heisman winner Hopalong Cassady and filled in admirably, leading the team in rushing in 1956 and '57, when the Buckeyes captured a national title. Clark finished his career with 2,116 yards, which at the time trailed only Cassady on the all-time list and is still in the top 20.

Harold "Champ" Henson was the fullback with a nose for the goal line in the early 1970s before Pete Johnson took over. Henson rushed for 20 touchdowns in 1972 and 36 for his career, tied with Spencer for fourth all time.

The 1980s and '90s saw a trio of backs who a casual Buckeyes fan might have trouble placing, but who are seventh, eighth, and ninth, respectively, on the career rushing list: Pepe Pearson, Carlos Snow, and Michael Wiley. Antonio Pittman, 10th on the list, ran for 2,945 yards before leaving for the NFL after his junior season in 2006.

Chris "Beanie" Wells and Carlos Hyde, both of whom possessed a deadly combination of size and speed, are two recent additions to the list. Both topped 3,000 yards for their careers, with Wells (who played from 2006 to 2008) sitting at fourth all time and Hyde (2010–13) at sixth.

The 2006 Season

The 2006 Ohio State Buckeyes were a talented but mysterious team as the season dawned, with several dynamic players returning on offense but significant holes to fill on defense. That didn't stop the preseason pollsters from voting them the top-ranked team in the country before play began, and for once the voters seemed to get it right.

The Buckeyes were led by Coach Jim Tressel, who had already won one national title in his five years in Columbus, and poised and athletic quarterback Troy Smith, who would win the Heisman Trophy that season as the nation's finest player. Ohio State rolled to a 12–0 regular season, including wins over two number-two-ranked teams: the University of Texas and the University of Michigan.

The Bucks were riding a 19-game winning streak as they headed to Arizona to play in the national championship game against Florida, which had lost once and struggled in some other games. To many pundits, it was a mismatch. Ohio State would roll over the Gators, they argued, making a mockery of the system (the Bowl Championship Series) that produced such a poor title contest. In fact, in the weeks leading up to the game, some questioned whether Florida deserved to be in the game and suggested that a better contest would be a rematch between Ohio State and Michigan, whose only loss was by three points at Ohio Stadium.

Apparently, the Gators were listening. They said as much before the game and then went out and proved it, after a brief hiccup at the start of the contest. Ted Ginn Jr., Ohio State's electrifying receiver and return man, took the opening kick and returned it 93 yards for a touchdown. It's a wonder the state of Ohio didn't split open at that moment from the tremors Ginn set off.

Looking back, they should have just called the game right there: "Thanks for coming everyone, but who's kidding who here?" Unfortunately, they didn't, and it immediately got worse for the Buckeyes—much worse. Ginn's jubilant teammates piled on him in the end zone, and he hurt his foot and wouldn't return.

It says something about the course of the game that it may not have even mattered. Ginn wasn't going to get in the way of the maniacal Florida rushers who were after Troy Smith all game, chase down the Gators running backs and receivers who carved up the Buckeyes defense, or design a scheme for the Ohio State coaches who appeared lost.

Ted Ginn Jr.'s return of the opening kickoff for a 93-yard touchdown at the BCS national championship game against Florida symbolized the Buckeyes' 2006 season—a promising start and disappointing finish.

Florida came right back to tie the game on a touchdown pass by Chris Leak, the much less-heralded quarterback who would play like a Heisman winner, and the rout was on. The Buckeyes seemed befuddled by Florida's spread offense, which used a variety of receivers and running backs and added athletic backup quarterback Tim Tebow to the mix.

The Gators rolled to a 34–14 halftime lead, and Buckeyes fans were stunned. The Florida scoring machine slowed a little in the second half, but Ohio State could never get going. The final tally, 41–14, told only half the story. Smith, continuing the supposed "Heisman jinx" that has seen several past winners flop in bowl games, completed just four of 14 passes for 35 yards with one interception. He was sacked five times, and Florida held him to minus 29 yards rushing on 10 carries. Leak, meanwhile, a frequent target of criticism from Florida fans, completed 25 of 36 passes for 213 yards and a touchdown. Overall, Florida outgained the Buckeyes 370 yards to 82 and led in time of possession 40:48 to 19:12. Florida showed complete dominance.

In ensuing days there was talk about how maybe the much longer gap between games for the Buckeyes, 51 days compared to 37 for Florida, had led to Ohio's sluggish play. And there was even criticism of the generally beloved Smith—was he too busy hitting the banquet circuit to prepare for the game? And didn't he look a little pudgy? And Tressel, who every time the camera caught him seemed to be staring down at his clipboard looking for answers, was also a target.

Florida head coach Urban Meyer and his players left little doubt that all the questions about whether they deserved to share the field with Ohio State had provided them with motivation. "I'd like to thank all those people," Meyer said afterward. "Our pregame speech was easy."

Tressel was still grasping for answers in the aftermath. "We scored on the first play of the game and from that point on, really couldn't keep the pressure where we needed it to be," he said. "Ohio State didn't get it done."

Fans, coaches, and players were left to seek some perspective. It had been a phenomenal season overall: a 12–1 record, a number-two final ranking, a Big Ten title, and a win over Michigan. A battered Smith tried to provide some perspective. "Not everything in life is going to go the exact way you want it," he said. "I don't have any regrets, though. I really don't. We came out and fought. We came up short. Sometimes you have great games, and sometimes you don't."

Well, that game was a "don't" that Buckeye fans will not soon forget. While it has happened before—Ohio State teams in 1970,

'75, and '79 went into the Rose Bowl undefeated and ranked first before losing—this loss seemed to sting like no other. The current 24/7 news culture that creates incredible hype for big sporting events had something to do with it, but even more significant was what happened on the field. A Buckeyes team that could have gone down as one of the greatest in the program's storied history was, for one night, simply outclassed. That was indeed stunning.

65 The Rising Cost of Success

Interest in Ohio State football seems to increase every year and fan passion surrounding the Bucks appears almost infinite. The 24/7 media environment feeds into this, with the program covered from all angles, even in the off-season. In truth, there really is no off-season for the Buckeyes, nor is there one for the blogs, talk radio hosts, and arm-chair quarterbacks who follow them from around the state and throughout Buckeye Nation.

All of this said, there's been a surprising development in the past few seasons: thousands of tickets still available for purchase for certain games as the season approaches and hundreds of empty seats at Ohio Stadium for some of the more unattractive matchups. It seems to be a confluence of events that includes rising tickets prices and a tough economy, tickets being readily available on the growing secondary market, and scheduled opponents that generate little excitement.

Major college football went to a 12-game schedule several years back, and Ohio State, like many other schools, took advantage of that to add a home game every year against a lesser-known opponent. It's a fairly easy way to fill athletics department coffers and almost always ends in a victory for the home team, except for the occasional Michigan–Appalachian State game. For Ohio State fans, however, Akron and Kent State just don't get the blood pumping like Michigan and Wisconsin.

But tickets have been available shortly before even some Big Ten games, and Ohio State also had trouble selling its allotment of tickets for the 2014 Orange Bowl. So this seems to point more toward the rising cost of these tickets, which are often not good seats, either.

"It is the new normal," according to a *Columbus Dispatch* analysis before the 2013 season. "As ticket prices have increased and the options to find tickets on the secondary market have expanded, a lot of fans no longer feel compelled to shell out big bucks to watch Ohio State hammer Florida A&M."

Ticket prices to Buckeye games have been on a steady climb over the years, as is the case with probably every major college team. But they took a significant leap before the 2013 season, rising 13 percent to $79—actually about $86 when service fees are included—for most seats.

The school, in a move approved by trustees, also initiated special pricing for so-called "premium games." So tickets for the 2013 contest with Wisconsin—and future ones against Michigan and likely one other opponent each season—will jump sharply. Tickets for the Michigan game are expected to top $150 in ensuing seasons and go up from there.

Men's basketball also has premium games, and such tiered pricing has been occurring at other schools and in professional sports for some time. For years Chicago Cubs fans have been paying much more to see a St. Louis Cardinals game in July as compared to an April matchup with the Miami Marlins. If anything, Ohio State is late to the game on this trend.

Athletics director Gene Smith said the increase was necessary to fund ongoing improvements at Ohio Stadium and to support the more than 30 non-revenue varsity sports at Ohio State. An encouraging development occurred when the Big Ten announced that starting in 2016 it was adding an extra conference game for a nine-game slate, meaning one less non-conference victim on the schedule.

Some Ohio State fans might gripe about the increases and premium pricing, but Ohio Stadium is still jammed with more than 100,000 people every home Saturday, even for the Florida A&Ms of the world.

"We do this because our people are passionate," Smith told the Associated Press. "We believe that they'll show up."

66 Time Runs Out at Michigan State

In the long history of Ohio State football there was never a game that ended in such controversy and confusion as the one on November 9, 1974, in Spartan Stadium. The undefeated and top-ranked Buckeyes were upset by Michigan State University that day, 16–13. Woody Hayes, however, had a more profane—and unprintable—description for what happened to his team. In the end, the loss spoiled Ohio State's perfect season and meant that it had to share the Big Ten title with the University of Michigan.

Ohio State and Michigan State were tied 3–3 at the half as neither one could get much going offensively. Ohio State built a 10-point lead in the second half on a Tom Klaban field goal and a Champ Henson touchdown run, and it led 13–3 with a little more than nine minutes to play. But the Spartans struck back with two scores of their own, including an 88-yard touchdown run by Levi Jackson that put Michigan State up 16–13, with the game nearing an end.

Ohio State stormed back, though, marching the ball down the field until a plunge by Henson left them at the Michigan State 1-yard line with 14 seconds to play. Ohio State had no time-outs left, and Buckeyes players scrambled to get into position for one final try as the final seconds ticked away. Not surprisingly, Michigan State players didn't seem to be responding with the same urgency, and Hayes would later accuse them of holding down Ohio State players at the end of Henson's run.

The Buckeyes got into position, kind of, but the ball was hurriedly snapped and went through the legs of quarterback Cornelius Greene. Wingback Brian Baschnagel scooped it up and ran in for the presumed game-winning touchdown.

But had the Buckeyes gotten the play off in time? One referee signaled touchdown, while another indicated time had expired before the ball was snapped. The referees huddled with each other and Big Ten Commissioner Wayne Duke, who was on hand, and a 46-minute delay ensued, with the Buckeyes' perfect season and number-one ranking hanging in the balance. Many of the 78,533 fans on hand stayed in their seats to await the verdict.

After what must have seemed an eternity to the players and fans, Duke announced the decision: the clock had expired and the touchdown didn't count. Michigan State had pulled off one of its greatest wins in school history.

The game may have been officially over, but the arguments were just beginning. Hayes was livid and reportedly confronted Duke, using a choice word to tell the commissioner what had been done to his team. Michigan State fans note that even if the ball was snapped just before the clock read 00:00, the Buckeyes weren't set the required one second, and therefore an offensive penalty should have been called. Buckeyes backers argue that they would have had time to get set and run one final play if the Spartans players hadn't intentionally dawdled after the previous play.

Ohio State recovered to beat Michigan a few weeks later to earn a share of the Big Ten championship with the Wolverines. The conference athletic directors voted to send Ohio State to the Rose Bowl, where they lost 18–17 to the University of Southern California. The Bucks ended the season 10–2, with the two losses coming by a total of four points, and a fourth-place ranking in the final Associated Press poll.

67 The Good Woody Hayes

Former Buckeyes quarterback Rex Kern remembers Woody Hayes occasionally calling him over after he'd finished up at the training table. "He'd say, 'Rex, you got any tests you are studying for?'" Kern recalls. "If I said no, he would say, 'Let's go.'"

Pop quiz on the new game plan? Film session? Extra work with the receivers? "You knew where you were going," Kern says. "You were going to the hospital with him."

Hayes was a regular at Columbus hospitals, so much so that the nursing staffs got used to seeing him walking the halls. Often he'd bring along boxes of chocolates or flowers and one of his star players, and they'd spend time visiting with complete strangers. He'd ask the nurses who hadn't had a visitor that day and pop in unannounced, sometimes after visiting with one of his own players who was recovering from an injury.

There was a compassionate side of Hayes that didn't jive with the image many saw on television of the raving, obsessive coach whose only concern seemed to be winning football games at all costs. And Hayes couldn't have cared less that few knew of his good deeds. One time a reporter overheard that Hayes was headed to the hospital after practice and asked to come along. Woody supposedly snapped and threatened him, saying he most definitely was not invited and better not write about it.

Hayes always preached to his players about their obligation to pay it forward, and it was something he tried to live. There were the innumerable visits to hospitals, and he was often on hand for big moments in the lives of his players and ex-players: weddings, funerals, births. "One of the best days of my life was October 18, 1981, when my son Jimmy was born," says former Buckeyes great Jim Otis. "I held him first, and Woody held him second, even before his mother."

When Ohio State returned from the 1969 Rose Bowl victory, which capped off a national championship season, Hayes didn't appear at a giant rally, hit the talk-show circuit, or take advantage of the exposure to cut some commercials. Two days later he headed to Vietnam to visit American troops there.

Hayes was a rock-ribbed conservative—he once spoke in support of the Vietnam War and U.S. troops at a campus rally—who had a particular interest in military history. He often related history back to football. He definitely fell into the camp of folks who felt the world was changing too fast, and not necessarily for the better.

But then again, he often defied stereotypes. Hayes recruited African American players and several of them were stars on his teams years before teams in the South would integrate. When Jim Parker found the Ohio State campus less than welcoming in the 1950s, Hayes let him move in with him. Just a few years after schools such as the University of Alabama grudgingly integrated, Hayes had a black player starting at quarterback.

Woody could be considered old-fashioned when it came to academics, too, because he thought all of his players should get their degrees, and he harped on it constantly. The pressure to achieve in school started before they even reached campus. Jim Stillwagon recalls his first meeting as a recruit with Hayes.

"I sat down with him, and he asked 'What was the last novel you read?'" Stillwagon says. "I'd never read a novel in my life. I told him *Moby Dick* because I'd just seen it on TV, and we talked about it for about an hour."

Linebacker Tom Cousineau said when Hayes recruited him he "talked to you about everything—everything but football. Sometimes he gave you the impression he wasn't interested in you for football because he never talked about it. He left that to the assistants."

Hayes' interest in schoolwork didn't stop when players reached campus. "He never let me forget that I was at Ohio State for an education first and to play football second," Jim Parker once said.

The NCAA thought Woody cared a little too much about his players. After acknowledging in a *Sports Illustrated* story that he sometimes gave down-on-their-luck players a few dollars from his own pocket, Ohio State was placed on probation. "We're not going to give these kids on the football team anything illegal, you can bet on that," he later said. "But we are going to give them an opportunity to get an education. And I am going to see they get that education. We certainly owe them that."

Former fullback and linebacker Bruce Elia says he's often heard the misconceptions about Hayes. "'Oh, you played for that crazy guy, Woody Hayes,' they will say. I just say, 'Let me tell you, he wasn't crazy. He was not only a good coach, but he was a great man,'" Elia says. "That man cared about people more than anybody I ever knew."

68 Put in the Super Sub

Ohio State visited the University of Illinois midway through the 1968 season, and after grabbing a 24–0 lead over the winless Illini, the Buckeyes allowed the home team back in the game. When Illinois scored with a little less than five minutes to play, the game was tied, and the Buckeyes' perfect season was in jeopardy. Ohio State got the ball back, but things went from bad to worse when starting quarterback Rex Kern went out with a head injury. Enter Ron Maciejowski.

One of the less-heralded members of that celebrated sophomore class, Maciejowski calmly led the Buckeyes on the game-winning touchdown drive to preserve their unbeaten season. He hit Larry Zelina for 10 yards and then ran for 12 himself. Maciejowksi then found Zelina down the middle on a 44-yard pass that put the Bucks on the Illini 4. Jim Otis scored a couple of plays later, and Ohio State had a 31–24 victory.

The following week Kern sprained an ankle in the second quarter, and Maciejowski was back under center. He promptly led Ohio State on an 83-yard scoring drive in a game the Bucks would win, 25–20, over a tough Michigan State University team. Maciejowski was earning the moniker "super sub," but the next week he started at the University of Wisconsin because Kern was still out. Maciejowski passed for 153 yards and one touchdown and ran for 124 yards and three scores as the Buckeyes won easily, 43–8.

Kern returned to close out the season, including a blowout of the University of Michigan and a Rose Bowl victory over the University of Southern California that clinched the national title. Kern was named Most Valuable Player of that game, received most of the accolades over the next two seasons, and is a Buckeyes legend. But Maciejowski played a vital role subbing for the injury-prone starter during the most successful three-year run in Ohio State history.

The "super sub" was far from the only underrated Buckeye over the decades. When you've had as many Heisman Trophy winners, All-Americans, and championship teams as Ohio State has had, there is bound to be an entire lineup of great players who have largely been lost to history. Doubtless they're remembered by their teammates and coaches, though.

Bruce Elia was a mainstay on both sides of the ball for the great Buckeyes teams of the first half of the 1970s, but he was overshadowed by guys named Griffin, Greene, and Johnson. All Elia did was lead Ohio State in scoring as a fullback in 1973, and then he made the switch to linebacker and led the team in tackles in 1974.

Wingback Brian Baschnagel was on those same teams and did all the little things while his backfield mates got most of the glory. He blocked, ran the occasional reverse, caught passes, and even was

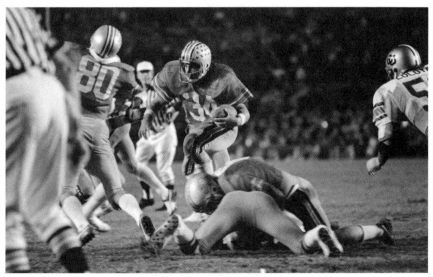

Jeff Logan, a 182-pound tailback working at fullback for the first time, crashes through the Colorado line in the Orange Bowl game in Miami on New Year's night, January 1, 1977. Ohio State won 27–10.

the holder on field goals and extra points. He was the steady fourth member of the greatest backfield in Ohio State history.

Jeff Logan came to Ohio State as a celebrated school-boy running back, but the Buckeyes had this Archie Griffin fellow holding down the starting tailback spot. So Logan bided his time until his opportunity came in 1976, his junior season. Griffin may have been irreplaceable, but Logan did a fine job trying, rushing for 1,248 yards that season to lead the team as Ohio State went 9–2–1 and won the Orange Bowl. He finished his career with 2,026 yards.

The 2002 national champion Buckeyes frequently had trouble moving the ball and so relied on their defense and placed great emphasis on always winning the field position battle. That's where punter Andy Groom came in. Groom was an All-American that season, and his punts were critical all year long, including in the Fiesta Bowl against the University of Miami. Coach Jim Tressel recognized Groom's important role and asked him to be the one to present President George W. Bush with an Ohio State helmet when the team visited the White House.

69 The 1976 Rose Bowl Upset by UCLA

The 1975 season played out to perfection for Ohio State: an 11–0 regular season and Big Ten championship, a number-one ranking, and a team stacked with talent that included two-time Heisman Trophy–winner Archie Griffin and Big Ten MVP Cornelius Greene. The requisite Rose Bowl berth seemed nothing more than a coronation for this team, led by Woody Hayes.

And the game itself looked like a mismatch. Pac 8 champion UCLA went 8–2–1 that season, and one of those losses was a

41–20 thumping at home to the visiting Buckeyes. There was no indication the Rose Bowl would be any different, especially after Ohio State pushed UCLA all over the field in the first half. The Bruins didn't get a first down until almost halftime and racked up only 48 total yards in the first two quarters. Ohio State, meanwhile, penetrated deep into UCLA territory repeatedly. The only problem was that the Bucks couldn't get in the end zone, mustering only a Tom Klaban 42-yard field goal to take a 3–0 halftime lead.

Whether it was the tight score that gave the Bruins confidence or the halftime strategizing of Coach Dick Vermeil, UCLA was a different team in the second half. Led by quarterback John Sciarra and running back Wendell Tyler, the Bruins put up 366 yards of total offense during the final 30 minutes. They scored 16 unanswered points in the third quarter on a field goal and two Sciarra scoring tosses to receiver Wally Henry to jump ahead 16–3.

The Buckeyes finally responded in the fourth quarter, with a 65-yard scoring drive that culminated with a Pete Johnson three-yard touchdown run, closing the gap to 16–10. But Tyler came back with a 54-yard touchdown run that sealed the upset before 105,464 fans. Ohio State's hopes for a perfect season and national championship were dashed.

The final score was 23–10, and the stats help tell the story: Tyler ended up with 177 yards on 21 carries. Game MVP Sciarra completed 13 of 19 passes for 212 yards, along with the two scoring passes to Henry, one of 16 yards and the other 67 yards. For the Buckeyes, Griffin fractured his hand on the first series of the game but still rushed for 93 yards on 17 carries, and Greene completed just seven of 18 passing for 90 yards and threw a pair of interceptions.

The Bucks finished fourth in the final Associated Press and United Press International polls that year, one spot ahead of UCLA, while Oklahoma, which had beaten the University of Michigan in the Orange Bowl, claimed the national title.

The game was the fourth consecutive Rose Bowl for Griffin, Hayes, and the Buckeyes, and it would be Hayes' last, as well as one of the most crushing defeats of his career. He was devastated afterward and shouldered the blame for the loss.

"We got out-coached and just got beat," he said. "Our defense played magnificently for the first half, but this UCLA staff just out-coached us."

Vermeil was just 39 years old at the time and moved on to the NFL after the season, where he would have a distinguished career that included a Super Bowl win with the Rams.

"It was probably the biggest upset in the history of the Rose Bowl," he said of that 1976 game.

He wouldn't get any arguments from Ohio State players or fans. "That was the most disappointing loss I ever experienced. Period," Griffin says. "That game really hurt."

70 One Point from Glory

There was every reason to believe the 1979 season would be one of rebuilding for the Buckeyes. Earle Bruce was starting his first season as head coach, following the abrupt departure of Woody Hayes after Hayes slugged a Clemson University player at the end of the previous season's Gator Bowl.

The Buckeyes lost that game to close out a 7–4–1 season that included a defeat to the University of Michigan and a fourth-place, Big Ten finish. Key players such as tailback Ron Springs and two-time All-American linebacker Tom Cousineau were gone. Art Schlichter returned at quarterback, but he was just a sopho-more and had thrown a school-record 21 interceptions in 1978.

The pundits certainly weren't expecting much, as Ohio State was unranked in preseason polls.

The pundits and almost everyone else were in for a surprise as Ohio State ripped off win after win on the way to a perfect regular season and number-one ranking. The Buckeyes then fell just short in the Rose Bowl, falling by one point to USC in a loss that cost Ohio State the national title. Still, that 1979 season remains one of the more unforgettable and unexpected ones in Ohio State history.

Bruce had a daunting challenge in replacing Hayes, but the former Ohio State player and assistant coach faced it head on. "I guess I'm a guy who goes for great challenges," Bruce said.

He had the Buckeyes ready to play as they downed Syracuse University 31–8 in the season opener at Ohio Stadium. Ohio State then fell behind the University of Minnesota 14–0 the following week and seemed completely outplayed, but Schlichter led them back for a 21–17 win.

A 45–29 home win over Washington State University followed, and then Ohio State traveled to Los Angeles to face 17th-ranked UCLA. The Buckeyes trailed 13–10 with a little more than two minutes to play when Schlichter directed the game-winning drive, capped off by a two-yard touchdown pass to Paul Campbell.

Schlichter was playing like the superstar Buckeyes fans had expected to see when he arrived on campus; Calvin Murray looked like the latest in a long line of great Ohio State running backs; and guard Ken Fritz was in the midst of an All-American season. The defense was coming together behind tackle Luther Henson, linebacker Jim Laughlin, and a tough and athletic defensive backfield that included Mike Guess, Vince Skillings, and Todd Bell.

The Buckeyes defeated Northwestern University16–7 and then ran off five straight blowout wins over Big Ten opponents, the closest of which was a 34–7 victory over the University of Iowa. Ohio was 10–0 and number two in the nation as it headed to Michigan to face the 13th-ranked Wolverines. Ohio State trailed

15–12 with approximately four minutes to play when Laughlin blocked a Michigan punt, and Bell picked up the ball and ran 18 yards for the touchdown. Ohio State would hold on for the 18–15 win and head to Pasadena for the Rose Bowl with an 11–0 record and ranked first in the nation.

The Buckeyes apparently still had doubters because they were underdogs to third-ranked USC. And those skeptics seemed right when USC jumped to a 10–0 lead in the first half. But Ohio State tied the game by halftime on a Vlade Janakievski field goal and a 67-yard Schlichter-to-Gary Williams touchdown pass. Janakievski added a couple of field goals in the second half, and Ohio State led 16–10 with five and a half minutes to play, a perfect season and national title in sight.

But USC's Heisman Trophy–winning tailback Charles White had been running all over the Bucks, and USC coaches knew to stick with what worked. It was White left and White right as USC marched 83 yards for the game-winning score, the tailback getting 71 of them, including the final one-yard plunge into the end zone. The extra point provided the final margin: USC 17, Ohio State 16. Apparently there was no Heisman jinx yet as White rushed for a Rose Bowl record 247 yards.

Ohio State finished the season ranked fourth, Bruce was named coach of the year, and Schlichter and Fritz were All-Americans. "That '79 team is a forgotten team," says Murray. "We had a great year and were Big Ten champions, and anniversaries come and go and nobody has any functions for us or mentions it. It just seems if you don't win a national championship, you are forgotten."

71 Great Nontitle Teams

In 1942 the Paul Brown–led Buckeyes went 9–1 and finished first in the final Associated Press poll to capture the school's first football national championship. Two years later Ohio State was 9–0, but the AP ranked the Buckeyes second to Army at season's end. Woody Hayes led the Bucks to a 10–0 record and the 1968 national title but said the following year's team that finished with one loss and ranked fourth in the country was his best ever. The 2002 Buckeyes put together a school-record 14–0 mark and won the first consensus national title since that 1968 team, but some Ohio State fans insist they weren't nearly as good as a couple of John Cooper's teams from the 1990s that had to settle for number-two rankings.

College football has never lent itself to closure. Without a playoff until 2014, the end of the season usually meant the beginning, or continuation, of the discussion over who had the best team. Many football historians and members of the media have put the word *mythical* in front of *national champion,* and the Bowl Championship Series did only so much to alleviate the confusion.

This imprecise system has benefited some "national champions" that maybe weren't truly challenged, and it has hurt some excellent teams that played one bad game or had one bad quarter and lost their shot at a title. Ohio State has had several teams suffer the latter fate, probably more than any school in college football. Ohio State claims seven national titles: 1942, '54, '57, '61, '68, '70, and 2002. But for an intercepted pass, a bad half of football, or a slip, the following teams would be among them:

1944—This team had Heisman Trophy–winner Les Horvath and three other All-Americans and was rarely challenged on the way to a 9–0 mark. But the Big Ten did not allow those Buckeyes to go to the Rose Bowl, and they finished second to 9–0 Army.

1969—This is the team Hayes called his best ever. It romped through the season until the 24–12 loss to the University of Michigan and Bo Schembechler. The Bucks had six interceptions that day, four by Rex Kern.

1973—The only blemish on this team's record was a 10–10 tie with undefeated Michigan. Ohio followed that by stomping USC in the Rose Bowl, 42–21. The result was a 10–0–1 record and number-two ranking behind Notre Dame University.

1974—They finished 10–2, but the two losses were a controversial three-point defeat at Michigan State University and an 18–17 loss to USC in the Rose Bowl. If a couple of plays had gone a different way, this squad might have been 12–0 and remembered as one of the best ever.

Woody Hayes Wasn't the First Choice

Woody Hayes may be the most iconic figure in the long history of Ohio State football, the veritable face of Buckeye football, but the reality is he was not the school's first choice when the job opened in 1950.

Ohio State football historian Jack Park says that after the resignation of Wes Fesler, a search committee interviewed seven finalists for the position, and the committee's top choice was the head coach at the University of Missouri, Don Faurot. Faurot had been considered for the job when Paul Brown was hired 10 years earlier, and this time it appeared to be a done deal. Faurot was offered the job and accepted it in February 1951, and Ohio State was planning a news conference to make the announcement. But then athletics director Dick Larkins received a call from Faurot saying he had changed his mind and was staying at Missouri. The committee turned to Hayes, the head coach at Miami of Ohio, and Hayes accepted.

The rest, as they say, is history.

1975—Archie Griffin and Cornelius Greene were seniors, and this team looked unbeatable…and it was, until the Bucks were upset by UCLA in the Rose Bowl, 23–10, a team they had beaten by three touchdowns earlier in the season.

1996—Undefeated Ohio State led Michigan 9–0 when All-American cornerback Shawn Springs slipped, allowing Tai Streets to score on a 69-yard pass play. It got the Wolverines back in the game, and they would pull the upset, 13–9. Ohio State went on to beat Arizona State University in the Rose Bowl and finish with a second-place ranking.

1998—A 28–24 upset loss to Michigan State at Ohio Stadium ruined the Buckeyes' title hopes. The Bucks led 24–9 in the second half, before the Spartans climbed back into it and took the lead. Ohio State had a final shot, but Joe Germaine was intercepted near the goal line. The Buckeyes beat Michigan two weeks later and then Texas A&M University in the Sugar Bowl, and for the second time in three seasons the Buckeyes were 11–1 and ranked second.

2006—The 12–0 Buckeyes and their Heisman Trophy–winning quarterback Troy Smith were favored in the BCS title game but were completely outplayed by the University of Florida in a shocking 41–14 loss. It was Ohio State's third No. 2 final ranking in a decade.

Wes Fesler

Wes Fesler was a three-time All-American, one of only seven in Ohio State history, and went on to become head coach and lead the Buckeyes to their first win in the Rose Bowl. But his tenure at Ohio

State would come to a premature and controversial end, clearing the way for a young coach from Miami of Ohio to take over and begin building a dynasty.

Fesler was an end and fullback who was named All-American in 1928–30, and he was the Big Ten's Most Valuable Player in his final season. He was an outstanding all-around athlete who also won three letters in basketball and baseball for Ohio State.

Fesler bounced around as a coach following his playing days, including stints at Princeton University and the University of Pittsburgh, before returning to Ohio State as head man in 1947. In four seasons he compiled a 21–13–3 record, won a share of one Big Ten title, and led the Buckeyes to their first Rose Bowl win, a 17–14 defeat of third-ranked California in the 1950 game.

The following season, a 6–2 Ohio State team hosted the University of Michigan in the season finale, with another shot at a conference championship, although the no-repeat rule meant Ohio wouldn't be going to Pasadena no matter what happened. It was November 25, 1950. Yep, that game—the Snow Bowl. With blizzard-like conditions, the teams basically gave up trying to move the ball and sometimes punted on first down.

Ohio State was leading 3–2 (Michigan had scored a safety on one of several blocked punts that day). The Buckeyes had the ball near their own goal line with less than a minute to go before halftime when Fesler decided to punt on third down. It was blocked, and the ball was recovered in the end zone by Michigan for a touchdown, putting them ahead 9–3, which would be the final score.

The loss cost Ohio State the Big Ten title, and critics jumped all over Fesler for his call. They said if the Bucks had run at least one more play they could have drained the remaining time off the clock before halftime. Fesler disagreed.

"We had two plays left but too much time to close out the end of the period," Fesler said. "So rather than take a chance of anything happening, I wanted to get the ball out of there."

Woody Hayes Too Conservative for His Staff?

Woody Hayes was fairly entrenched when it came to his conservative offensive schemes, but that doesn't mean his assistants didn't try to rebel every once in a while.

One of the most famous cases was in the 1973 game against Ohio's eternal rival, the University of Michigan. Both teams came in undefeated and battling for the Rose Bowl (there was no alternative) and a possible national title.

Ohio State jumped out to a 10–0 first-half lead but never scored again. Buckeyes quarterback Cornelius Greene had an injured thumb on his throwing hand, so Hayes was even more run-oriented than usual. Michigan tied it up, and Hayes finally lifted Greene. Hayes put in backup Greg Hare with a little more than one minute to play, but Hare's first pass was intercepted. The game ended 10–10.

In the book "Then Tress Said to Troy...," former Ohio State assistant coach Ed Ferkany describes a "near mutiny" among Hayes' staff. "Woody was so stubborn sometimes," Ferkany said.

The assistants were planning to boycott a coaches' meeting the next morning, but cooler heads prevailed after it was announced that Big Ten athletics directors, in a surprise move because Ohio State had been to Pasadena the year before, had selected the Buckeyes over Michigan to go to the Rose Bowl.

Apparently his explanation didn't quiet the critics enough because Fesler resigned two weeks later, saying the pressure of coaching at Ohio State was too much on him and his family. He actually had considered the move a year earlier but was talked into staying by school officials. The uproar over the Snow Bowl loss was the final straw.

What happened next was even more surprising. Fesler had said he wanted to go into business, but less than two months later it was announced he had taken the job at Big Ten rival University of Minnesota. He spent three seasons there and went 10–13–4.

In the end, things worked out for Ohio State. Fesler's resignation created the opening that was filled by Woody Hayes. Ohio State football was in good hands.

73 Ernie Godfrey and Esco Sarkkinen

"You win with people." It was a favorite saying of Woody Hayes, an acknowledgment that although his name was always out front, he couldn't and didn't do it all by himself. He was referring to the players and the support staff that kept the program running, especially the assistant coaches a head football coach so often leans upon.

And while some of his assistants went on to great success as head men—Bo Schembechler, Lou Holtz, Earle Bruce—two lesser names stand out for their contributions to Ohio State football, as well as their longevity: Ernie Godfrey and Esco "Sark" Sarkkinen. Both served on the coaching staff at Ohio State for more than 30 years, and both have been inducted into the Ohio State Hall of Fame.

Godfrey played for Ohio State and earned a letter in 1914, but he is remembered for serving as an assistant coach for the Buckeyes from 1929 to 1961, the last 11 seasons under Hayes. Godfrey worked for seven different head coaches and was a coach on four different national championship teams.

During his tenure, he served as defensive backs coach, helped develop 11 All-Americans as line coach, and was head coach of the freshman team for nine years. He also worked with the kickers and continued to do so after his formal retirement. Prior to returning to Ohio State in 1929, Godfrey was head coach at Wittenberg University in Springfield, Ohio, where he compiled a 63–24–8 record and coached two undefeated teams. He was inducted into both the Ohio State and the College Football halls of fame. He was 88 when he passed away in 1980.

Sarkkinen was an All-American end on the 1939 team that captured the Big Ten championship. After serving in the Coast

Guard during World War II, he returned to Ohio State in 1946 as an assistant football coach. Sark was on staff for 32 years, until 1978, although he spent much of that time on the road as a scout, checking out upcoming Buckeyes opponents.

He was known for his sense of humor and philosophical outlook on life, and he used to attend Buckeyes games and the occasional practice well into his seventies.

Once asked about Woody Hayes, he said, "You don't describe Woody Hayes in one word, one sentence, or one paragraph. You describe him with chapter after chapter."

Sarkkinen died in 1998 at the age of 79.

Another one of those people that Hayes depended on was Ernie Biggs, Ohio State's head football and basketball trainer from 1945 until 1972.

Biggs served as president of the National Athletic Trainers Association and held a patent on a knee brace he designed. He was inducted into the Ohio State Hall of Fame in 1980. The Ernie Biggs Athletic Training Facility is named in his honor.

74 All-Time Great Receivers

Jim Karsatos faded back to pass in the 1985 Citrus Bowl against Brigham Young University but came under pressure and decided to throw the ball away. The football, however, never made it out of bounds. It was also in the general vicinity of sophomore wide receiver Cris Carter, and what he did next left teammates, fans, and others astonished.

"When I finally saw it on film, he was tip-toeing the sidelines, and he jumped up and caught the ball left-handed by the point of the football at least a yard out of bounds," Karsatos says. "Then he somehow levitated back in bounds to get both his feet in bounds. I swear to this day he actually levitated to get back in bounds. When I saw it on film, it just blew me away."

It was probably the greatest catch in Ohio State history made by a player who should be a starting split end on anybody's all-Buckeyes team. Carter had incredible hands, great leaping ability, and made the highlight-reel catches look routine, but he was also known for running precise routes and his football smarts. He was a two-time All-American (1985–86), who set single-season records in 1986 for receptions (69), yardage (1,127), and touchdowns (11). Despite playing just three seasons, he also set career marks for receptions (168) and touchdowns (27), and he remains second in both categories to David Boston.

Carter, a native of Middletown, Ohio, was declared ineligible for his senior season after admitting taking money from sports agents. It was a big blow to Carter and also to the team. The Buckeyes would struggle to a 6–4–1 record, and coach Earle Bruce would be fired in the season's final week.

Carter left for the NFL and, after some inconsistent seasons in Philadelphia, latched on with the Vikings and became a perennial All-Pro. He was inducted into the Ohio State and Pro Football halls of fame.

Carter was just one in a long line of great receivers at Ohio State, a fact that demonstrates better than anything how quickly the team moved away from Woody Hayes' "three yards and a cloud of dust" philosophy.

If Carter is one of the starting wideouts on an all-time Ohio State team, Boston is the other. He too played only three years (1996–98), departing after his junior season for the NFL, but he set new career records for receptions (191), yardage (2,855), and touchdowns (34). In 1998, hooking up with Joe Germaine, Boston set single-season marks for catches (85) and yards (1,435), and a year earlier he set the record for most grabs in one game with 14 at Penn State.

Boston was a confident player who sometimes aggravated opponents and even Buckeyes fans with his on-field antics. His most famous catch was fairly routine but won the 1997 Rose Bowl when Germaine hit him on a five-yard touchdown pass with about 20 seconds to play.

Terry Glenn exploded onto the scene in 1995 with one of the finest seasons ever for a Buckeyes receiver. He was unknown outside Columbus coming into the season but ended up winning the Biletnikoff Award as the nation's top receiver after catching 64 passes and a school-record 17 touchdowns. Glenn was a speedster and had eight catches of longer than 45 yards.

There were other great ones along the way: Doug "White Lightning" Donley, who led Ohio State in receptions three years running (1978–80), and was followed by Gary Williams, who remains fourth all time with 154 catches; John Frank (1980–83) is 10th on the list with 121 receptions and is number one among tight ends; Joey Galloway thrilled Buckeyes fans by catching 19 touchdown passes in the early 1990s, including 11 in 1993; Ted Ginn Jr. caught 135 passes in just three seasons (2004–06), with 15 touchdowns, and also made a name for himself as a dynamic return man.

Besides Carter, only one other former Ohio State receiver so far has made it into the Pro Football Hall of Fame, and that's Paul Warfield. Warfield, however, was used mostly as a halfback by Woody Hayes in the early 1960s, and only occasionally as a receiver. He did lead the team in receiving in 1962 and '63, when he had eight and then 22 receptions.

75 The Last Line of Defense

With Ohio State and the University of Michigan tied at 14 points each, and with just minutes to play in their 1975 game, the Buckeyes got key plays from a pair of defensive backs with famous last names. Those plays lifted the Bucks to a 21–14 win and preserved their undefeated season. First, sophomore Ray Griffin, little brother of Archie, intercepted a pass and returned it to the 3-yard line to set up the go-ahead touchdown. Then on the ensuing drive, Craig Cassady, son of former Buckeyes great Howard "Hopalong," picked off a pass of his own to clinch the victory.

It was Cassady's second interception of the day, and he would have a school record nine on the season. Ray Griffin never gained the fame of his older brother, but he would go on to earn All-American honors at safety in 1977. Ohio State may be better known for churning out Heisman Trophy–winning backs on the other side of the ball, or even award-winning linemen and linebackers, but there has been a slew of defensive backs who have carved a significant space in Buckeyes history.

Howard Cassady is actually one of the greats. He is better known as an elusive running back who won the Heisman Trophy in 1955, but Cassady also picked off 10 passes in his career. The biggest came in a showdown with the University of Wisconsin during the national championship season of 1954, when he intercepted a pass deep in Buckeyes territory and returned it 88 yards for a touchdown.

Jack Tatum is first and foremost among the best of all time, though. A member of the Ohio State and College Football halls of fame and a two-time All-American, his combination of size, speed, and fierce tackling made him pretty much the perfect defensive back.

But he was far from alone as the last line of defense on teams that lost just two games in three seasons from 1968 to 1970. There was Mike Sensibaugh and Tim Anderson, both of whom, along with Tatum, were members of the celebrated class of '70, and a year ahead of them was Ted Provost. All four earned All-American honors at some point in their careers, and their position coach was a young man named Lou Holtz. Talk about a dream defensive backfield.

Provost made one of the biggest plays of that memorable season of 1968 when he picked off a pass against top-ranked Purdue University and returned the ball for Ohio State's first touchdown. The Buckeyes would win 13–0 and go on to capture a national title, and Provost would be an All-American the following season. Anderson was an outstanding cornerback who was named All-American in 1970, while Sensibaugh was also an All-American that season and holds the record for most interceptions in a career (22) and season (nine in 1969, tied with Craig Cassady).

Ohio State had a pair of All-American defensive backs in the mid-1970s in cornerback Neal Colzie ('74) and safety Tim Fox ('75). Colzie intercepted eight passes in 1974 and had 15 in his career, and he also was an excellent return man. Shawn Springs, son of former Ohio State star running back Ron Springs, was an All-American cornerback in 1996, despite not having a single interception that season. Teams simply refused to throw his direction, and he proved that strategy was prudent when he limited star Arizona State University receiver Keith Poole to one catch in the 1997 Rose Bowl.

Antoine Winfield is another defensive back who had relatively few interceptions (three for his career), but is considered one of the top cornerbacks in Ohio State history. Winfield was just 5'9" and 175 pounds, but he was extremely fast and a devastating tackler. He was the first cornerback in school history to lead the team in tackles when he did so in 1997, and his 82 solo tackles that year are the fifth-most ever.

Winfield was named All-American in 1997 and '98, and he won the Jim Thorpe Award as the nation's top defensive back as a senior, the only Buckeye ever to do so since the award was first handed out in 1986. Finally, there is Mike Doss, the three-time All-American safety (2000–02) who decided to return for his senior year in 2002 and became one of the key leaders of a team that would go 14–0 and win a national title.

# 76 Maurice Clarett

Maurice Clarett was an incredibly gifted running back who broke Archie Griffin's freshman rushing record, led the Buckeyes offense throughout their 2002 national championship season, and scored the winning touchdown in the Fiesta Bowl win over the University of Miami that clinched the school's first title in more than three decades. Coach Jim Tressel and university administrators probably wondered, at times, if it was all worth it.

Clarett never played another down after that glorious freshman season. A bitter divorce from the school ensued that included Clarett acknowledging accepting payments from boosters and making accusations of special treatment and academic fraud. After a failed attempt at professional football, Clarett was back in Columbus, when authorities announced on January 1, 2006, that they were seeking him in connection with a robbery outside a nightclub. He was later charged in that robbery and faced weapons charges and other violations from another arrest. He pled guilty and was sentenced in 2006 to seven and a half years in prison. It was a swift and precipitous fall from, if not grace, than glory.

The relationship between Clarett and Ohio State started to sour even before that national championship game. Just days before the game with Miami, a friend of Clarett's was killed in a shooting, and Clarett complained publicly that school officials wouldn't allow him to fly home to Ohio for the funeral. Administrators insisted that wasn't the case and that it was only a matter of Clarett failing to fill out the proper forms. Clarett said he had completed the paperwork, and he accused the school of lying. It was an awkward public spat so close to the biggest Ohio State game in decades.

Apparently it didn't affect the team, though, and they captured a stunning double-overtime victory over favored Miami, with Clarett diving over for the final score. Earlier in the game he had authored one of the most spectacular plays in Ohio State history. In the third quarter, Miami's Sean Taylor picked off a Craig Krenzel pass in the end zone and started up the sideline. But Clarett came out of nowhere to chase Taylor down and strip him of the ball as they fell to the ground (five years after that play, Clarett was in prison and Taylor was fatally shot inside his home during a burglary in 2007). It was Buckeyes ball again, and shortly thereafter a Mike Nugent field goal put them up 17–7.

Clarett finished the 2002 season with 1,237 yards rushing, easily topping Griffin's freshman record of 867 yards, and scored 18 touchdowns. But things went bad from there. He was charged with filing a false police report in 2003, and at about the same time, allegations of academic fraud involving Clarett were aired from a former Ohio State teaching assistant. Clarett was suspended for the 2003 season, and it was soon clear that the relationship had been irreparably damaged.

Clarett would make his own accusations of special and improper benefits given to him by coaches at Ohio State and boosters, many of them detailed in an *ESPN Magazine* piece. But an

Ohio State faculty committee investigated allegations of academic fraud and could not substantiate them.

Athletics Director Andy Geiger made it clear he was fed up with Clarett. "He vowed to me that he would do something to try to get us, and this may be what he's trying to do. So he's on his own," Geiger told the magazine. "We dealt with this guy for 18 months. I just hope you've checked into the background and history of who you're dealing with."

Clarett applied for early entry to the NFL draft but was denied, and with time on his hands, things continued to spiral downward. By the time he got his NFL shot he was in no shape to play football and was cut by the Denver Broncos. Back in Columbus he faced the robbery allegations, and then in August 2006, he was arrested after leading police on a chase. Officers had to use mace and a stun gun to subdue him, and they found an assault rifle, three handguns, a hatchet, and an open bottle of alcohol in the car. And Clarett was wearing body armor.

It was going from sad and frightening to bizarre. There were rumors of an association with an Israeli mobster and reports that Clarett was in the neighborhood of one of the witnesses in his robbery case when he was arrested. As Ohio State prepared for and played in another national championship game to wrap up the 2007 season, the 24-year-old Clarett was spending his days at the Toledo Correctional Institution.

Clarett was released in 2010 and began taking steps to put his life back together. In 2012, he returned to Ohio State to celebrate the 10th anniversary of the 2002 team's undefeated season.

77 Coaches Not Named Hayes

Ohio State fans remember Woody Hayes, of course, and there was John Cooper and Earle Bruce and Wes Fesler and Paul Brown and John Wilce. All left their mark on Buckeyes football and built it into what it is today. But there were other coaches, lesser known and not as well remembered, who played important roles along the way.

John Eckstrom took the helm in 1899 after a stint at Kenyon College, where he had led the tiny school from Gambier, Ohio, to a 29–0 win over Ohio State the previous season. He promptly led the Buckeyes to a 9–0–1 mark in his first season and a championship of the Ohio colleges. Unbelievably, the team shut out every opponent except for one, and that was a 5–5 tie with Case Western Reserve University. Five points allowed remains an Ohio State single-season record. The Bucks then shut out their first six opponents of the 1900 season on the way to an 8–1–1 record. The one loss was to Ohio Medical College, for which Eckstrom would depart after one more season (5–3–1). His overall mark in three seasons, 22–4–3, places him third of all time in winning percentage at .810.

A.E. Herrnstein was a star at Michigan as a player and took over as head coach at Ohio State in 1906, leading the Bucks to a 28–10–1 record in four seasons. He led Ohio State to an 8–1 mark in his first season and an Ohio colleges championship. He was the first coach to incorporate the forward pass at Ohio State, and he led the team to the 100th victory in program history, a 17–6 win at Vanderbilt University in 1908.

Francis Schmidt led Ohio State to its highest ranking at that time—fourth in 1939 before a loss to Cornell University—and

Schmidt's Trickery

Francis Schmidt coached at the University of Tulsa, the University of Arkansas, and Texas Christian University before landing at Ohio State in 1934, and his teams were known for their intricate offensive schemes that often used trick plays and multiple laterals. His teams were so consistently high scoring that the press dubbed him Francis "Close the Gates of Mercy" Schmidt. Tippy Dye, an Ohio State quarterback under Schmidt, said the team had more than 300 plays that were run from seven different formations. Dye said it was so complicated that the quarterbacks would write plays on index cards and keep them in their helmets while they were playing so that they could consult them during breaks in the action. Dye said he was hit so hard during the 1936 Michigan game that his helmet flew off, and the cards scattered on the field. Michigan players started to try to decipher what was on them before Dye could collect them all.

was on hand for other important firsts. He was the first Ohio State coach to receive a multiyear contract, symbolizing the growing importance of football and the school's commitment to the sport. He coached Ohio State to four straight shutout wins over Michigan, including the 1935 game that established the tradition of a season-ending game between the rivals. He is also responsible for creating the gold pants tradition, where a gold charm in the shape of football pants is given to players if they beat Michigan. Schmidt, known as an innovative offensive coach who frequently used trick plays, won Big Ten titles in 1935 and '39, and he finished with a 39–16–1 record from 1934 to 1940. His first two teams both went 7–1, but he never matched that again and resigned following a 4–4 mark in 1940 that included a 40–0 loss to Michigan.

Carroll Widdoes took over when Paul Brown departed for the military in 1944 and had one of the most unique coaching careers at Ohio State. Widdoes, playing mostly with freshman because of war enlistments, went 9–0 in that first season to capture a Big Ten title, and he ended the season ranked second to Army nationally. The Buckeyes went 7–2 the next season, after which Widdoes switched spots with assistant coach Paul Bixler. That arrangement lasted just one season, then both Bixler and Widdoes were gone following the 1946 campaign. Widdoes' overall record of 16–2 places him first of all time in winning percentage at .889.

78 Gaylord "Pete" Stinchcomb

Chic Harley was gone when Ohio State gathered for preseason practice in 1920, but the team didn't miss a beat. The unprecedented enthusiasm Harley had helped to generate remained and even grew in no small part because of Harley's backfield mate, Gaylord "Pete" Stinchcomb. Stinchcomb and Coach John Wilce would lead Ohio State to a 7–0 regular season record and another Western Conference championship. Ohio State would also play in the school's first Rose Bowl, although that game ended in a 28–0 loss to California.

Stinchcomb was a year behind Harley in school but played halfback alongside him in 1917 as Ohio State went 8–0–1 and captured the conference title. He and Harley and others missed the 1918 season because of a military service commitment, but Stinchcomb returned in 1919 to play quarterback on another conference champion team. He was named an All-American along with Harley.

Stinchcomb moved back to halfback for his senior season in 1920 and repeated as All-American. Like Harley, Stinchcomb not only was the playmaker on offense but also played defense and occasionally handled the kicking duties. In a 13–7 win over the University of Wisconsin at Ohio Field that would determine the conference title, Stinchcomb caught two touchdown passes from Harry Workman, and the second pass was a 48-yarder with less than a minute to play.

All the All-Americans

Boyd Cherry, an end, was Ohio State's first All-American. He earned the honor in the 1914 season after helping lead the Buckeyes to a 5–2 record. He wouldn't be the last. Nearly a century later Ohio State has had over 130 first-team All-Americans through the 2013 season, when junior linebacker Ryan Shazier made the list.

Ohio State has had more than two dozen two-time All-Americans, and eight who made the team three times: running back Chic Harley, 1916–17 and '19; end Wes Fesler, 1928–30; halfback Lew Hinchman, 1930–32; end Merle Wendt, 1934–36; tailback Archie Griffin, 1973–75; punter Tom Skladany, 1974–76; safety Mike Doss, 2000–02; and James Laurinaitis, 2006–08.

Ohio State had several nail-biters that season but kept winning, and interest in the program seemed to have no ceiling. Approximately 21,000 fans packed Ohio Field for the home finale against the University of Michigan, which was another come-from-behind win. The timing was perfect as the funding campaign for Ohio Stadium was launched that fall.

Also like Harley, Stinchcomb was small, 5'10", 165 pounds, but a quick and elusive runner. He was a great athlete who also played basketball and ran track at Ohio State, and he went on to play five seasons in the new National Football League. Stinchcomb is in the Ohio State Hall of Fame and was inducted into the College Football Hall of Fame in 1973, the same year he passed away.

While Harley's name and number adorn the upper-deck façade at Ohio Stadium and he is credited with generating the enthusiasm that made construction of a new stadium necessary, he was far from the only star on teams that ran up a record of 28–2–1 in four seasons (1916–20, excluding the war-depleted team of 1918). There was Stinchcomb, but also lineman Robert Karch, ends Charles "Shifty" Bolen and Harold Courtney, and center Kelley Van Dyne—All-Americans all.

Iolas Huffman was a two-time All-American (1920–21) at guard and tackle, and in consecutive games against Michigan he blocked punts that resulted in touchdowns. The second time, he fell on the ball himself in the end zone to provide the winning margin in a 14–7 victory in 1920. If he did that today they'd probably retire his number on the spot.

One of Huffman's linemates was John "Tarzan" Taylor, a "very high-spirited tackle, who would occasionally toss his helmet to the sideline and play bare-headed for a few downs," according to *The Official Ohio State Football Encyclopedia*. Lucky for Taylor, in those days they didn't flag for excessive celebration or removing your helmet.

Stinchcomb, Huffman, Karch, and others are names largely lost to history, but along with Harley they formed the foundation of Ohio State football.

79 Jim Marshall and Jim Houston

The Ohio State offense was struggling mightily to move the ball and score points in the middle of the 1958 season. After defeating Indiana University 49–8 to raise their record to 4–0 on the year, the Buckeyes could muster only one touchdown in a tie with Wisconsin. Ohio State was shut out the following week against Northwestern University. In the next game, Purdue University kept the Ohio State offense out of the end zone again, and if not for the play of a pair of Buckeyes defensive linemen, it would have been another shutout loss.

Jim Marshall scored two touchdowns, both set up by teammate Jim Houston, and Ohio State came away with a 14–14 tie.

In the first quarter, Houston blocked a Purdue punt, and Marshall picked up the ball and rumbled 22 yards for the score. Then in the second quarter, Houston deflected a Boilermakers pass, and Marshall snatched it out of the air before running 25 yards for another touchdown.

Defensive linemen spend a lot of their time taking up space and drawing blockers so that the guys behind them can make plays, but Marshall had lived a lineman's dream that day. While his performance was indeed unique, Ohio State has had plenty of game-changing players on the defensive line. Jim Stillwagon set the standard as winner of the Lombardi Award and Outland Trophy in 1970 from his middle guard position, but there have been many others.

Houston is one of the best defensive ends ever for the Buckeyes, playing a key role as a sophomore on the 1957 national championship team and earning All-American honors in 1958 and '59. He also played end on offense and led the team in receiving his senior year, with 11 catches. Houston was inducted into the College Football Hall of Fame in 2006.

With Houston holding down one of the end spots on an all-time Ohio State defense, the other would have to go to Mike Vrabel. Known for his quickness and tenacity, Vrabel was the most feared pass rusher in the country in the mid-1990s, and he holds all the significant Ohio State records for sacks and tackles for loss. Vrabel had a school-record 13 sacks his junior season and 36 for his career, also the most ever; the next closest player has 27.5. He had 66 tackles for loss for minus 349 yards in his career, both records.

Those rankings do come with a caveat, in that for many years sacks weren't regularly counted, and teams in Vrabel's era threw the ball much more than in decades past, creating many more opportunities for sacks. That does nothing, however, to discount what he accomplished at Ohio State. Vrabel was a two-time All-American

(1995–96), made All–Big Ten three straight seasons, and was the Big Ten's Defensive Lineman of the Year twice (1995 and 1996). He moved to linebacker in the NFL and has been a mainstay for New England Patriots teams that have captured multiple Super Bowl titles.

Van Ness DeCree was another two-time All-American (1973 and 1974) at defensive end, who was overshadowed by better-known teammates on both sides of the ball but who wreaked havoc on Big Ten champion and Rose Bowl teams of the early 1970s. He would be first-string on any all-name team, too.

The 1970s also saw All-Americans on the defensive line in tackle Pete Cusick ('74), end Bob Brudzinski ('76), and nose guard Aaron Brown ('77). In the early 1990s, Dan "Big Daddy" Wilkinson was a disruptive force at defensive tackle for two seasons and made All-American in 1993 before leaving for the NFL.

As for Marshall, he was an All-American, too, but at offensive tackle. He did go on to a successful and long NFL career playing defensive end, mostly for the Minnesota Vikings teams known as the Purple People Eaters.

Going Bowl-ing

After falling behind 10–0 to the University of Colorado in the first quarter of the 1977 Orange Bowl, Woody Hayes inserted sophomore Rod Gerald at quarterback. The speedy Gerald had been out since the season's seventh game with an injured back, but he ripped off a 17-yard run on his initial play in the bowl game to set up Ohio State's first touchdown. By halftime the Bucks had gone ahead 17–10 on their way to a 27–10 win.

It was a nice comeback win over the Big 8 champion Buffaloes, and it lifted Ohio State to a 9–2–1 final record and rankings of five (United Press International) and six (Associated Press) in the final polls. It was also Hayes' last bowl win.

Even more significant was the fact Ohio State was there at all. Just one year prior, the Big Ten had decided to allow teams to play in bowls other than the Rose Bowl, and this was Ohio State's first such foray into postseason play outside Pasadena.

It was a turning point for the program. Since that Orange Bowl win, Ohio State has appeared in more than 30 bowl games, only a few of them the Rose.

While the Rose Bowl remained goal number one (until the Bowl Championship Series title game was created and now the season-ending playoff), the Fiesta, Cotton, Holiday, and other bowls provided fine consolation prizes and more than a few highlights. There was the Mike Tomczak-to-Thad Jemison 39-yard touchdown pass with 39 seconds left in the 1984 Fiesta Bowl for a 28–23 win over the University of Pittsburgh; Chris Spielman intercepted two passes and returned one for a touchdown in a 28–12 win over Texas A&M University in the 1987 Cotton Bowl; there was a 24–14 win over eighth-ranked Texas A&M in the 1999 Sugar Bowl that left the Bucks 11–1 and ranked second in the nation; and there were four straight bowl wins from 2003–06, including the Fiesta Bowl national title game.

There were some low moments, too. The 35–6 pasting by the University of Alabama in the 1978 Sugar Bowl was the only time Hayes and Bear Bryant ever faced each other. The Gator Bowl loss to Clemson University in 1978 ended Hayes' career. There were six defeats in seven bowl trips from 1990 to 1996, including a 23–11 loss to Air Force in the 1990 Liberty Bowl. And there was the 24–7 Outback Bowl loss in 2001 that was John Cooper's last game.

Ohio State has appeared in 14 Rose Bowls (7–7), followed by six trips to the Fiesta Bowl (5–1) and four to the Citrus Bowl (1–3).

The Bucks have been in each of the other major bowls, too: Sugar (2–2), Cotton (1–0), and Orange (1–1).

Ohio State has an overall bowl record of 20–24 through the 2013 season:

Ohio State's Bowl Record

Year	Bowl	Result
1921	Rose Bowl	California 28, Ohio State 0
1950	Rose Bowl	Ohio State 17, California 14
1955	Rose Bowl	Ohio State 20, Southern California 7
1958	Rose Bowl	Ohio State 10, Oregon 7
1969	Rose Bowl	Ohio State 27, Southern California 16
1971	Rose Bowl	Stanford 27, Ohio State 17
1973	Rose Bowl	Southern California 42, Ohio State 17
1974	Rose Bowl	Ohio State 42, Southern California 21
1975	Rose Bowl	Southern California 18, Ohio State 17
1976	Rose Bowl	UCLA 23, Ohio State 10
1977	Orange Bowl	Ohio State 27, Colorado 10
1978	Sugar Bowl	Alabama 35, Ohio State 6
1978	Gator Bowl	Clemson 17, Ohio State 15
1980	Rose Bowl	Southern California 17, Ohio State 16
1980	Fiesta Bowl	Penn State 31, Ohio State19
1981	Liberty Bowl	Ohio State 31, Navy 28
1982	Holiday Bowl	Ohio State 47, Brigham Young 17
1984	Fiesta Bowl	Ohio State 28, Pittsburgh 23
1985	Rose Bowl	Southern California 20, Ohio State 17
1986	Citrus Bowl	Ohio State 10, Brigham Young 7
1987	Cotton Bowl	Ohio State 28, Texas A&M 12
1990	Hall of Fame	Auburn 31, Ohio State 14
1990	Liberty Bowl	Air Force 23, Ohio State 11
1992	Hall of Fame	Syracuse 24, Ohio State 17
1993	Citrus Bowl	Georgia 21, Ohio State 14
1993	Holiday Bowl	Ohio State 28, Brigham Young 21
1995	Citrus Bowl	Alabama 24, Ohio State 17
1996	Citrus Bowl	Tennessee 20, Ohio State 14
1997	Rose Bowl	Ohio State 20, Arizona State 17
1998	Sugar Bowl	Florida State 31, Ohio State 14
1999	Sugar Bowl	Ohio State 24, Texas A&M 14

2001	Outback Bowl	South Carolina 24, Ohio State 7
2002	Outback Bowl	South Carolina 31, Ohio State 28
2003	Fiesta Bowl	Ohio State 31, Miami (FL) 24
2004	Fiesta Bowl	Ohio State 35, Kansas State 28
2004	Alamo Bowl	Ohio State 33, Oklahoma State 7
2006	Fiesta Bowl	Ohio State 34, Notre Dame 20
2007	BCS Title	Florida 41, Ohio State 14
2008	BCS Title	Louisiana State 38, Ohio State 24
2009	Fiesta Bowl	Texas 24, Ohio State 21
2010	Rose Bowl	Ohio State 26, Oregon 17
2011	Sugar Bowl	Ohio State 31, Arkansas 26
2012	Gator Bowl	Florida 24, Ohio State 17
2014	Orange Bowl	Clemson 40, Ohio State 35

81 Hitting the Books

Amid the pageantry and fanaticism of Ohio State football, it's often easy to forget that these young men are, after all, college students. It has always been incomprehensible to some people that institutions of higher learning would dedicate so much time, money, energy, and emotion to the fate of a football team. And the relationship between academics and athletics has been an uneasy one, probably since the first college sports team was formed.

At Ohio State it's no different. When plans were in the works for Ohio Stadium, many professors and administrators balked at the idea of such a large and prominent building dedicated solely to athletics. The argument that a vigorous football program could energize students and alumni and raise the university's profile won out and still does today.

But there have been some highly publicized bumps along the way that the university would just as soon forget. Robert Smith was

Paul Keels

Paul Keels is the popular voice of the Buckeyes as the play-by-play announcer for Ohio State football and basketball games on the Ohio State Buckeyes Radio Sports Network, which can be heard on 77 affiliates across the state.

What fans tuning in might not know—and what they won't find out from reading his bio on the network's website— is that Keels was the voice of the Michigan Wolverines for several seasons in the 1980s. He announced games for Michigan from 1981 to 1987, and also did Detroit Pistons games. Keels then moved back to his home town of Cincinnati, where he announced games for the University of Cincinnati, the Bengals, and hosted a sports talk show. He came to Ohio State in 1998.

Keels was inducted into the Radio Television Broadcaster's Hall of Fame of Ohio in 2007.

an excellent running back for the Buckeyes in the early 1990s and also a good student, who said he had aspirations of going to medical school. Sounds like the perfect poster boy to promote students' athletics at Ohio State, right? The only problem was that Smith complained that the demands of football didn't allow him enough time to pursue academics, and he did so publicly.

Although he was considered one of the top running backs in the country, he quit the team prior to the 1991 season, forcing the university into defense mode about its priorities. Smith returned the following season to lead the Buckeyes in rushing before leaving early for the NFL. He had a productive career with the Minnesota Vikings before retiring at the age of 28, following his best season. He now does some work as a television football analyst, among other pursuits.

Then there was the Maurice Clarett saga. A star running back on the 2002 national championship team as a freshman, Clarett never played again for Ohio State after he found a whole mess of trouble, including robbery and weapons charges and reports that he accepted benefits from a booster. Amid the messy break from the university, a teaching assistant went public with accusations that Clarett and other players frequently received preferential treatment on their schoolwork, and Clarett and a couple of other players later made similar allegations. A faculty committee investigated the assistant's allegations and could not substantiate them, but again the university found itself defending its integrity.

But for every Maurice Clarett, there are heartening stories about players like Craig Krenzel, Troy Smith, Archie Griffin, and a host of Academic All-Americans over the years. Krenzel pursued a degree in molecular genetics as he shared a backfield with Clarett on that 2002 national title team, was named first-team Academic All-American, and won several other top national honors for student-athletes.

Smith already had one degree and was pursuing a second as he led Ohio State to a 12–1 record in 2006 and won the Heisman Trophy. Griffin is just as likely to talk about the degree he received from Ohio State as his two Heismans. And wide receiver Mike Lanese was a two-time Academic All-American and 1985 Rhodes Scholar.

Ohio State has had more than 30 Academic All-Americans, and we're not talking about benchwarmers here. There is Krenzel, wide receiver Anthony Gonzalez (2006), defensive back Ahmed Plummer (1999), linebacker Greg Bellisari (1995–96), tight end John Frank (1982–83), linebacker Marcus Marek (1980), running back Jeff Logan (1977), fullback Pete Johnson (1976), wingback Brian Bashnagel (1974–75), and linebacker Randy Gradishar (1973). That's a veritable all-star team of ex-Bucks just in the last 35 years. And talk to almost anyone who played under Woody Hayes, and they'll tell you the great emphasis he placed on academics and getting a degree.

"In the first meeting I was ever in at Ohio State, Woody told us that if we were there for any other reason than getting an education that we should leave," Griffin says.

It is no doubt an enormous and ever-shifting challenge to balance academics with such a high-profile football program. Ohio State has responded by creating the Student-Athlete Support Services Office with tutors, academic counselors, and life skills coordinators, and the school believes it's on solid footing. "We want to create an environment that allows our student-athletes the opportunity to receive their degrees, achieve success in their athletic careers, and grow as young men and women," says athletics director Eugene Smith.

Scandal

Woody Hayes was renown for his temper, which got him in trouble many times and led to his firing from Ohio State. But he was otherwise known for his conservatism both on the field and off, a law-and-order type who was the epitome of the 1950s football coach.

So it would probably be surprising to Buckeyes fans still trying to digest the details of the 2010–11 scandal to know that it was the actions of Hayes that in part got Ohio State put on probation in 1956. A *Sports Illustrated* story on the program that year revealed that Hayes occasionally loaned money to players out of his own pocket. That and supposed no-show jobs held by some players led to the probation. Woody acknowledged giving money to players but said he only did it to help truly down-on-their-luck young men, not to reward players or entice recruits to come to Ohio State.

Like many other big-time college football programs, Ohio State has experienced the occasional scandal and suffered NCAA sanctions. Woody's offense seems to pale in comparison to the more recent transgressions that led to coach Jim Tressel resigning and the school being placed on probation.

Tressel, known as "The Senator" for his staid demeanor and sweater-vests, apparently didn't learn anything from Richard Nixon or any number of other scandals: the cover-up is often worse than the crime.

Tressel found out that some of his players were exchanging autographs and memorabilia—including jerseys and championship rings—for cash and free tattoos, and he didn't tell school officials or the NCAA. He said he didn't do so because the owner of the tattoo parlor in question was also the target of an FBI investigation. But as the players' actions started to come to light over the next year Tressel still didn't come clean, and he played key players in the scandal, including star quarterback Terrelle Pryor, in the 2011 Sugar Bowl. That win and all the others in the 2010 season were later vacated.

Other revelations about supposed no-show jobs for players came to light during the investigation. Overall, it appeared Tressel's main concern was losing Pryor and other key players—and hence probably losing games—rather than protecting the integrity of the school and the program. And in the end he lost his job and Ohio State took a serious hit to its reputation.

The scandal garnered significant national attention but was followed by ones involving child sex abuse at Penn State and an out-of-control booster at Miami (Florida) allegedly providing money, cars, and even prostitutes to players. In comparison, memorabilia-for-tattoos seemed tame.

Other pundits downplayed the transgressions, noting that the players had been given the rings and other items, so who's place was it to say they couldn't sell them? And have you noticed how the schools themselves profit immensely from merchandise sales, including pedaling "game-worn" jerseys online?

Then–Ohio State president Gordon Gee said he believed the school reacted properly to the scandal.

"Any president hopes that what they have done is to put in place a process that will assure our integrity," he said. "Saying that, I feel very confident that we have done the things that we need to do to assure that further problems will be identified early and taken care of."

Showing that the drama was not limited to the football field or athletics department, Gee himself was frequently getting himself into trouble with his off-the-cuff comments, and was out of a job in 2013 after he poked fun at Notre Dame and the Southeastern Conference. Ohio State's board of trustees was not humored and Gee abruptly retired.

It was ironic and showed the great influence Buckeye football has at Ohio State. So did another comment Gee made, this one as the Tressel scandal unfolded. It was in response to whether he was considering firing Tressel, and was another attempt at humor.

"No, are you kidding? Let me just be very clear: I'm just hopeful the coach doesn't dismiss me."

Buckeyes Roadtrips

When Ohio State played the University of Miami in the Fiesta Bowl for the 2002 national title, Sun Devil Stadium in Arizona was a neutral site in theory only. In reality, the underdog Buckeyes emerged from their locker-room to "a sea of scarlet," as punter Andy Groom saw it. "Everything about the game was breathtaking," Groom says.

Another Buckeye, defensive lineman Kenny Peterson, said it felt like a typical Saturday afternoon in the Horseshoe. "When we went out for warmups that night, we knew it would be a home game," he said. "We were thousands of miles from home, but we felt we were at home."

It was an amazing turnout, and Buckeyes fans who made the trip were rewarded with an Ohio State victory in double overtime that many have called the greatest college football game ever played. But the turnout really wasn't all that surprising as Ohio State fans have always traveled to see the Buckeyes.

"I think they're very supportive," says Archie Griffin, who recalls large Ohio State crowds on the road in his playing days. "You can tell by the way they travel; there's great support wherever we go. And that's not new. The state of Ohio loves football."

Support on the road even predates Griffin. Special trains used to shuttle Buckeyes fans to games decades ago, particularly up to Ann Arbor for the always-anticipated game with rival University of Michigan. And according to an anecdote in *The Official Ohio State Football Encyclopedia*, approximately 4,000 Ohio State fans made the trip to Champaign, Illinois, for a season-ending showdown with the University of Illinois in 1920, with some of the students commandeering army trucks that were stored near campus and creating a convoy.

Seeing the Buckeyes in a bowl or on the road creates a unique bonding experience for those who do it, like scarlet-clad agents who have snuck behind enemy lines. Unless, that is, it's a complete takeover.

"The sports information director at Indiana told me one time when Ohio State plays there they make sure to get an aerial shot of the stadium because it's full and everyone's wearing red," says Ohio State football historian Jack Park. From that distance it's impossible to distinguish Ohio State's scarlet from Indiana's crimson, and Indiana gets a shot of a packed stadium for school publications.

Northwestern University is another location where Buckeyes fans often make up about half the crowd or more, but the examples are endless. Notre Dame University fans are known to travel en masse to see the Irish play and are boosted by a dedicated base of "subway alumni," but at the 2006 Fiesta Bowl the Irish fans were equaled and maybe outnumbered by Buckeyes supporters. Fans at the 2007 Michigan game in Ann Arbor got some nice chants of "O-H-I-O" going around the Big House. And the 2008 Bowl Championship Series national championship game in New Orleans was played in Louisiana State University's backyard, but Ohio State fans made an impressive showing.

Travel agencies around Columbus and Ohio have seen the trend and offer package trips to road and bowl games. For the BCS title games in 2007 and '08, airlines added flights from Columbus to Phoenix and New Orleans to meet demand. And Ohio State's vast alumni network also helps boost crowds at road games, as there are Buckeyes spread out all over the country.

One of the most heartwarming examples of this dedication, at least to Ohio State fans who enjoy a beer or two before kickoff, was when the Varsity Club took over a bar in Tempe, Arizona, about a block from Sun Devil Stadium before the 2003 Fiesta Bowl. Owners of the famed Ohio State hangout rented the place out and hung up a "Varsity Club" sign, and Buckeyes fans lined up to get in.

Former Ohio State running back Maurice Hall was playing in a college All-Star game in Florida several years ago when he commented on the trend. "Doesn't matter where you are, there's always a bunch of Buckeye fans," Hall told the *Orlando Sentinel*. "Our fans are the best. They love us."

84 Pete Johnson

No Buckeye may have personified the "three yards and a cloud of dust" offense of the Woody Hayes era as well as fullback Pete Johnson. Okay, Ohio Stadium had Astroturf by the time Johnson was around so there was no literal dust cloud in his wake, but there was usually a pile of bruised and battered defenders.

Johnson was a bull, 6'1" and nearly 250 pounds, who opened holes for Archie Griffin during Griffin's two Heisman Trophy–winning seasons, and a goal-line specialist who graduated as the all-time leading scorer in Ohio State history. Besides his blocking duties, Johnson was devastating between the tackles when running the ball.

Johnson was a three-year starter (1974–76) and finished his career with 2,308 yards rushing on 534 carries, a 4.3-yards-per-carry average, and an amazing 56 rushing touchdowns. That's still the school record (the next closest is Keith Byars with 46), and Johnson's 58 career touchdowns also remain the record. He is tied with Byars for most rushing touchdowns in one game, with the five Johnson had against the University of North Carolina in 1975. He is second on the all-time scoring list since he was passed by kicker Mike Nugent.

In his junior year, when Griffin was a senior and on his way to collecting his second straight Heisman, Johnson rushed for 1,059 yards and 25 touchdowns, a then–Big Ten record and still the school record. Johnson was hobbled by ankle injuries his senior year but still rushed for 724 yards and 18 touchdowns while also blocking for tailbacks Jeff Logan and Ron Springs.

The Buckeyes won or shared the Big Ten title every year Johnson was on campus, and he played in three Rose Bowls and the Orange Bowl. They were dominant teams that reflected Hayes' "run first and run often" philosophy. And when the offense neared the goal line, everyone watching from the fans in the last row of C deck to the opposing defense knew who was getting the ball. And it didn't matter.

Johnson, who was an Academic All-American in 1976 and was voted a member of the Ohio State Hall of Fame in 2007, was selected by the Cincinnati Bengals in the second round of the NFL draft following his senior year, where he again teamed up with Griffin. But this time it was Johnson who was the featured back. While Griffin had a respectable career both running and catching the ball, Johnson led the Bengals in rushing for seven straight seasons and left as the franchise leader in rushing (5,421 yards) and touchdowns (70).

85 Jim Otis and Bob Ferguson

Before Pete Johnson there was Jim Otis. And before Otis there was Bob Ferguson. All were battering-ram fullbacks, the blunt instruments in Woody Hayes' straight-forward attack. Ferguson led Ohio State in rushing three straight seasons, was a two-time All-American (1960 and 1961), and finished his career with 2,162 yards, which at the time was second in Ohio State history to Howard "Hopalong" Cassady.

In his senior year, Ferguson rushed for 938 yards and scored 11 touchdowns in helping lead Ohio State to an 8–0–1 record and a share of a national title. He capped off his career by going for 152 yards and four touchdowns in a 50–20 win over the University of Michigan. He was second to Syracuse University's running back

Ernie Davis in the Heisman Trophy voting that season, resulting in one of the closest Heisman votes ever.

Ferguson, whose professional career was shortened by a head injury, is a member of the Ohio State and College Football halls of fame. He passed away in 2004.

Otis was the featured back on the great Ohio State teams of the late '60s, including the national championship squad in 1968. He led the team in rushing all three years he played, scored 35 touchdowns, and closed out his career with 2,542 yards, which is 10th of all time and still tops among Buckeyes fullbacks.

Otis' matriculation at Ohio State may have been preordained. He was born in Celina, Ohio, and his father was a roommate and good friend of Woody Hayes when both were at Denison University in the 1930s. That friendship was put on hold once Otis was on campus, though, as Hayes didn't want even the appearance of impropriety.

As a sophomore, the 6', 220-pound Otis led the 1967 team with 530 yards rushing. The following year, on a team dominated by sophomores, the junior Otis ground out 985 yards on the season. He had 144 yards in the huge win over then top-ranked Purdue University and 143 yards and four touchdowns in the 50–14 romp over Michigan. He then rushed for 101 yards against the University of Southern California in the Rose Bowl and scored a first-half touchdown to get the Buckeyes on the board after they'd fallen behind 10–0. They would of course go on to win 27–16 to capture the national championship.

Otis followed that with a stellar senior year, rushing for 1,027 yards to become the first player in Ohio State history to top the 1,000-yard mark. He was selected an All-American and was seventh in the vote for the Heisman Trophy in 1969. Besides his career rushing totals, Otis is second all-time to Archie Griffin in average rushing yards per game at 94.1. Otis was inducted into the Ohio State Hall of Fame in 1996.

Otis was drafted by the New Orleans Saints and also played for the Kansas City Chiefs, but he had the most success with the St. Louis Cardinals, where he played for six years. In 1975 he rushed for 1,076 yards and was selected to the Pro Bowl. Otis' son, James John Otis II, was a walk-on at Ohio State and played on special teams, lettering in 2003.

Take a Tour

Athens has the Acropolis, Rome the Coliseum, Paris the Eiffel Tower, and Columbus...the Horseshoe. Ohio Stadium may not rival those landmarks for history and romance, but try telling that to a die-hard Buckeyes fan. The Stadium is indeed a landmark on par with any in the state, and tours are offered for those wanting a behind-the-scenes look at this historic place. Even longtime season-ticket holders who think they've seen and done it all will likely pick up some new Buckeyes lore or learn something about the 'Shoe they didn't know before.

The tours take fans through the Huntington Club level and one of the suites, the Yassenoff Recruit Center, with its walls filled with giant photos of former and current Buckeyes greats, and the Steinbrenner Band Center. The latter is so named because of a large donation from New York Yankees principal owner George Steinbrenner on behalf of his wife Joan, a graduate of Ohio State. Fans will enjoy a message to band members on one wall that encourages them to "Pick Up Your Feet, Turn Your Corners Square, and Drive, Drive, Drive!!!"

Fans also get to see the expanded press box; interestingly, it's the highest point in the entire stadium. But probably the best part

Game Suspended for Lightning

Ohio State was hosting the University of Southern California at Ohio Stadium on September 29, 1990, when a furious thunderstorm blew through central Ohio and led to the game being called early, the only such time this has happened in modern history.

As the second-half wore on, officials had become increasingly concerned about the threatening weather and had consulted with Buckeyes coach John Cooper and USC's Larry Smith about possibly suspending the game. After Ohio State's Raymont Harris scored with 2:38 to play in the game to cut USC's lead to 35–26, the officials again huddled with the coaches. Cooper told them he planned to attempt an on-side kick, and all agreed that if it didn't work they'd head to the locker rooms. USC recovered the kick, and the Trojans had a victory nearly two and a half minutes short of regulation.

It is not, however, the only time an Ohio State game has failed to go the distance. In a November 16, 1912, game with Penn State at Ohio Field, Ohio State coach John Richards pulled his team from the field with approximately nine minutes to play, complaining of the rough play of the opponents and the failure of the officials to properly police the action on the field. Ohio State was also getting pounded 37–0 at the time. Tempers were running high, and after the game was called, an Ohio State student burned the Penn State colors from one of the goal posts. Ohio State apologized for the incident, but the two teams wouldn't meet again for more than 40 years.

for most fans is when they get to go down on the field and stroll the sideline where Woody Hayes and other Buckeyes legends once roamed.

Tours are $4 for adults and $2 for students, and children must be in the sixth grade or older to take part. The tours last approximately 90 minutes and can be scheduled year-round, Monday through Thursday, between 9:00 AM and 3:00 PM; they must be set up two weeks in advance and have at least 10 people. Not surprisingly, the stadium is often booked during the season. There is a good deal of walking involved, but the tours can be made accessible for those with disabilities.

Another way to get a behind-the-scenes peek at the stadium is to hold an event there. Fans get married inside the Horseshoe and hold wedding receptions and rehearsal dinners there. There are also corporate luncheons and meetings and Christmas parties. Ohio Stadium hosts approximately 100 events annually, and the entire stadium can be rented, starting at $3,000. Other facilities, such as the Yassenoff Recruit Center, Huntington Club, press box, University Suite, and Varsity O Room, are also available, ranging in price from $750 to $1,000 for three hours. One of the most popular spots is the President's Suite, which overlooks the 50-yard line.

87 Magical Moments

Almost exactly seven years to the day after Ohio State fullback Bob Ferguson scored four touchdowns in a 50–20 romp over archrival University of Michigan in 1961, Buckeyes fullback Jim Otis also scored four touchdowns against the Wolverines as Ohio State again ran up 50 points on its rival. That sounds like an incredible and fortuitous coincidence for the Buckeyes. But it doesn't end there.

Ferguson rushed for 152 yards and four scores against Michigan on November 25, 1961, in a win that closed out an unbeaten season for the Buckeyes. According to a story detailed in *The Official Ohio State Football Encyclopedia*, as Ferguson walked off the field after his destruction of the Wolverines, a young fan asked him for his chin strap as a souvenir, and Ferguson obliged.

Seven years later, Otis says that same fan approached him at the pep rally the night before the Michigan game and handed him the chin strap. The fan told Otis the story behind it, and Otis was so moved that he taped the chin strap to the inside of his shoulder pads for good luck the next day, November 23, 1968. He then went out and rushed for 143 yards and four touchdowns as Ohio State won 50–14 to cap off an unbeaten season.

To this day, 50 points remains the most ever scored by Ohio State in the series. In more than a century of football there are moments like these that seem almost magical, or at the very least to defy convention. Another such moment occurred in 1975 when undefeated and top-ranked Ohio State trailed Michigan 14–7 midway through the fourth quarter of the game at Ann Arbor. The Buckeyes had been outplayed most of the day, and their vaunted offense completely shut down early in the game. Their perfect season, number-one ranking, and shot at a Big Ten title and Rose Bowl berth were all in serious jeopardy.

After Michigan scored to go ahead with a little more than seven minutes to play, Ohio State got the ball back on its own 20, but the struggling offense hadn't recorded a first down since early in the second quarter. That's when quarterback Cornelius Greene decided a little divine intervention might be needed. He asked the players to hold hands and say a prayer.

"When we got to the huddle and brought the offense together, he said, 'We've got to do it right here,' and he said a prayer asking the Lord to give us the strength to play to the best of our ability," Archie Griffin recalls. "And we drove that ball down the field and scored and tied that thing up."

That they did, a key play coming right after the prayer when Greene hit Brian Baschnagel with a 17-yard pass on third-and-long. Ohio State marched down the field, and Pete Johnson plowed over from the 1 on fourth down. The scored was tied 14–14 with approximately three minutes to play.

Michigan needed a win for a Rose Bowl berth because Ohio State had the better overall record, so the Wolverines started throwing the ball when they got it back. Ray Griffin intercepted a pass and returned it to the Michigan three, and Johnson scored again to give Ohio State a 21–14 win. Woody Hayes called the game "our greatest comeback, and the greatest game I've ever coached."

Then there is this: the night of top-ranked Ohio State's historic 42–39 victory over Michigan in 2006, the much-hyped contest in which both teams came in undefeated and ranked first and second, the winning numbers in the Ohio Lottery's Pick 4 game were 4, 2, 3, and 9. The drawing was held about a half hour after the game ended, and lottery officials estimated that most of the winning bets were placed in that window.

88 A Rose Bowl Invitation Declined

The 1961 Ohio State team was one of the finest in the history of the school, but the conclusion of that season left coach Woody Hayes and his players deeply bitter. And it had nothing to do with an outcome on the field.

The team that year opened with a 7–7 tie with Texas Christian University but then rolled off eight straight wins, powered by a dream backfield of Matt Snell, Bob Ferguson, and Paul Warfield. No other team came within a touchdown of the Bucks, and they closed out the season with a 50–20 destruction of Michigan. The Buckeyes were 8–0–1 and won the Big Ten title outright. The requisite Rose Bowl invitation arrived, and that's when things started to go bad.

The Buckeyes had been to the Rose Bowl four times previously, but now a contentious debate erupted within the Ohio State faculty council over whether to accept the invitation. At the time, the Big Ten didn't have a formal contract with the Rose Bowl because the conference had failed to renew it a couple of years earlier, with Ohio State among those opposing renewal. Nonetheless, the invitation came, and the faculty council was left to mull it over.

In a debate almost as old as college football itself, some council members argued that football had become too consuming at Ohio State and was damaging the school's academic reputation. Others also argued that the Rose Bowl was becoming too commercial. When the final vote was tallied, the council narrowly rejected the invitation, leaving Hayes and Buckeye fans everywhere disillusioned.

Second-place University of Minnesota went to the Rose Bowl instead. Ohio State finished at number two in both the final Associated Press and United Press International polls, one spot behind the University of Alabama, which had defeated the University of Arkansas in the Sugar Bowl. The Buckeyes were number one in the Football Writers Association of America poll, and the school counts 1961 as one of its seven national titles.

Hayes was at a booster club get-together in Cleveland when he received word of the faculty council's vote. Whoever delivered the news probably anticipated a world-class blow-up, but instead Hayes went on a long walk and was composed when he returned. "I respect their integrity, if not their intelligence," he said.

He may have been uncharacteristically calm that day, but he remained bitter about it for years. Hayes would claim that the decision affected his recruiting in coming years because competing schools were telling high school players not to bother going to Ohio State if they wanted to play in the Rose Bowl. He strongly believed that he was losing players from Ohio to rival schools.

There is evidence to support his claim. Ohio State didn't win another Big Ten title until 1968 and suffered through its only losing season during Hayes' tenure, 4–5, in 1966. Or maybe it was just an excuse for some atypical seasons. Either way, Hayes made it clear it was a snub he would never forget.

89 Hineygate

Tens of thousands of fans descend on the Ohio State campus and the surrounding neighborhoods on game days to tailgate, crowd into area bars, and join the party leading up to kickoff. And the single biggest gathering is Hineygate, which bills itself as the world's largest tailgate party.

Held game-day morning in the parking lot of the Holiday Inn on Lane Avenue near the stadium, Hineygate has grown into a massive and raucous event since it was created in the early 1980s. For fans who like their pregame experience to be loud and crowded, and occasionally crude, this is the place.

It's not advisable to bring children to Hineygate, and fans who favor khakis and a scarlet-and-gray tie rather than a Buckeyes jersey and baseball cap might feel out of place. Also, anyone wearing the colors of that day's opposing team, particularly if they involve the combination of maize and blue, are sure to be on the receiving end of heaps of verbal abuse.

But on fall Saturdays Hineygate is nirvana to several thousand Buckeyes fans. There is beer, lots of it, and grills put out burgers and sausages and brats for the masses. The Danger Brothers band has provided the sound for years. A bunch of middle-aged guys cranking out rock-and-roll classics, as well as Ohio State favorites including "Hang on Sloopy," they're more wacky than dangerous.

A guy who's spot-on for Woody Hayes, with the glasses and the black *O* hat, is certain to make an appearance, and he may even take the stage to give the crowd a pep talk. Young women in the crowd are frequently encouraged to reveal, um, themselves, and some of them do.

And the party doesn't end at kickoff: fans without tickets to the game stick around to watch it on a giant screen that's set up, and the band revs it back up post game.

Hineygate—*hiney* is another word for *tail,* hence the name—has actually been reined in somewhat in recent years. Lane Avenue used to be shut down to vehicular traffic on game days, and the party would spill out onto the street. Now there's a fence surrounding the party that keeps it enclosed and prevents revelers from walking out carrying beers. The changes have done little to slow the party inside the fence, though.

It may sound like decadence to the greatest degree, but partiers can soothe their consciences with the knowledge that it's all in the name of altruism. Hineygate organizers have donated several hundred thousand dollars to various charities over the years. So, party on.

There are other such organized tailgates in the area, including one outside Tommy's Pizza and the Rockin' at Riverwatch event. Both are also along Lane Avenue, just down the street from Hineygate. The food and drink options vary depending on the party sponsors, but the method is basically the same: scarlet-and-gray-clad fans by the thousands drinking their fill and getting fueled up to cheer on the home team.

90 The Other Team Up North

There is, of course, the bitter and long-standing rivalry with the team that dons the famed winged helmet and plays in the Big House, the school whose name Woody Hayes wouldn't deign to utter. Then there is Michigan State University.

Located approximately 40 miles northwest of Ann Arbor in East Lansing, Michigan State has a proud football tradition that, while not as storied as its in-state neighbor's, is still scattered with great teams and great moments. Just ask any Ohio State fan with a decent memory. The Spartans have been responsible for four of the biggest upsets in the history of Ohio State football, losses that ruined perfect seasons for the Buckeyes and derailed national championship hopes.

The first occurred November 11, 1972, at Spartan Stadium. Ohio State came into the game 7–0 and ranked fifth in the country, while Michigan State was scuffling along at 3–4–1 in legendary coach Duffy Daugherty's final season. The Spartans gave him the perfect going-away present.

Daugherty had announced his planned retirement prior to the previous week's game, an upset of Purdue University, and apparently the Spartans were still on a high from the win. They dominated the game statistically and forced three fumbles and intercepted two passes. Hayes' postgame press conference lasted perhaps 15 seconds because he took no questions but simply said Ohio State deserved to lose after making so many mistakes. It was the second straight win for Michigan State over Ohio State, although the Bucks had gone 6–4 in 1971, and the loss wasn't nearly as significant.

Michigan State has proved to be a stubborn foe for the Buckeyes through the years. Here Greg Cooper tries to stop Ohio State's Antonio Pittman in their October 2006 game.

The Buckeyes recovered to defeat Michigan two weeks later and earn a share of the Big Ten title and a Rose Bowl berth, where they were whipped by the University of Southern California.

Almost two years later to the day, Ohio State returned to Spartan Stadium, this time carrying an 8–0 record and number-one ranking. The unranked Spartans were 4–3–1 but had won two straight and were in the midst of what would become a season-ending, five-game winning streak. The largest crowd of the season, 78,533, was on hand, and they would witness a game that would go down as maybe the most memorable—and certainly the most controversial—in the history of the Michigan State–Ohio State series.

The two teams had battled back and forth, then Spartans running back Levi Jackson ripped off an 88-yard touchdown run that put Michigan State up 16–13 with a little more than three minutes to play. Ohio State got the ball back and marched down the field, a run by Champ Henson getting them to within inches of the Michigan State goal line with seconds to play. Ohio State couldn't stop the clock and hustled to get into position. The ball was snapped and went through the legs of quarterback Cornelius Greene, but an alert Brian Baschnagel picked it up and ran it into the end zone. But had time expired?

One referee said it was a touchdown, while another indicated the game had ended prior to the snap. A huddle ensued that included Big Ten Commissioner Wayne Duke, and after 46 minutes it was announced that the touchdown didn't count. Hayes was livid and confronted Duke afterward, saying the game had been stolen from him.

Ohio State beat Michigan two weeks later for a share of the Big Ten championship and then lost to USC 18–17 in the Rose Bowl.

The scene then moves ahead 24 years and shifts to Columbus, but the results were sadly the same for the Bucks. Ohio State again came to the game undefeated, with an 8–0 record, and again ranked first in the nation. Additionally, Ohio State was a

The Illibuck Trophy

Everyone associated with Ohio State football knows the season finale against Michigan is the game to circle on the schedule every year. And while nothing rivals that, ahem, rivalry, Ohio State and the University of Illinois have been going at it almost as long. Their series features something the Ohio State–Michigan one lacks: a trophy.

The Illibuck Trophy, a wooden replica of a turtle, has been awarded to the winner of the Ohio State–Illinois game since 1924. Actually, in the first few years it was a live turtle that changed hands, but the turtle passed away in 1927 and a replica has been used ever since. Ohio State and Illinois first met in 1902, and for many years it was the last game of the season, until Michigan took that slot starting in 1935. Ohio State has played Illinois more times than any other team but Michigan, and Ohio leads the series 65–30–4 through 2013.

28-point favorite. Michigan State came in with a 4–4 record and nothing to lose. Unlike the previous games, Ohio State seemed in control of this one, leading 17–3 early and going ahead 24–9 in the fourth quarter on a Damon Moore interception return for a touchdown.

That's when things went south. Ohio State started turning the ball over, and Michigan State scored on four consecutive possessions to move ahead, 28–24. But Ohio State had its chances. The Bucks were stuffed on a fourth-and-1 with less than four minutes to play to kill one drive, and then they drove to the Spartans' 15 before quarterback Joe Germaine was intercepted in the end zone on another fourth down with just over a minute to go.

Again Ohio State recovered to beat Michigan a couple of weeks later and earn a Big Ten co-championship. The Bucks then defeated Texas A&M University 24–14 in the Sugar Bowl to finish 11–1 and ranked second in the nation. That team, coached by John Cooper and loaded with talent, was probably one of the best in school history, but an upset at the hands of Michigan State kept it from immortality.

Fast-forward to 2013, and an undefeated Ohio State team headed into the Big Ten Championship Game against a tough Michigan State team. The Buckeyes needed a win to secure a spot in the final BCS Championship Game and a shot at another national title.

Again, the Spartans failed to cooperate, delivering Urban Meyer his first loss as Buckeyes coach, 34–24, after 24 straight wins. Ohio State headed to the Orange Bowl while Michigan State went to the Rose Bowl with an identical 12–1 record.

This one was not really an upset—Ohio State had looked vulnerable the week before in a close win over a mediocre Michigan team, and Michigan State was undoubtedly good—just another in a series of disappointments at the hands of that other team up north.

 **Terrelle Pryor**

Terrelle Pryor was the most sought-after high school recruit in the country and Jim Tressel probably did his best sales job as coach when he landed Pryor over many other top schools, including Joe Paterno and Penn State. Pryor, from Jeannette, Pennsylvania, was a phenomenal athlete with size and speed who excelled at football and basketball in high school, and he landed at Ohio State amid much anticipation over what he would do for the Bucks as their quarterback.

In some ways he delivered on that promise, leading Ohio State to three straight Big Ten titles, wins in the Rose Bowl and Sugar Bowl, and finishing 12th all time in total offense (4,815 yards) despite playing just three seasons. But he also left a sad and bitter legacy that saw the departure of Tressel and the team put on probation.

Terrelle Pryor led the Buckeyes to a 31–26 victory over Arkansas in the Sugar Bowl following the 2010 season.

That was not all due to the actions of Pryor but he was a key figure in a scandal that saw players trading memorabilia and autographs for tattoos. Tressel found out about the scheme in the spring of 2010 but failed to notify school and NCAA officials, and when that surfaced the following spring he was out of a job. Pryor and other players were suspended for the first five games of the 2011 season, so he decided to leave, too. He was selected in the NFL supplemental draft by the Oakland Raiders and had an up-and-down first few years in the pros.

That was the thing about Pryor. Despite his incredible athleticism—he was almost 6'5", weighed about 230 pounds, and supposedly ran a sub-4.4 40-yard dash—he never seemed a true fit at quarterback. Pryor played college ball before the read-option offense saw athletic quarterbacks racking up incredible stats all over the country, and Tressel never seemed entirely sure how to best deploy him.

He did have great success at Ohio State, however, which now seems overshadowed by his ugly exit. He was MVP of that Rose Bowl win over Oregon, the Bucks' first victory in Pasadena in more than two decades. Pryor beat Michigan three times and led them to that win in the Sugar Bowl, too, over Arkansas at the end of the 2010 season.

But that last accomplishment is also under a cloud. The fact Pryor and some other players were even playing was controversial at the time because the scandal had surfaced and it was announced they would be suspended for games the following season. So why were they allowed to play in the Sugar Bowl, pundits asked? Cynics suggested it was because Tressel needed Pryor and the others for a win over a Southeastern Conference team in a high-profile game.

He got his win with Pryor but it would be the last Ohio State game for both men. And in the fallout from the scandal Ohio State would end up vacating the win anyway, as well as all the other victories that season and the Big Ten title.

So while he may be one of the most athletic and dynamic players in Ohio State history, and one of its most successful, the record book isn't even sure how to handle him. On the Ohio State website, where it lists statistics and recaps for previous seasons, under 2010 it just says "Season Vacated."

Pryor, speaking in the fall of 2013 while a member of the Raiders, was clear the bitterness remains on both sides.

"That's my school, but they don't really accept me," he said. "I've moved on to what I have now, and that's just football.... Those guys kicked me out of school after all those things I did for them."

Cornelius Greene

Ohio State won a Big Ten title in 1972, and one of the key components heading into the following season was returning quarterback Greg Hare, a senior and co-captain. But in spring practice Hare was challenged by a fleet sophomore from Washington, D.C., named Cornelius Greene, and by the opening game that fall Greene was the starter.

The replacement was a bold move by coach Woody Hayes, but Greene rewarded Hayes for his faith in him. He would go 31–3–1 as a starter over the next three seasons, and the Buckeyes would win a Big Ten title each year. Greene would team with tailback Archie Griffin and fullback Pete Johnson, as well as wingback Brian Baschnagel, in probably the most talented and potent backfield in Ohio State history.

The slender and athletic Greene also made history as the first African American player to start at quarterback for Ohio State.

More than three decades later, African American quarterbacks are commonplace, and one at Ohio State—Troy Smith—was awarded the Heisman Trophy in 2006, but Greene's achievement was a significant moment. Greene told the *Columbus Dispatch* in a 2007 story that he received racist hate mail but didn't make it public.

"I went through that hardship myself because if I threw that out into the press it would just get worse," he said. "But I did feel pressure because I was playing for my race."

The pressure didn't show on the field or off. Greene earned the nickname "Flam" for his flamboyant dress and personality, and he found immediate success running the Buckeyes offense. He rushed for 12 touchdowns for that 1973 team, which didn't win the national championship but is considered among the handful of greatest Buckeyes teams ever. It still holds the school record with an average of 355 rushing yards per game and finished the season 10–0–1. Besides a 10–10 tie with undefeated University of Michigan, the next closest game was the 42–21 defeat of the University of Southern California in the Rose Bowl.

In that Michigan game, Greene had an injured thumb that limited his ability to throw the ball, and he was replaced by Hare with just a minute or so to play in an unsuccessful attempt by Hayes to get something going offensively. Greene returned for the Rose Bowl, completing six of eight passes for 129 yards, running for 45 yards and a score, and being named game MVP.

Greene and the Buckeyes would beat Michigan the following two seasons, although they would lose in the Rose Bowl at the end of each season. 'Corny' was All–Big Ten both his junior and senior seasons, and in 1975 he was named team and conference MVP, even as Griffin won the Heisman that season. Those were obviously ground-oriented teams, and Greene attempted just 46 passes in the entire 1973 season. Hayes would open it up a little more the following two years, and Greene completed 68 of 121 passes for

1,066 yards his senior season. As a junior he had 1,781 yards of total offense, 842 running, and 939 passing.

Most impressively, Greene finished in the top 20 in Ohio State history in both career passing (2,348 yards) and rushing (2,066 yards). He was inducted into the Ohio State Hall of Fame in 1998.

Beat Michigan Week

When the University of Michigan players entered their locker room prior to the 1994 game with Ohio State at the Horseshoe, star Wolverines running back Tyrone Wheatley and several other players discovered something missing, something very important, actually: their helmets. Pranksters, or thieves depending on your point of view, had made off with the famed winged helmets of Wheatley and four other offensive players, including starting quarterback Todd Collins.

During the game that day, the Buckeyes rolled to a 22–6 win to snap a six-game winless streak against their rivals. The Michigan offense failed to score a touchdown for the first time in a decade, and Wheatley suffered a minor concussion that he suggested was caused by an ill-fitting helmet. "I can't blame (my performance) on that," Wheatley said afterward. "But whoever has my helmet, I would please like it back."

The culprits were eventually found, with an Ohio State band member among those charged in the thefts. Pranks surrounding what is called Beat Michigan Week are nothing new, but this might be the only one that possibly had an affect on the outcome of the game. There is the story, apocryphal maybe, of the car with Michigan plates that was pushed into the Olentangy

River following one Ohio State–Michigan game. Michigan online message boards contain complaints of verbal abuse, threats, and even assaults suffered by Wolverines fans in Columbus.

The stories may be embellished, but Michigan issued an email ahead of the 2006 game with some warnings. Here is a sampling:

- If possible, drive a car with non-Michigan license plates.
- Keep your Michigan gear to a minimum, or wait until you are inside the stadium to display it.
- Stay with a group.
- Stay low-key; don't draw unnecessary attention to yourself.
- If verbally harassed by opposing fans, don't take the bait.

Then there was this: "If at any time you feel unsafe, you should call 9–1–1 for assistance. U-M campus police also will be available in Columbus to support our fans." They brought their own cops.

Michigan fans might be surprised or pleased to learn that there are many harmless and even charitable traditions that have sprung up surrounding the game. The Thursday night before the game each year, Ohio State students take a dip in Mirror Lake no matter the temperature outside in an effort to bring the Bucks luck. Some wear costumes, some nothing at all.

There is the Beat Michigan Blood Drive, a long-standing blood battle between the schools, and the Buckeye Wolverine Challenge for Life, a campaign to get fans to commit to being organ or tissue donors. And the Rivalry Run—fraternity brothers from both schools holding a relay that delivers a game ball to the site of the game from the opposing team's stadium—raises money for cancer. WolverBuck is the annual contest between the two schools' crew clubs, held the morning of the game in whatever city is hosting the game.

The excitement and anticipation infects the entire city of Columbus and state of Ohio, really: grade schools hold Buckeyes spirit days the week of the game; Michigan Avenue is temporarily renamed Buckeye Way by the mayor of Columbus; a prisoner in Franklin County agrees to plead guilty if the judge will let him watch the game Saturday. That was the famous story surrounding the 2003 game. Ohio State fan Jeff Renne pled guilty to forgery but in return asked the judge to delay his transfer to a state prison so he could stay in the local lockup, where he knew he'd be able to watch the game. The judge agreed.

"If they win, I will be on cloud nine for a few months that I'm incarcerated," said Renne, who was facing a two-year prison term. Alas, it was hard time for Mr. Renne right away: Michigan 35, Ohio State 21.

As for the judge who granted the request, he had a simple explanation: "It's Michigan week, and it's Columbus, Ohio," said Judge Richard Sheward. "And I thought I should do my part for the Ohio State Buckeyes."

94 Football Families

There was a bumper sticker that could be seen on cars in central Ohio in the mid-1970s that contained a simple expression of gratitude: "Thank You, Mrs. Griffin." It was a reference to the fact that three Griffins played for Ohio State in the decade: Archie and his little brothers Ray and Duncan. All were on the 1975 team, Archie as the Heisman Trophy–winning running back, Ray a sophomore defensive back, and Duncan as a freshman who played on special teams.

In that season's University of Michigan game Archie struggled with just 46 yards rushing, snapping his streak of 100-yard games at 31, so Ray picked him up. With the score tied at 14–14 and about three minutes to play, Ray intercepted a Rick Leach pass and returned it to the 3-yard line. Ohio State scored on the next play and won 21–14, preserving an undefeated season and earning another Rose Bowl berth. Ray, No. 44, would go on to captain the 1977 team, and he was a first-team All-American that season at safety.

One of the most overused clichés in all of sports is when players and coaches refer to their team as "family," but at Ohio State it rings true. Besides the Griffin brothers, there are numerous other examples of siblings, fathers and sons, and other blood relatives who have worn the scarlet and gray. The 2005 team alone had a half-dozen legacies: fullback Dionte Johnson (father Pepper Johnson lettered 1982–85); cornerback Shaun Lane (Garcia, 1981–83); linebacker Ryan Lukens (Bill, 1974–76); wide receiver Kyle Ruhl (Bruce, 1973–76); fullback Stan White, Jr. (Stan, 1969–71); offensive guard Doug Datish (Mike, 1975).

There are some other Buckeyes family ties.

The 1917 team, which went 8–0–1 and captured the Western Conference (Big Ten) title, was the only one captained by brothers, Harold and Howard Courtney. Both played tackle, and Harold was an All-American.

Former quarterback and current ESPN personality Kirk Herbstreit and his father James are the only father-and-son duo to serve as captains at Ohio State (Kirk in 1992, James in 1960).

Craig Cassady, a starting defensive back in 1975, was the son of Howard Cassady, the 1955 Heisman Trophy winner. Craig had two interceptions in the 21–14 Michigan win that year.

Brothers Lin and Jim Houston were both All-Americans (Lin in 1942, and Jim in 1958–59), and both won national titles (Lin in 1942, and Jim in 1957).

Chic Harley's great-great nephew Rob Harley was a defensive back and special teams player who lettered from 2003 to 2005 and who now does some radio and TV work for Buckeye games.

Cornerback Dustin Fox, who graduated in 2005, is the nephew of 1975 All-American safety Tim Fox.

All-American cornerback Shawn Springs (1996) is the son of former Buckeyes running back Ron, who led the team in rushing in 1977 with 1,166 yards.

Fred Pagac played at Ohio State and later became defensive coordinator, where he coached his son, linebacker Fred Pagac Jr.

Ohio State once fielded twins, Dale and David Bonnie, who played together in 1947.

95 Retired Numbers

Ohio State surprised Archie Griffin at halftime of the game against the University of Iowa on October 30, 1999, when the school handed him a large frame containing his jersey and announced that no Buckeye would ever again wear his No. 45. Griffin was the first to have his jersey retired by Ohio State, and six others have joined him since, the names and numbers adorning the upper-deck façade in the closed end of Ohio Stadium.

Those so honored include all the Buckeyes to have received the Heisman Trophy, except for Troy Smith, who just won the award in 2006, as well as Charles "Chic" Harley and Bill Willis. Here they are, with year the number was retired noted in parentheses:

No. 31, Vic Janowicz (2000)—Hailed by many as the most spectacular athlete in Ohio State history, he won the Heisman Trophy in 1950.

No. 40, Howard "Hopalong" Cassady (2000)—Cassady snuck into Ohio Stadium as a kid to watch the Buckeyes and later starred for them on both sides of the ball as a running back and defensive back. He won a national title in 1954 and the Heisman Trophy the following year.

No. 22, Les Horvath (2001)—Horvath was in dental school at Ohio State when a wartime rule allowed him an extra year of eligibility. He returned in 1944 and led Ohio State to its first undefeated season in 27 years, becoming the only Heisman Trophy–winner who hadn't played the previous season.

No. 27, Eddie George (2001)—George put up incredible numbers in his Heisman season of 1995: a school record 1,927 yards rushing, 25 touchdowns, and even 47 passes caught.

No. 47, Charles "Chic" Harley (2004)—Ohio State's first three-time All-American, Harley didn't win the Heisman Trophy because it wasn't around yet. He actually only wore No. 47 for his final game, which was also the only game he lost in his career.

No. 99, Bill Willis (2007)—Ohio State's first African American All-American, Willis was a star two-way lineman who played on the school's first national championship team in 1942, coached by Paul Brown. Willis was All-American in 1943–44. The 86-year-old Willis attended the number retirement ceremony at halftime of the University of Wisconsin game on November 3, 2007, and passed away less than a month later.

Troy Smith won the Heisman Trophy and beat Michigan as a starting quarterback three times, so it would seem his No. 10 would join the others. Smith had an outstanding career, but the memories of his final game in an Ohio State uniform aren't positive. That was the blowout loss to the University of Florida in the Bowl Championship Series title game in 2007, when he and the rest of the team looked overwhelmed. With time should come some perspective, though, and it would be surprising if Ohio State made him the only Heisman Trophy–winner not to have his jersey retired.

If the school does retire Smith's jersey they could do so with a nod to two other All-American quarterbacks at Ohio State who have worn No. 10: Rex Kern and Art Schlichter.

A couple of other jerseys at Ohio State stand out for the unusual number of stars who have worn them: Cornelius Greene, Chris Gamble, Joey Galloway, Joe Germaine, and Ted Ginn Jr. all wore No. 7, while No. 36 was favored by a trio of All-American linebackers: Tom Cousineau, Marcus Marek, and Chris Spielman.

And then there is Griffin's No. 45, which star linebacker Andy Katzenmoyer requested when he came to campus in the mid-1990s. The number was not yet retired, but no one had worn it

Chic Is Welcomed Home

Chic Harley had been away from campus for decades, living at the Veteran's Administration Hospital in Danville, Illinois, apparently suffering from depression and other ailments, when he planned a return in the fall of 1948 for the season finale against Michigan. He was feeling up for the trip for the first time in years, and he received a hero's welcome in Columbus.

Harley was greeted at the train station downtown by Ohio State and city officials, and then thousands of people lined High Street for a ticker-tape parade. He was the guest of honor at the Captain's Breakfast before the game and, although shy, he did several interviews for radio and newspaper reporters. One quoted the modest Harley, in reference to the parade: "I am not deserving of that."

Another great honor came from the Ohio State marching band, which while performing a Script Ohio at halftime, opened up the right side of the Os to spell Chic. It's believed to be the only time Script Ohio has been altered.

Harley did not, however, bring the Bucks any luck: they lost to Michigan that day, 13–3.

since Griffin left two decades earlier. When Katzenmoyer put it on it raised some hackles among Buckeyes fans.

Katzenmoyer had worn that number since junior high school, but he may not have helped his case among Buckeyes fans by admitting he originally wanted the number not in honor of Griffin but because the number (44) of a star linebacker at Oklahoma at the time, Brian Bosworth, was unavailable, and he wanted something close to it. Ohio State consulted with Griffin when Katzenmoyer was still a recruit, and Griffin gave his consent, saying the request didn't bother him and that the hoopla surrounding it made him know people still cared about him and his accomplishments.

Brutus Buckeye

When the Buckeyes take the field at Ohio Stadium to the deafening roar of more than 100,000 fans, at the head of the charge is a sprinting mascot carrying aloft an Ohio State flag: Brutus Buckeye. Players say the moment is almost indescribable, but what about Brutus?

"It was a feeling like no other. The adrenaline rush was incredible," says Emily Moor, who was Brutus during the 2001 and 2002 seasons. "I've never had my heart beat so fast." Along with the excitement was some anxiety. "If I drop the flag, I'm done. The whole team will run over me," Moor said.

Brutus Buckeye has been revving up fans at Ohio Stadium since 1965, when an art student designed the first mascot. There had been attempts to introduce a mascot prior to that, but none took hold. There was a German police dog at one point, but that didn't last long. Other ideas were bandied about involving a male deer (a

Brutus Buckeye does one-armed pushups at a fan rally in January 2007.

buck), a moose, an elk, and a ram. Instead, the school bowed to the reality that, unlike schools with names like Wildcats or Spartans or Seminoles, there just was no obvious way to represent a nut.

Then Brutus came along. The name was chosen in a contest, and the first incarnation was a large papier-mâché shell designed to look like a Buckeye. It was a bulky costume, and any sort of physical movements beyond simply walking were out of the question. In the mid-1970s a new Brutus was introduced that had a smaller, prune-like head, but that was met with derision from the home fans. Finally, there is the current edition: a more athletic Brutus with a soft, lightweight head that allows the mascot to run and jump and lead cheers and storm the field at the front of the team.

Brutus is played by a student, and there are tryouts each spring, with a handful making the cut and rotating appearances, sometimes during the same game. Judges look at personality and school spirit, but they also question Brutus hopefuls on how they'd react if they accidentally ran over a child or were offered booze by a fan. Another possible hazard can be opposing fans. "I heard every cuss word in the book," Moor said of some of her fan interactions.

Brutus is considered a member of the cheerleading squad, so beyond energy, the students are expected to know cheers and be prepared for the game. Moor said it's all worth it when you take the field. She performed at the 2003 Fiesta Bowl and said it was the thrill of a lifetime, especially after she received a national championship ring.

In a 2005 story in the *Lantern,* Ohio State's school newspaper, another former Brutus, Ty Schlegel, told about the thrill of leading the charge onto the field.

"(Coach) Tressel's getting the troops ready and then he looks straight at you and points, and you just go," he said. "It's got to be adrenaline: you're running so fast, you fly down the field."

97 Tom Skladany and the Kickers

The excellent Buckeyes teams of the mid-1970s had powerful running games, of course, hard-hitting defenses, and were disciplined and efficient squads molded in the image of their leader, Woody Hayes. As if they needed another advantage, they almost always won the field position battle, too, and that was because of Tom Skladany.

When Skladany came to Ohio State it was not too far removed from the time when the kicking and punting duties were given to the position player with the strongest leg. But Hayes was a believer and made Skladany the first kicking specialist at Ohio State to receive a scholarship. Skladany rewarded him by being named All-American at punter three years in a row (1974–76), one of just seven players in Ohio State history to achieve that feat. He was captain of the 1976 team, the first specialist to earn that honor as well.

Skladany was a good all-around athlete who supposedly could throw a golf ball from one sideline of Ohio Stadium into the upper deck on the opposite side (kicking specialists have a lot of down time during practice). He was the number-one punter all four of his years at Ohio State, and by his senior year he was doing it all: punting, kicking extra points and field goals, and kicking off. He averaged 45.6 yards per punt his sophomore year and led the country that year and the next when his average was 46.7 yards per boot. He was named to the Football Writers All-America team as a sophomore and was a consensus All-American his final two seasons. While he made his name and earned the scholarship as a punter, Skladany kicked the longest field goal in Ohio State history, 59 yards, during a 1975 game at the University of Illinois.

Skladany was drafted in the second round by the Cleveland Browns, a high pick for a punter or kicker, but he held out his entire rookie year over a contract dispute. He then signed with Detroit and punted for the Lions for five seasons, making one Pro Bowl, and he played part of a sixth season with Philadelphia.

Skladany was the first in a growing line of kicking specialists to make a name for themselves at Ohio State. Place-Kicker U. and Punter U. don't exactly have the same ring as Linebacker U., but they are apt for Ohio State. Punter Tom Tupa, who also played quarterback, was an All-American in 1987, when he averaged 47 yards per punt, and he set a school record in 1984—that still stands today—with an average of 47.1 yards per punt.

Kicker Dan Stultz (1997–2000) is third on the all-time scoring list with 342 points, and Vlade Janakievski (1977–80) is fifth (295 points). Both were first-team All–Big Ten selections. Punter B.J. Sander won the Ray Guy Award as the nation's best punter in 2003, and Andy Groom was an All-American for the 2002 national champions. Groom's booming punts were critical for a team that often relied on defense and special teams to win.

Kicker Mike Nugent was also an All-American on that team and repeated in 2004, when he won the Lou Groza Award as the nation's top place-kicker. "Nooooge," as he was known to the Ohio Stadium faithful, was simply the greatest kicker ever to don a pair of cleats at Ohio State. He is the leading scorer in Ohio State history (356 points) and holds or shares more than 20 Buckeyes kicking records, including most field goals in a season (25) and career (72), and best field goal percentage in a season (25–28, .893 in 2002) and career (72 of 88, .818).

At different points Nugent made 83 straight extra points and 24 consecutive field goals. In 2004 he made five field goals of longer than 50 yards and was eight of nine on such long-distance attempts in his career. Also in 2004 Nugent was the first kicking specialist named captain since Skladany, and at the end of that season Nugent's teammates selected him as team MVP.

Nugent was taken by the New York Jets in the second round of the 2005 draft, and finished his ninth season in the NFL with the Cincinnati Bengals in 2013.

Wacky Wins

There have been plenty of games in the nearly 120-year history of Ohio State football where the ending seemed to defy belief: the confusing and controversial loss at Michigan State University in 1974, the see-saw battle and last-second loss to the University of Oklahoma in 1977, the triple overtime win against North Carolina State University in 2003 when officials had to confer over whether a Wolfpack running back had stretched far enough to score the tying touchdown on the final play, and of course the double overtime win against Miami in the 2003 Fiesta Bowl that brought a national championship home to Columbus.

But none of those compares to two games in the 1940s when Ohio State pulled out victories after time had expired. In both instances fans had begun departing Ohio Stadium and players had retired to their locker rooms only to be brought back on the field to finish it out.

In the first game, Ohio State and the University of Illinois were tied 26–26 on November 13, 1943, when the Buckeyes had the ball on the Illini 23 with one final shot at the end zone. A pass, however, fell incomplete, the final gun sounded, and it appeared the two teams had played to a tie. The players headed to their respective locker rooms, and many of the more than 36,000 spectators in attendance started home.

What hardly anyone realized, including most of the officials, was that the head linesman had signaled that one of the Illinois linemen was off-sides on the final play. The referees huddled and, after determining the Buckeyes deserved one more play, went to the locker rooms to tell the coaches, Paul Brown for Ohio State and Ray Eliot for Illinois. Some of the players had already begun

Ohio State's Biggest Win

Ohio State took on Oberlin College at Ohio Field on October 14, 1916, and it was bad for the visitors from the get-go. Frosty Hurum and Chic Harley scored touchdowns on Ohio State's first two offensive plays, and the score was 33–0 after the first quarter. The Buckeyes were just getting warmed up. By halftime the score was 67–0, and Ohio State would almost double that by game's end. The final was 128–0, the most points ever scored by a Buckeyes team and the largest margin of victory in school history. In fact, it's the only time a Buckeyes team has scored in triple digits.

Halfback Fred Norton scored five touchdowns, and fullback Dick Boesel added four. The score looks absurd but was not a complete aberration for this team. Led by Harley and All-American tackle Bob Karch, they outscored their opponents 258–29 that season, went 7–0 to become the first unbeaten and untied Ohio State team, and won the Western Conference. And although Oberlin was a smaller school, the disparity wasn't as great back then, and it was common for Ohio State to play other small colleges from around the state. Oberlin had beaten Ohio State several times before that game and would do so again five years later before being dropped from the schedule shortly thereafter.

taking their uniforms off, so they hastily redressed and returned to the field.

Brown decided to attempt a field goal, and kicker Johnny Stungis, a 17-year-old freshman, booted it through from 33 yards out—but just barely. It was the only field goal of his career, and Ohio State had a surprising 29–26 victory. It was one of the few highlights in a season that would see the Buckeyes go 3–6.

That was a textbook ending compared to the game against Northwestern University on November 8, 1947. The Buckeyes trailed 6–0 late when they drove to the Wildcats' 1-yard line, only to be stopped on downs with just 1:47 to play. Many fans headed for the exits at that point. thinking the game was over.

But Ohio State held Northwestern and forced a punt, getting the ball back at the Wildcats' 36 with 31 seconds to play. But a couple of plays later a pass from Pandel Savic was picked off as time expired. Game over, right? Fans who were still around began to depart, and the Ohio State band started to take the field. But what went unnoticed was that officials had called Northwestern for having 12 men on the field.

Ohio State would get another shot, but a run by Rodney Swinehart was stopped at the 2. Northwestern was off-sides on the play, however, and on the ensuing down Savic hit Jimmy Clark in the end zone for the tying touchdown. But the extra point was blocked, meaning a tie game.

Not so fast. The officials again penalized Northwestern for being off-sides. Emil Moldea nailed his second attempt, and Ohio State had a 7–6 win. For real.

Woody-isms

Woody Hayes may have been obsessed with football, but he had opinions on most everything, and he wasn't bashful about sharing them. He would discourse on military history, the fate of western civilization, and the pitfalls of the forward pass. It's one of the things that differentiates him from many of the coaches of today, who would no more talk about social issues than they would admit to liking Broadway musicals. Hayes could even be funny on occasion. Here's a sampling of Woodyisms.

Woody-isms on Life

"Without winners, there wouldn't be any civilization."

"I don't like nice people. I like tough, honest people."

"I see my job as a part of American civilization and a damn important part. I see football as being just so much above everything else."

"You can never pay back, but you can always pay forward."

"Football is about the only unifying force left in America today. It is certainly one of the few places in our society where teamwork, mental discipline, and the value of hard work still mean anything. We stick to the old-fashioned virtues, and if the rest of the country had stuck to them, it would have been a different story in Vietnam."

Woody Hayes was not afraid to express his opinion on or off the field.

Woody-isms on His Football Philosophy

"There are three things that can happen when you pass, and two of them are bad."—This is one of his most famous Woody-isms, but it is also credited to a couple of other football coaches.

"You don't get hurt running straight ahead."

"I will pound you and pound you until you quit."

"Eliminate the mistakes, and you'll never lose a game. To eliminate mistakes, you have to pick the right quarterback. And the pass is a weapon of surprise—don't overuse it."

"No back in the history of football was ever worth two fumbles a game."

"I love football. I think it is the most wonderful game in the world, and I despise to lose."

"I don't motivate the players. I get them to motivate themselves."

"The only meaningful statistic is number of games won."

"There's nothing that cleanses your soul like getting the hell kicked out of you."

"The will to win is not as important as the will to prepare to win."

"Son, women give birth to babies every day of the year, but we will only once play this game against SMU."—This statement was delivered to Buckeye Mike Radtke, whose wife had just had twins, before a 1968 game.

"Tell him he's going to have to wait. I'm talking to my team right now."—This was Hayes' response upon being told his friend President Nixon was on the phone after the 1970 Michigan game.

Woody-isms about Himself

"Nobody despises to lose more than I do. That's what got me into trouble over the years, but it also made a man with mediocre ability a pretty good coach."

"I don't live in the past. I'm a student of the past, and I try to learn from the past, although some people will say, 'You haven't done a very good job of it.' But for me to live in the past? Hell, no."

"I don't apologize for anything. When I make a mistake, I take the blame and go on from there."

"I'm not trying to win a popularity poll. I'm trying to win football games."

"I try to get six to seven hours sleep at night and try not to miss any meals. What time is left goes to football."

"Just remember one thing. I can do your job, but you can't do mine."—These words were spoken to a professor.

"Should I apologize for all the good things that I've done?"—This was Hayes' reply to advice that he should apologize for punching a Clemson University player at the 1978 Gator Bowl.

100 The Buckeye

Woody Hayes was a renowned recruiter, but he usually left the football talk to his assistants. Instead, Hayes would work on the recruit's parents, stress his own commitment to education, and throw in an emotional appeal about the tradition and uniqueness of Ohio State football.

"You can go become a tiger, a bear, a lion, or any other animal that is a mascot at schools across this country, but there is only one place in this world you can become a Buckeye," he was reported to have said to at least one recruit. "Are you ready to be a Buckeye?"

Woody was acting as a salesman, but he wasn't embellishing: There is only one place in college football where the Buckeyes play. The nickname actually wasn't officially adopted by Ohio State until 1950, but it had been in use in reference to the school and its athletics teams for decades by then. Mascot Brutus Buckeye was created in 1965, and it was in 1968 that Hayes and trainer Ernie

Biggs came up with the idea to plaster buckeye-leaf stickers on helmets as rewards for good play. It's a tradition that has become one of the most recognizable and cherished symbols of the school's nickname.

So where did the name come from? The buckeye tree is the state tree of Ohio and was apparently called such because its nuts resemble a "buck's eye." Native Americans are credited with naming the tree and also with first using it to describe a settler, when they encountered Colonel Ebenezer Sproat in the late 1700s, according to the university news office. Sproat led a legal delegation at the first court session in what was then the Northwest Territory. He was a large, outgoing man, and the apparently impressed Native Americans referred to him as "Hetuck," their word for "buckeye."

The nickname became popular to describe other white settlers of the area, and common usage came after William Henry Harrison, who had adopted Ohio as his home state, used the buckeye tree and nuts as campaign symbols in his winning presidential bid in 1840.

The nut is described as mildly toxic, so it's not eaten. The soft wood isn't of much use, and the distinctive five-fingered leaflet somewhat resembles the leaf of another plant that's illegal in the United States and most other countries. But according to lore, carrying buckeyes in your pocket can bring good luck and ward off rheumatism. And the university proudly notes that the buckeye tree is "native, tenacious, attractive, and unique."

Didn't know a tree could be tenacious? "The tree has grit," the university says. "It grows where others cannot, is difficult to kill, and adapts to its circumstances." Put that way, it sounds like a fine symbol for a school and football team.